D0443219

TO LOOSE THE BANDS
OF WICKEDNESS

*International Intervention
in Defence of Human Rights*

Also available from Brassey's

BROWN
The Strategic Revolution

GOW
Iraq, the Gulf Conflict and the World Community

IISS
Military Balance

IISS
Strategic Survey

ROGERS/DANDO
A Violent Peace

RUSI/BRASSEY'S
Defence Yearbook

SAYIGH
Arab Military Industry

TO LOOSE THE BANDS OF WICKEDNESS

International Intervention in Defence of Human Rights

Edited by

NIGEL S. RODLEY

Published in association with

THE DAVID DAVIES MEMORIAL INSTITUTE OF INTERNATIONAL STUDIES

BRASSEY'S (UK)

Copyright © 1992 Brassey's (UK) Ltd

All Rights Reserved. No part of this publication
may be reproduced, stored in a retrieval system or transmitted
in any form or by any means: electronic, electrostatic, magnetic
tape, mechanical, photocopying, recording or otherwise, without
permission in writing from the publishers.

First English edition 1992

UK editorial offices: Brassey's, 165 Great Dover Street,
London SE1 4YA
orders: Marston Book Services, PO Box 87, Oxford OX2 0DT

US orders: Macmillan Publishing Company, Front and Brown Streets,
Riverside, NJ 08075

Distributed in North America to booksellers and wholesalers by the
Macmillan Publishing Company, NY 10022

Library of Congress Cataloging in Publication Data
available

British Library Cataloguing in Publication Data
A catalogue record for this book is
available from the British Library

ISBN 1–85753–047–0 Hardcover

Typeset by Florencetype Ltd, Kewstoke, Avon
Printed in Great Britain by BPCC Wheatons, Exeter.

To loose the bands of wickedness, to undo the heavy burdens, and to let the oppressed go free.

Isaiah 58:6

Contents

Preface

As early as 1988 the director of the David Davies Memorial Institute of International Studies, Sheila Harden, began to contemplate the desirability of mounting a study to consider, against the background of the profound changes taking place in Soviet foreign policy and East–West relations, whether there should not be a more vigorous international response to gross violations of human rights, including the development of the international capacity to intervene in matters traditionally excluded from United Nations action by article 2(7) of the Charter. By the following year she was thinking in terms of enlarging this study to include the question of international intervention in civil conflicts in the light of the frequent linkage of such conflicts with human rights violations, in particular the displacement of peoples.

It was not until the beginning of 1991 that the Institute decided to proceed with this study. By that time Miss Harden's prescience had been fully justified. The communist system in Eastern Europe had collapsed and the Soviet Union was close to involuntary decolonisation. Ethnic nationalism, with its potential for intra-state conflict and human rights abuse, was on the upsurge. Most of the 20 or so armed conflicts causing death and destruction from Burma to El Salvador were civil rather than inter state. On the positive side, with the end of the Cold War, the United Nations was already demonstrating by its response to the Iraqi aggression against Kuwait that it could act quickly and decisively, not only to persuade but also to coerce.

Accordingly, a study group was formed comprising the following individuals:

Sir Anthony Parsons (Chairman)

UK Permanent Representative to the UN in New York from 1979–1982, UK Ambassador to Iran 1974–1979.

Sydney Bailey

Represented the Quakers at the UN from 1954–1958. Author of a number of books on the political function of the UN.

Peter Calvocoressi

Former Reader in International Relations at Sussex University and author of a number of books on international affairs.

Colonel Richard Connaughton

Until July 1992 he was Colonel, Defence Studies at the Staff College, Camberley. He is the author of Military Intervention and the Logic of War (Routledge, 1992).

Paul Fifoot

Former deputy legal advisor to the FCO and former legal advisor to the UK Mission to the UN in New York. Member (Chairman 1989–1990) Steering Committee on Human Rights, Council of Europe.

Lawrence Freedman

Professor of War Studies, University of London.

Nigel Rodley

Reader in Law, Human Rights Centre, University of Essex.

During the meetings of the group (from June 1991 onwards), it was agreed that the study should consist of separate chapters dealing, *inter alia*, with the history of the relationship between the international community and the sovereignty of its individual members, the legal background, and the instruments of persuasion and coercion at the disposal of the United Nations.

Case histories would also be included, the obvious ones being first the response by the Allied Coalition and the UN Security Council and the UN Secretariat to the humanitarian crisis precipitated by the reaction of the Iraqi government to the rebellion which broke out following the rout of the Iraqi armed forces in the Gulf War; and secondly the international reaction to the civil strife in Yugoslavia which exploded in September 1991. A final chapter would draw the threads together and advance conclusions and recommendations.

The need for such a study has become accepted by all except the most diehard adherents to the doctrine that national sovereignty is inviolate against external interference in all circumstances. Heads of government, foreign ministers and the UN Secretary-General himself have publicly questioned this doctrine. As early as 1968 Michael Stewart (the then UK foreign secretary) in his address to the General Assembly stated that:

> If we want men to love peace we shall want to make sure that peace means something more to them than the continuation of poverty, oppression and discrimination. Well, we try to tackle that, we try to tackle it in the field of human rights. And article 56 of the Charter makes it clear that no country can say that the human rights of its citizens are an exclusively domestic matter. A country that denies its citizens the basic human rights is by virtue of article 56 in breach of an international obligation. (HMSO Cmnd 4123, para.17)

Under the article cited, 'All Members pledge themselves to take joint and separate action in co-operation with the Organization for the achievement of the purposes set forth in article 55.' These purposes include the promotion of 'universal respect for, and observance of, human rights and fundamental freedoms for all without distinction as to race, sex, language, or religion' (article 55c). In April 1991 the British foreign secretary Douglas Hurd stated that the division between the internal and external policies of a nation is 'not absolute'. Similar statements have been made by American congressional leaders. President Mitterrand has pledged a new French initiative to expand the international community's duty to intervene to protect the rights of minorities. The then UN Secretary-General, Pérez de Cuéllar, put the issue clearly in an address at the University of Bordeaux on 22 April:

> But one could – and I would even say, should – inquire whether certain . . . texts . . . later adopted by the United Nations, in particular the Universal Declaration of Human Rights, do not implicitly call into question this inviolable notion of sovereignty. Has not a balance been established between the rights of states, as confirmed by the Charter, and the rights of the individual, as confirmed by the Universal Declaration? We are clearly witnessing what is probably an irresistible shift in public attitudes towards the belief that the defence of the oppressed in the name of morality should prevail over frontiers and legal documents.

Such has been the effect on international attitudes of the dramatic events of the last two or three years.

Method of Work

At its first meeting the members of the group, after a wide-ranging discussion, approved the draft outline (with some structural changes to the format) and agreed who should undertake the individual subjects. It was also agreed that all chapters should be signed, including the final chapter by myself as Chairman. The chapters were circulated in draft and discussed at two further meetings to allow the authors to take into account written or oral comments and suggestions by other members of the group, but were not agreed line by line.

Our book is thus a study to which each member contributed special expertise in individual chapters, but for which we all are jointly responsible. There is inevitably some overlapping between the chapters as each of us has approached the same set of objectives from different points of departure. There was no serious disagreement with the final version and we all support the conclusions and recommendations set out in the final chapter.

Sir Anthony Parsons

Postscript to Preface

This book was completed too early to take into account the important report by UN Secretary-General Boutros Boutros Ghali, An Agenda for Peace, submitted to the Security Council on 17 June 1992. It is included as an appendix. Readers will be interested to note the high degree of convergence between the conclusions in our book and those of the Secretary-General.

CHAPTER 1
A problem and its dimensions

PETER CALVOCORESSI

What do you do, what are you entitled to do, and what ought you to do if you repeatedly hear your neighbours beating their children? Similar questions arise in international affairs.

For 'you' read 'the state'. The state is the outstanding feature and dominant actor on the international scene. It possesses identity, legitimacy, legal definition, machinery for taking decisions and the capacity for action. The international community consists of states, and for most people dissatisfaction with a particular state is expressed by wanting to belong to or create a different state.

The state is not a fact of nature but a product of history, more especially Western European history. It arose in a conflict over authority between the universal and the particular, a conflict in which popes and emperors claimed universal authority which the state successfully denied. The principal features of this state were natural frontiers and a communications system effective for the transmission of orders and despatch of troops. These features altered with time as geographical obstacles became less formidable and communications more efficient. Techniques of communication set the limits to the state's effective scope; techniques of war enabled the state to transcend these limits, if only temporarily. Underpinning the very existence of the state was the evolving doctrine of sovereignty which proclaimed the state's pre-eminence against universal pretensions and its absolute right to resist the encroachment of other states.

The European state has been copied throughout the world – even in modern China where an imperial universalism akin to that of medieval European popes and emperors has had a far longer life. An important part of the success of the European state has been its adaptability to changing circumstances: it has moved with the times. Its greatest test occurred in the early modern age. The medieval state was a piece of real estate more or less owned by its lord the king. Louis XIV of France famously declared that he was the state. This

1

claim was both correct and outdated. When a King's operations, notably wars, ceased to be financially viable, he was obliged to seek contributions from others, first from his immediate tenants and ultimately from his more numerous subjects or – as they began to style themselves – fellow citizens. At the point where he could levy these contributions only by making promises and concessions, the state, while it might remain a kingdom, ceased to be a monarchy. The modern state therefore acquired a new and necessary characteristic: it became a 'nation state'. The homogeneity implied by this definition was to be found practically nowhere, but the term adequately expresses the transition from a personal to a popular basis for the state's identity and legitimacy. This profoundly important switch blurred the outline of the state since a nation is only what some people say it is, but at the same time the nationalism of the nation state gave it fresh impetus and reinforced it both against other states and against assaults on its sovereignty from supra-state organisations or principles.

The heyday of the sovereign state lay between, at its beginning, the prevailing of the idea of the state over the idea of empire in the Middle Ages and, towards its conclusion, the resurrection of the idea that there is after all something above the state. This idea was never completely obliterated. It has been most persistently displayed in the laws of war which, although external to the state and 'above' it, have been accepted by the state in theory, even when not observed in practice. In a world comprising a multiplicity of states, war means mainly war between states: it must therefore be either unregulated or regulated by something other than the state. The laws of war – part product of judicial notions of natural law and part product of the rise of a bourgeoisie for which war meant the destruction of commercial opportunities – affirmed that the state was free neither to make war merely because it wished to nor to conduct war in any way it pleased.

These laws – *jus ad bellum* and *jus in bello* – are constraints on the rights and on the status of the state. What precisely the constraints are is the subject of debate which still continues, but that there are constraints has never been denied. With the passage of time and with the enormous changes in the impact of war on societies, the constraints formulated in medieval Europe ceased to satisfy. Whereas, for example, medieval *jus ad bellum* decreed that only the prince might make war (thus invalidating the use of violence to settle private feuds), modern international law seeks to restrict the rights not of subjects but of the state itself. The state has taken the place of feudatory baron as the object of necessary prohibition and, since 1945, the state's right to use violence otherwise than in self-defence has been transferred to the Security Council of the United Nations.

Simultaneously international conventions and international organisations have been developed, primarily in order to reduce the incidence of war in international affairs, on the grounds that war is evil and harmful. In doing so they have presented a creeping challenge to the sovereignty of the state, for if the state is not free to wage war when and how it pleases perhaps there may be other matters – including domestic behaviour – in which its own omnicompetence is limited in theory and ought to be restrained in practice.

Sovereignty is furthermore limited not only by law or custom but also in its appeal. Sovereignty relates to status and not to capacity, and without capacity status loses much of its savour (it is not so easy to enjoy a title if you do not have the income to go with it). Sovereignty is a legal notion and to a considerable degree a legal fiction. Like all legal fictions it serves a useful purpose by providing ground rules or touchstones, but by affirming that all states are sovereign and equally sovereign it purports to confer upon them something which most of them neither have nor can have: immunity from restraint or reproach and, in particular, immunity from interference in their domestic affairs. Such immunity, where it exists, derives not from sovereignty but from power. States with sovereignty but a deficiency of power have the right to do things which other states have the power to prevent them from doing, or the right to do things which they have never wanted to do or have ceased to want to do. These states – the majority – are less enamoured of sovereignty than their more powerful neighbours and the readier to cede, either temporarily or permanently, sovereign rights which they cannot exercise. (But weaker states which are also new tend to prize their sovereignty until they have the time to weigh appearances against realities.)

Nor are the weaker states alone in having to take account of the gap between the right to do something and the ability to do it. Even powerful states are constrained in the exercise of their sovereignty. A British chancellor of the exchequer, for instance, may insist on his right to raise or lower interest rates as he pleases but if he thinks that that is what he is doing he deludes himself (and others), for he cannot in practice ignore shifts in German interest rates and is normally obliged, however unwillingly, to raise British rates if German rates go up. Such restraints have become increasingly potent throughout the world ever since states came to be in permament contact with one another and particularly since the huge transformation in communications technology in this century (air transport, television, the fax machine, etc.). All of which shows that economic policies have become, like making war, an exercise of national rights which is subject to international interference.

Sovereignty therefore means different things to different states, because the exercise of sovereignty – sovereignty in action as distinct from sovereignty on paper – varies from state to state. It also varies from period to period. This variability is a function of changing circumstances which change the climate of opinion and so change the current interpretation of rules of law and of the legal instruments which express these rules. At any given moment the law is both static and mobile – static in the sense that it has objective prescriptive authority in terms to be made explicit by licensed interpreters (mainly judges), but also mobile in the sense that the interpretation is likely to vary with the climate of opinion: law is relative to the spirit of the times (as Montesquieu most notably argued) and laws fall into desuetude or are repeatedly violated unless they are adjusted by interpretation. So, on the particular issue of the division of authority between the state and international bodies, two sets of questions have to be examined: first, what are the legal rules and, secondly and no less significant, what is the political and cultural context in which the rules have to be interpreted and applied?

The Charter of the United Nations is a multilateral treaty voluntarily subscribed to by its original signatories and subsequent adherents. Because of the undoubted predominance of the state in international affairs the Charter is essentially a record of voluntary but permanent concessions by the state to the international body which is the creation of these states, and it affirms at the outset the fundamental immunity of the state to intervention in its domestic affairs, in these words:

> Nothing contained in the present Charter shall authorize the United Nations to intervene in matters which are essentially within the domestic jurisdiction of any state or shall require the Members [of the UN] to submit such matters to settlement under the present Charter; but this principle shall not prejudice the application of enforcement measures under Chapter VII (article 2(7)).

The UN Charter contains two other articles which need to be cited at this point. Its very first article defines 'the purposes of the United Nations' including:

> To achieve international cooperation in solving international problems of an economic, social, or humanitarian character, and in promoting and encouraging respect for human rights and fundamental freedoms for all without distinction as to race, sex, language or religion . . . (article 1(3)).

And article 55 reads, in part:

> With a view to the creation of conditions of stability and well-being which are necessary for peaceful and friendly relations among nations based on respect for the principle of equal rights and self-determination of peoples, the United Nations shall promote . . . (c) universal respect for, and observance of, human rights and fundamental freedoms for all without distinction as to race, sex, language or religion.

In neither of these articles is the obligation to 'promote' accompanied by any indication of how such things may legitimately *be* promoted. However, the articles and the whole tenor of the Charter demonstrate a serious and substantial intention actively to engage in the establishment and protection of human rights and this aspect of the commitment of the United Nations was reinforced a few years after its inauguration by the adoption without dissent of the Universal Declaration of Human Rights (1948). In the ensuing half-century a series of formal documents has further defined humanitarian law, international human rights law and the UN's role in promoting them: international humanitarian law applicable in armed conflict in the tradition of the Geneva and Hague Conventions; human rights law applicable in peace as well as war. The most notable documents in the latter category, the two Covenants on Civil and Political Rights and on Economic, Social and Cultural Rights, came into force in 1976. Moreover, the United Nations, in adopting these Covenants, did not rest content with their promulgation but charged the Human Rights Committee with monitoring the implementation of the first of them within member states by means of reports by states via the Economic and Social Council to the General Assembly and – where the optional protocol had also been accepted – individual complaints. And the Economic and Social Council has since set up a committee to consider similar reports on implementation of the latter Covenant. (The European Convention on Human Rights and the European Convention for the Prevention of Torture and Inhuman or Degrading Treatment contain provision for individual complaints and investigatory visits.)

The United Nations, like the League of Nations before it, has been regarded primarily as an instrument or mechanism for the prevention of wars. Both organisations were created in the immediate aftermath of a great and ghastly war and largely because of it. But the prevention of war is not an isolated or self-contained aim. It is part of a wider purpose. The essential horror of war is the killing and maiming and bereaving of people on a large scale but these evils are not confined to war. Their occurrence in other contexts is of equal international concern and has become more prominent and more pressing. One of the principal differences between the Covenant of the League and the Charter of the United Nations is the more specific and explicit concern of the latter with inhumanity outside war. The League of Nations was charged with specific obligations in relation to certain minorities but the Covenant of the League made no mention of human rights in its preamble, contained no articles such as those cited above from the UN Charter, and created no body equivalent to the UN's Economic and Social Council which in turn created the UN Human Rights Commission.

Immediately after the Second World War the wider purpose of preventing and castigating internationally recognised crimes against the person, whether perpetrated in war or not, was ventilated before the Nuremberg and Tokyo trials of major war criminals (and a number of other trials, notably the 12 trials conducted in the American zone of occupied Germany under Control Council Law No. 10). These proceedings were the judicial and forensic counter-part to the adoption of the UN Charter, a two-pronged attempt to affirm and apply rules of law in international affairs which had been so calamitously and horrifyingly broken in the 1930s and 1940s. After the Second World War some 10,000 individuals were brought before national and international tribunals on charges which related mainly, but not exclusively, to war crimes traditionally so called.

The defendants at Nuremberg, for example, were indicted on four counts. The first count alleged a common plan or conspiracy to commit the crimes particularised in the further counts and was designed as a comprehensive indictment of the entire Nazi regime and its principal figures from 1933 onwards. This count was followed by two more which amounted to modern versions of *jus ad bellum* and *jus in bello*: starting wars without just cause and waging war in contravention of the laws and customs of war. These charges rested, in the first case, principally on the Covenant of the League of Nations, the Kellogg–Briand Pact of 1928 (adhered to by 63 states by 1939) and numerous inter-war treaties, many of which had been adhered to by Germany; and, in the second case, on the Hague Conventions of 1899 and 1907 and the Geneva Conventions of 1925. There was also a fourth count charging crimes against humanity which was drafted with a view to incriminating individuals who had been guilty of murder, torture and other such crimes committed within as well as outside Germany and before as well as after the onset of war in 1939.

The Nuremberg Tribunal declared itself incompetent to entertain these last charges unless they were associated with charges under the other counts in the indictment – that is to say, unless the atrocities alleged could be shown to be part of the crime of planning and initiating aggressive war or the crime of misconducting the war. The Tribunal did not rule against the existence in law of crimes against humanity, or against the justiciability of such crimes before an international tribunal. It ruled that it was itself precluded by its own terms of reference from entertaining the charges. The Tribunal had been established *ad hoc* in 1945 by an agreement signed by the four principal anti-German allies and in exercise of the several sovereign rights of each of these states to establish courts; and it had been adhered to by 19 of Germany's foes. This agreement creating the Tribunal contained a charter defining the Tribunal's functions and competence. In the view of the Tribunal itself the charter was a declaratory instrument and not an attempt to make new law, but it was also a limiting instrument inasmuch as it restricted the Tribunal's role to those aspects of the law specifically mentioned in its charter. On this ground crimes against humanity, other than crimes committed after 1939 and in the prosecution of Germany's operations against its external enemies, fell outside the Tribunal's *ad hoc* jurisdiction.

If, however, a permanent international court with criminal jurisdiction were to be established, the category of crimes against humanity could, and should, be included in its standing terms of reference; at least so far as such crimes had been declared and defined in formal international instruments. The lack of a permanent court of this nature is a serious gap in the international system. However fair the conduct of the Nuremberg and Tokyo trials, and however just their sentences, the fact that the judges were chosen and appointed *ad hoc* and exclusively by and from victorious states was a flaw which the Tribunals could not escape. A permanent court composed of judges drawn from many countries and esteemed for their professional and personal qualities is a requirement of natural justice. Its competence would not be restricted to crimes committed in association with acts of international aggression. If, for example, such a court had been in existence, the unseemly proceedings in Kuwait against alleged quislings, which followed the recovery in 1991 of that country from its Iraqi invaders, might have been inhibited. (This is not to underrate the problems, practical and juridical, of creating and operating an international criminal court. In international cases the nostrum 'First catch your criminal' is peculiarly difficult to realise and a trial *in absentia* peculiarly unsatisfactory. Saddam Hussein, for example, might have been indicted before a competent court in 1991 or several years earlier and such a court might have decreed sanctions against Iraq in default of his surrender to justice. But this course would have come uncomfortably close to visiting the crimes of one man on numberless innocents.)

The course of events since the Nuremberg trials and the signing of the UN Charter has emphasised the lesson that international war is not necessarily the context in which the worst international crimes are committed and the worst international calamities are suffered. Since 1945 wars between states have been numerous – at least 150 by reputable calculations – but they have been matched in horror by domestic tyranny and civil war. The civil wars in Sudan alone have taken more than a million lives; the mere recital of the names of Idi Amin, Bokassa, Macias Nguema and Pol Pot suffices to make the point that Hitlerite atrocities need no war; and the stifled cries from hellish jails and police cells in South Africa, Iraq, Israel, China and elsewhere have rubbed in the lesson that forces of 'law and order' have killed, maimed and tortured people on a scale and with a barbarity comparable to the sufferings inflicted in the Vietnam, Iraq–Iran and Central American wars. These doings are clearly criminal, and since additionally they infringe specific international conventions, what – to revert to this chapter's initial questions – does the international community do, what is it entitled to do and what ought it to do?

The easiest answer is that, however horrible and however criminal these doings may be, they must be left to those within the boundaries of the states where they are perpetrated: in other words, suffer or rebel (which essentially was President George Bush's message to the Kurds in Iraq). The justifications for this attitude are well known and may be summed up by emphasising, first, that international affairs are sufficiently intractable without attempts to rectify wrongs of this kind and, secondly, that intervention against one established regime becomes an awkward precedent for unwelcome calls for intervention against another, or against oneself. Article 2(7) of the Charter is the outward and visible sign of this minimalist attitude. But article 2(7) has in practice been eroded or reinterpreted under the impact of events since its adoption in 1945. At that date it was widely, perhaps universally, believed that even inscription on the agenda of a UN body, let alone discussion, of a domestic matter was tabu. In effect, a state was entitled to get away with every kind of bad behaviour within its own borders. This view, immediately challenged at Nuremberg, was next and more successfully challenged by the opponents of apartheid in South Africa. Apartheid did not threaten international peace and might therefore be adjudged an essentially domestic matter. Some campaigners against it tried to maintain that it did endanger peace and should in consequence be put on the international agenda; but their arguments were more ingenious than compelling, and what forced a breach in the conventional interpretation of article 2(7) was not argument so much as outrage. The UN General Assembly and Security Council agreed to discuss apartheid because not to do so seemed an intolerable abdication of responsibility. (The arrival in the 1960s of many new black states at the United Nations was another factor. Not only did they have voices and votes; some also had clout because they occupied strategic locations or possessed crucial mineral resources. But the hostility to apartheid among whites was palpable even before this adventitious shove.) And the mere discussion of apartheid was followed by action in the shape of economic and other sanctions.

Article 2(7) was from the outset, and expressly, to have no operation in situations permitting 'enforcement measures' under Chapter VII of the Charter. Very soon its impact in other situations was likewise limited: as early as 1968 the United Kingdom declared that it would not invoke the article in any human rights context. Rationally these glosses on article 2(7) amounted to saying that the word 'domestic' was not to be interpreted as purely and simply geographical. An issue might cease to be 'essentially domestic' on account of its import and regardless of its location.

Yet article 2(7) remained potent. If it was no longer held to inhibit debate or invalidate economic and other sanctions, it was still regarded as a bar to more direct action. In 1979 Tanzania invaded Uganda to put an end to Idi Amin's activities. Virtually everybody thought this was a good thing. But in order to justify his action, Julius Nyerere invoked the right of self-defence under article 51 of the Charter which had nothing to do with the case. Nyerere felt he had to find a legal pretext for an act which on the face of it contravened article 2(7).

The deposition of Idi Amin by the apparently illicit use of external force was an embarrassing demonstration of the uncertainty concerning the UN's right to uphold the law in a particularly gruesome case. The Ugandan case was embarrassing because Idi Amin's behaviour, although abominable and illegal, appeared immune from external correction while Nyerere's intervention, although salutary, appeared illegal too. It was an act of war, and since 1945 acts of war not only required to be justified by *jus ad bellum* but, if undertaken by a state, were *a priori* illegal except in severely circumscribed circumstances (in effect self-defence, which was nowhere defined in the Charter). The Charter had transferred the right to make war from the state to the community of states, a bold step for which many were emotionally unprepared. The Charter did not outlaw war but it did go far towards outlawing war by the state. As a corollary the Charter promulgated machinery for the exercise of armed force by the United

Nations but the temper of the times – more specifically, the Cold War – vitiated this machinery with the result that the use of armed force in international affairs fell into a legal limbo: the state was not entitled to use it and the United Nations was neither equipped nor minded to do so. So radical a change as the abrogation of the state's right to make war – perhaps the most startling change in a thousand years of international intercourse – required a climate of exceptional, indeed unnatural, equanimity and collaboration among states. But what in fact transpired was the reverse: a period of intense and worldwide suspicion, mistrust and hostility between the super-powers, aggravated by a period of obsessive distrust between older and newer states. These conflicts – the Cold War and the North–South divide – turned the Security Council and the General Assembly of the United Nations into arenas for the prosecution of disputes in the worst style of *dialogues des sourds*. The United Nations could neither assume the responsibilities envisaged for it by the Charter nor grasp the nettle of re-examining the Charter in the light of a situation which was unforeseen. Nor is it reasonable to suppose that, given this situation, the United Nations would be likely to do otherwise.

But the situation has changed. The Cold War has abated to a point and for reasons which render its recrudescence in anything like its pristine form impossible. It is now evident that there are not two superpowers and that the bipolar world presupposed by Cold Warriors does not exist (and may never have existed). A 'great power' conflict, if one were to arise, must be entirely different from the Cold War of *circa* 1945–85. The bipolar pattern which dominated minds in the first post-war period has faded, not only because the leading powers are less militantly opposed to one another, but also because they are no longer two: they may be many or there may be only one, but they are not two. The rigidity of the bipolar pattern was the chief cause of the neutering of the United Nations, and the disappearance of this pattern, by restoring diplomatic mobility to the centre of international affairs, has simultaneously enhanced the use-fulness and relevance of international organisations. The interpret-ation of the Charter becomes a matter of practical importance instead of academic interest and politicians working at the United Nations acquire a common interest in arriving at a workable interpretation of its rules instead of tolerating inanition in a moth-balled organisation.

The North–South clash has abated too, at least for the time being. The multiplicity of new states resulting from decolonisation, most of them terribly poor and resentfully aware of the comparative wealth of older states, created a community of the poor which, dubbed the

Third World, was united by indignation as well as deprivation, and was ruled by leaders whose prime function was to get a better deal out of the rest of the world, and who regarded the United Nations as a route to a substantial redistribution of resources and a radical change in the rules set by the richer states for international commerce. The method chosen was solidarity and frontal assault combined with attempts to play one side in the Cold War off against the other. But the ensuing confrontation brought little gain to the new states: the Third World states, in spite of their common economic plight, proved insufficiently united (and not all the members were poor); the richer countries, particularly members of the European Community, learned to mitigate their irritation with what they regarded as unfair criticism; and the poorer learned the fruitlessness of reacting with obsessive and almost automatic scorn to whatever the richer proposed. Rational discourse gradually displaced simplistic attitudinising on both sides. By good fortune this shift from confrontation to debate, from challenge to haggling, coincided with the waning of the Cold War.

Together these two shifts have altered the climate of international affairs and have created opportunity. They are the necessary precondition for the examination of the problems posed in this chapter and pursued in the chapters which follow – problems central to the evolving distribution of authority between the state on the one hand and, on the other, international bodies created by states for purposes and with powers defined by states and voluntarily vested by states in the international body. The overriding purpose is to protect people, whether by preventing wars between states or civil wars or tyranny within states, and at the root of the discharge of these duties are two key concepts regulating the activities of the United Nations: the enforcement of international law including the law of the Charter, and non-intervention in a state's 'essentially domestic' affairs. The crux is the conflict between law enforcement and non-intervention.

Enforcement is the ultimate stage in intervention and the sanction through whose existence the purposes of intervention may be accelerated without enforcement. Non-forcible intervention is common and continuous, if often veiled or unavowed – diplomatic pressures, cultural boycotts, economic squeezes, discreet or not so discreet warnings or threats, sabre-rattling. But enforcement, overt coercion, is more than just a stage in intervention since the use of force transports international action on to a different plane. The Charter itself recognises the crucial distinction by separating the measures designated in Chapter VII into the two distinct articles 41 and 42. The dividing line is the use of military force against a member state. All members are obliged to comply with the measures prescribed by the Security

Council short of the use of force, but when it comes to force each member is entitled to abstain from participating. Hence the exceptional significance of Security Council resolution 688 of 5 April 1991 which, albeit without expressly invoking Chapter VII, is felt to have sanctioned international intervention within Iraq and led to the injection of armed forces into Iraq without its consent. This action at least suggested that its purpose – the protection of Iraqi Kurds, a humanitarian issue – might legitimately be pursued without invoking Chapter VII, at least explicitly, without posing a threat to international peace or security and without transgressing article 2(7).

The use of armed force by an organisation created primarily to avoid wars and keep the peace is inherently repugnant, but so too are the abdication of responsibility and the recoil from action in the face of inhumanity and breaches of international humanitarian laws. Intervention may proceed through non-coercive, non-violent stages but if ultimate steps are barred *ab initio* the sequence is atrophied, since an organisation committed to stopping after it has got half-way ceases to command or deserve respect or attention. The claim of the sovereign state to immunity from intervention in its essentially domestic affairs (whatever 'domestic' may be taken to mean at any given time) is deeply ingrained, hallowed by time, reinforced by propaganda and buttressed by vested interests. The enforcement of international law by intervening in a sovereign state, whether to stop or prevent a civil war or to stop officially organised or inspired brutality, has not as a rule been thought to be sufficient reason for breaching this immunity, but where the activities in question amount to breaches of law formally encoded and declared by competent international bodies and recognised juridical procedures, the question that arises is this: are illegal and criminal acts to be condemned and prohibited but not redressed or punished?

The United Nations is not a merely declaratory body. It is a political body which has by its very nature a role beyond codification and declaration. It has powers of intervention and enforcement specified in its Charter. But there is confusion over the exercise of these powers in certain situations: in particular, situations which have become, contrary to expectation, the most urgent instances of illegal and criminal behaviour by states and their officers – a development which has made human rights law as crucial, and the enforcement of human rights law as imperative, as the definition and application of the laws of war.

Crimes against humanity are nothing new, although the terms coined to describe them are new and so give an air of hazardous radicalism to attempts to tackle them. Crimes against humanity are crimes against the person (and perhaps also certain crimes against property and the environment) on a multiple scale and officially conceived and executed. Their location, domestic or external to the state accused, is secondary. Although frequently associated with breaches of international peace or with war-crimes strictly so called, they constitute a distinct swathe in international affairs. Their prevention and prosecution, as well as their definition, are matters of international concern and international competence. What is lacking is, first, any measure of how extensive a crime has to be before it passes from domestic to international purview; secondly, settled procedures and mechanisms for taking action, diplomatic or judicial or military, to forestall or redress such crimes; and finally, consensus regarding the effect in this sphere of article 2(7) of the Charter and its reconciliation with the UN's obligations, formulated elsewhere in the Charter and subsequently, in relation to human rights.

CHAPTER 2

Collective intervention to protect human rights and civilian populations: the legal framework

NIGEL S. RODLEY

There are two kinds of situation that pose the question whether the organised international community must stand aside and leave hapless populations to an appalling fate or whether it may step in to rescue them. The first is where populations are subjected to an unconstrained terror visited on them by their governments, for example, the Cambodians under the Khmer Rouge in the late 1970s. The second is where populations are at the mercy of an anarchy unleashed by the collapse of government, as happened in the Lebanon at about the same time. The question raised by the first type of situation can be restated as asking: when, if at all, may the violation of human rights justify external collective intervention? The question raised by the second situation may be formulated as asking: when, if at all, may the absence of government justify collective action to restore order? This chapter aims to assess the legal issues relevant to answering these questions. It will concentrate on the first of these, but give some consideration also to the second. Its main focus will be on collective action through the United Nations, especially enforcement action undertaken or authorised by the Security Council. While reference will be made to the debate on the lawfulness of 'humanitarian intervention' undertaken by one state or a group of states, no attempt will be made to resolve the debate. Similarly, reference will be made to instances of intervention by regional inter-governmental organisations, but no full examination of their lawfulness will be undertaken, other than in situations where the United Nations may authorise or otherwise offer legitimation of such intervention.

Four articles of the Charter of the United Nations may be said to

14

be the pillars of the UN structure and are relevant to our inquiry. Two of them are addressed to individual states:

Article 2(4):

All Members shall refrain in their international relations from the threat or use of force against the territorial integrity or political independence of any state, or in any other manner inconsistent with the Purposes of the United Nations.

Article 51:

Nothing in the present Charter shall impair the inherent right of individual or collective self-defence if an armed attack occurs against a Member of the United Nations, until the Security Council has taken measures necessary to maintain international peace and security . . .

The other two articles are addressed to the United Nations itself:

Article 39:

The Security Council shall determine the existence of any threat to the peace, breach of the peace, or act of aggression and shall make recommendations, or decide what measures shall be taken in accordance with Articles 41 and 42, to maintain or restore international peace and security.

Article 2(7):

Nothing contained in the present Charter shall authorize the United Nations to intervene in matters which are essentially within the domestic jurisdiction of any state or shall require the Members to submit such matters to settlement under the present Charter; but this principle shall not prejudice the application of enforcement measures under Chapter VII.

For our purposes the questions raised by these articles are: when, if at all, can coercive action (or the threat thereof) directed at a state and aimed solely at the protection of the civil population of that state, not be considered a threat or use of force 'against the territorial integrity or the political independence' of the target state? Are human rights problems matters falling 'essentially within the domestic jurisdiction of any state'? To the extent that they are, what actions constitute improper 'intervention' in such matters? In any event, can a situation characterised by human rights violations amount to a threat to international peace and security sufficient to justify enforcement action by the Security Council? This is a problem of interpretation.

One of the reasons the problem has eluded a generally agreed answer is that the very criteria of interpretation are unclear, with no definite weight to be given to each of them. This is partly because the issues straddle the two principal sources of international law. These sources are, first, customary (or general) international law, and, secondly, treaty (or conventional) law. The principles contained in Charter articles 2(4) (non-use of force against a state), 51 (right to self-defence) and 2(7) (non-intervention in internal affairs) are commonly and authoritatively held not only to be what they are *prima facie*, that is rules laid down by a particular treaty (the Charter itself), but also to reflect rules of customary international law, binding on all states in the international community.[1] Indeed, they may well be rules of *jus cogens*, that is, rules of customary international law that may not be varied by special agreement between states. Also, because the Charter serves a special purpose, namely being the organic instrument of the organised world community – a sort of constitution of the world – it is, in any event, thought to have a status distinct from that of an ordinary treaty. This leads to the notion that the canons for its interpretation should be more analogous to those used at the national level, to interpret national constitutions, than to those used to interpret statutes or contracts, which the ordinary rules for treaty interpretation more closely resemble.

It is easier to describe the elements that go into determining a rule of customary international law than those applicable to the interpretation of a treaty rule. One simply looks at state practice – consisting of official acts *and* statements – to determine whether a particular pattern of behaviour (the practice) is engaged in with sufficient uniformity and consistency and is explained in terms appropriate to consider the practice as one dictated by or in accordance with a rule of law (*opinio juris*). The problem – and it is a formidable one – is to make messy, political reality fall comfortably within these notions.

It is harder to describe the elements that go into the interpretation of treaties, even though treaties are often held to have the merit, being in black and white, of circumventing the difficulties of establishing the existence or scope of a rule of customary international law. The words of a treaty article need to be considered on their own and in the context of the treaty as a whole; the object and purpose of the treaty may be relevant, as may state practice at the time the treaty was concluded and even state practice *after* its conclusion.[2] On the other hand, it may be understood that, subject to certain exceptions that do not concern us here,[3] state practice that is manifestly irreconcilable with the words of a treaty cannot be seen as being an aid to interpretation of the treaty; indeed the practice will probably be seen as violating it.

It will be seen immediately that state practice is *a* key element in the interpretation of ambiguous treaty provisions, as well as *the* key element in determining a rule of customary international law. Furthermore, as far as the UN Charter is concerned, it has been understood from the time of its drafting, that the United Nations itself and, indeed, each of its organs would have the responsibility of interpreting the Charter. The analysis of state practice both within and outside the United Nations will therefore be central to the consideration of our problem.

Human rights and domestic jurisdiction traditionally

While article 2(7) is formulated in terms applicable to the United Nations as a body, it contains a notion with deep antecedents in international law. As international law evolved in Europe, it was that body of rules applicable to the relations of sovereigns with each other. Those relations did not traditionally encompass the relationship of the sovereign with his (or occasionally her) subjects. That was something within the *domaine réservé* of the state. It is true that Grotius would not have given an unreservedly free hand to the sovereign,[4] influenced as he was by doctrines of natural and church law, but the positivism of the eighteenth and nineteenth centuries relegated his caveats to the realm more of nostalgia or, at best, political aspiration than accepted law – at any rate as far as governments were concerned. It is also true that in the nineteenth century the movement against slavery, the very origins of the modern human rights movement, succeeded in limiting international legal acquiescence in the slave trade. The post-First World War twentieth century saw the conclusion of the 1926 Slavery Convention aimed at abolishing slavery and the establishment of the International Labour Organisation. The latter especially was a major breakthrough, as it clearly concerned itself with what had previously been an internal social (and human rights) problem. On the other hand, not too much should be made of the minorities treaties which clearly only protected certain minorities as part of a political adjustment of frontiers to secure the peace. Nor were the human rights clauses of the mandate system much more than a political price for the transfer of control over colonial territories from one metropolitan power to another. Subject to these exceptions, human rights remained throughout the League of Nations period, in the language of article 15(8) of its Covenant, 'solely within the domestic jurisdiction' of individual states. Whether this meant that unilateral armed intervention was thereby ruled out will be considered in the following section.

The human rights clauses of the UN Charter quoted in the introductory chapter, together with article 56, laid the basis for a radical review of the role of human rights in international relations. UN members were now pledged 'to take joint and separate action in cooperation with the Organization' (article 56) for the achievement of 'universal respect for, and observance of, human rights and fundamental freedoms for all' (article 55). The issue of human rights as such was now a matter of international concern. It did not necessarily follow that the human rights situation in any particular country was a legitimate subject of international action or even examination. After all, whereas Covenant article 15(8) had excluded the League Council from making recommendations on matters 'solely' within states' domestic jurisdiction, the Charter, within whose purview entered a broad array of economic and social matters, including human rights, by article 2(7) relieved states from having to submit to settlement under the Charter matters 'essentially' within domestic jurisdiction. A potential broadening of the *domaine réservé* seems to have been contemplated here. Moreover, the Charter drafters had eschewed explicit reference to the protection of human rights as opposed to its promotion.[5]

The early practice of the United Nations clearly veered towards a broad interpretation of the 'domestic jurisdiction' rule and a narrow interpretation of the human rights promotion clauses. Thus, the first two decades of the organisation were characterised by a strict practice by which private complaints could not be formally debated, much less acted upon, even by the UN Commission on Human Rights.[6] And states were comprehensively inhibited – probably on a mixture of legal and political grounds – from submitting each other's human rights sins to debate or scrutiny.

There were occasional exceptions. There was discussion of Franco's Spain in the early days of the United Nations. The association of that state under that government with the Axis powers, against which the allies who formed the United Nations had fought, was invoked to justify the raising of the issue as a matter of international peace and security, not just an internal Spanish one.[7] Consideration by UN organs of other human rights questions, such as Hungary (1956) and Tibet (1959), was in the context of external armed intervention against those countries. When, in 1963, the General Assembly sent a team to inquire into human rights issues in South Vietnam, it was at the request of the government of that country which was not a UN member. There was also consideration of human rights issues, pursuant to Chapters XI and XII of the UN Charter, in non-self-governing and trust territories and, eventually, other colonial territories. As far as the UN majority was concerned, interest in the human rights situation had to stop, however, once self-determination had been achieved. The only coercive action to have been undertaken, towards the end of this period, was the embargo ordered by the Security Council against Rhodesia after its unilateral declaration of independence (UDI) in 1965. Even here the action was justified on the dual and related basis that the UDI was not a proper act of self-determination and the 'lawful' UK government itself sought the action. The final relevant exception was that of South Africa, an independent founder member of the United Nations. The situation there was subjected to sporadic debate from as early as 1946 (in respect of its Indian population) and later as regards the apartheid system, which was itself portrayed as a threat to international peace and security. This notion will be returned to later.

Outside the United Nations, inter-governmental concern for human rights was being manifested within the Council of Europe and the Organization of American States (OAS). Action in the former centred on the conclusion of the European Convention on Human Rights (1950) and its implementation. Here it has to be noted that only states party to the Convention were to be subject to its rules and implementation machinery. And even such states parties did not have to respond to individual complaints unless, by making a special declaration (under article 15 of the Convention), they chose to do so; nor could cases be submitted to the Court without a further optional declaration being made under article 46. In the OAS, an Inter-American Commission on Human Rights was set up in 1959, like the UN Commission it had a promotional, rather than a protective function. In the 1960s, however, it started taking up individual cases, despite the absence of a mandate to do so; the mandate followed in 1967.[8]

Up to the mid-1970s little serious claim was made for a legal right of individual states to take up human rights issues bilaterally in other jurisdictions. There might be the occasional *démarche*, usually not made public, and probably couched in terms that refrained from claiming a legal right to intercede. Indeed, the informality of such initiatives – probably the rule rather than the exception up to the late 1980s – tends to confirm a lack of consensus as to the availability of a legal basis to intercede, at least about individual cases. Certainly, countries likely to receive such *démarches* were no more willing at the bilateral than at the multilateral level to admit a *right* of other states to scrutinise their human rights performance.

Human rights and intervention traditionally

If human rights issues traditionally fell within a state's domestic jurisdiction, it might be thought to be axiomatic that other states could not intervene, in the sense of taking coercive action or even otherwise expressing formal interest in a particular human rights situation. Yet there are examples of state practice and written doctrine tending to argue for the existence, at any rate until early in the present century, of a claimed right of humanitarian intervention to protect oppressed populations, particularly where the oppression was characterised by widespread killing. Most of the interventions in question involved the protection of Christian populations in the eastern Mediterranean from apparent oppression by Turkish rulers. The basis for the doctrine of humanitarian intervention has never been clear. It was more a response triggered by a humanitarian impulse to alleviate a human disaster than an attempt to uphold individual *rights* as against the oppressive state authorities. It can probably best be founded, if at all, on the notion of a need to take account of fundamental 'laws of humanity and the dictates of the public conscience',[9] a sort of extralegal or metalegal notion somehow aimed at reconciling the rigours of the law with the irresistible demand of a conflicting morality. No doubt an important condition for the justifiability of the doctrine resided in the fact that, before the 1928 Pact of Paris (Kellog–Briand Pact), the law did not, in any event, prohibit unilateral resort to war as a means for settling disputes between states. Interestingly, there were doubts even at the time about the legal propriety of such interventions, these being reflected in a tendency for the interventions to be made by a number of states as a means of shoring up the legitimacy of the actions.

Meanwhile, the extent to which the interventions were free from challenge on their own moral–legal grounds has been questioned. Usually, only certain minorities seemed to be able to benefit from the doctrine (e.g. the Christian populations mentioned above); only certain (stronger) powers could apply it (e.g. the large, Christian European powers); only certain (weaker) powers could be subjected to it (e.g. the Sublime Porte); the interventions usually had the effect (and therefore the purpose?) of advancing the broader political/strategic interests of the intervening state(s) at the expense of those of the target state; and, especially tellingly, there were numerous atrocities that were blithely overlooked by potential rescuing states (e.g. the Jews in Europe and Armenians in Turkey) – often precisely on the formal grounds that these were domestic matters![10]

Assuming the earlier existence of a doctrine of humanitarian intervention, the question arises whether it survived the conclusion of the UN Charter. This has been the subject of vigorous academic debate. Those who would defend the doctrine[11] argue that UN Charter article 2(4) does not prohibit a 'pure' humanitarian intervention, as such an intervention does not constitute an assault on the territorial integrity or political independence of the affected state. Article 51 should not be read as restricting any unilateral use of force to self-defensive purposes. A number of interventions could best be justified by the doctrine, notably those of India in Bangladesh, of Tanzania in Uganda, of Vietnam in Kampuchea, of the United States and members of the Organization of Eastern Caribbean States in Grenada and of the United States in Panama.

Opponents of the doctrine[12] contend that Charter article 2(4) intended to encompass the inviolability of national frontiers, leaving self-defensive operations, individual or collective, as the only permitted basis of unilateral resort to armed force. They consider as corroboration of this view the language and thrust of the 1970 General Assembly Declaration on the Principles of International Law Concerning Friendly Relations and Cooperation among States in Accordance with the Charter of the United Nations (General Assembly resolution 2625 (XXV), 24 October 1970): paragraph 1 of the Declaration explicitly defines the language of Charter article 2(4) to mean that '[e]very State has the duty to refrain from the threat or use of force to violate the existing international boundaries of another State . . .' World Court dicta condemning earlier policies of intervention – in general terms in the *Corfu Channel* case, in terms straightforwardly applicable to humanitarian intervention in the *Nicaragua* case[13] – are further cited. So are the actual justifications for the interventions mentioned offered by the intervening states; these tend to refrain from explaining the interventions as being aimed at protecting the human rights of the population of the state intervened against. Moreover, the comprehensive denunciations of most of the interventions by the General Assembly are seen as further indications of the general *opinio juris* on the matter. The misgivings about who could intervene against whom and the bases for the selection of appropriate cases for intervention remained a source of scepticism about the asserted doctrine. Finally, to the extent that the United Nations was itself held to be debarred from considering, without the agreement of the state in question, any specific human rights situation, it seemed subversive of the world order system it embodied to permit individual states to take the extreme action of armed intervention.

Developments in the doctrine of domestic jurisdiction regarding human rights

While there remain protagonists, especially among affected governments, of the traditional strict doctrine that a human rights problem concerns none but the state where it takes place, this is becoming an increasingly eccentric position. Until recently it was sturdily defended by the Soviet Union and its allies with general but not uniform and largely tacit support from the so-called Group of 77 (G77). Yet even before the fundamental changes in Eastern Europe in 1989, multilateral and bilateral practice had evolved significantly.

Parallel with, and probably as a result of, G77 pressure to take up the human rights situation in South Africa, the UN Commission on Human Rights, in 1967, sought and obtained authorisation to consider 'consistent patterns of gross violations of human rights'.[14] While it was decided in 1970 that private complaints had to be considered in closed sessions,[15] states could call publicly for studies on systematic, serious human rights violations in specific countries. Thus, in 1967, the Commission set up an *ad hoc* working group of experts on southern Africa, whose mandate included territories still entitled to self-determination (i.e. the Portuguese colonies, Rhodesia and South-West Africa), as well as South Africa itself. Pending the establishment of the General Assembly's own 'Special Committee of Three' to consider the human rights situation in the Territories occupied by Israel during the 1967 'Six-Day War', the Commission's *ad hoc* working group on southern Africa undertook this task for a year. By definition, such territories could not be considered as falling within a state's domestic jurisdiction. It was not until 1975 that the next study was mounted: an investigation into the human rights situation in Chile after the 1973 military coup. This was the first case where there was no suggestion of any transborder implications of the situation or even an express claim that it threatened (directly or otherwise) international peace and security. Over the years a further 10 such studies were initiated. Even then, the studies would only include on-the-spot investigations where the consent of the affected government was obtained.

In 1980 the Commission began developing 'thematic' mechanisms to study particularly grave violations of human rights, which were empowered to engage governments in dialogue about individual cases of alleged 'disappearance' (1980), summary or arbitrary execution (1982), or torture (1985). By 1986 there was a mechanism on the, arguably, less gross problem of religious intolerance and in 1991 a working group on arbitrary detention was established.[16] The mechanisms report annually and publicly to the Commission on their communications with governments. In general, they do not make formal findings of fact and, like the country studies, only visit relevant countries with their agreement. Meanwhile, the UN's 1966 International Covenants on Human Rights came into force in 1970 and have now been adhered to by over 100 states, half of which have ratified the Optional Protocol to the International Covenant on Civil and Political Rights; this allows the Human Rights Committee to consider individual complaints of violations committed by states party to the Protocol.

So UN practice has put states' actual human rights practices ever more persistently on the organisation's agenda, albeit with the limitation that no direct action not agreed to by the offending government can be undertaken. Indeed, it is difficult to conceive of anything more calculated to undermine the still fragile consensus behind these mechanisms (G77 countries have evinced a distinct restiveness about them in the last two or three years) than to portray them as a basis for potential coercive action should the human rights situation not improve. This would be true even of coercive action falling short of resort to armed force.

The legal basis for the action (beyond that provided for in the Covenants in respect of states parties) is unclear. It used to be argued that such action was incompatible with respect for Charter article 2(7). How has it now become compatible? One possible answer could be that the nature or extent of the human rights violations could at least potentially threaten international peace and security; and since enforcement action by the Security Council could override the 'domestic jurisdiction' bar in such a case, action short of enforcement should be permissible, as a means of averting enforcement. This is not an analysis likely to command the support of most UN members at this stage. A more likely explanation is that the notion of 'intervention' has changed so as to exclude non-coercive action from its scope. Thus, discussion, study, findings of fact, expressions of opinion and the making of recommendations would not amount to intervention ruled out by article 2(7). This begs the question of why only certain human rights violations, characterised by the gravity of their nature or extent, should be subject to such activity. A third explanation is that (at least serious) human rights violations have simply become over the years matters of international concern and no longer ones 'essentially within the domestic jurisdiction' of states. The second and third explanations may well both capture some of the reality of current UN practice.

There have been developments also at the regional level. Already, after the European Convention on Human Rights came into force, with virtually all of the Council of Europe's member states eventually adhering to the Convention, any state party could make a complaint against another such party. In practice, such conflicts have been the exception rather than the rule. However, the optional individual complaints procedure has flourished. Under the OAS system, the Inter-American Commission on Human Rights has, since the 1960s, been able to take up cases and situations of human rights violations even at the motion of the Commission. More recently, the human rights performance of a majority of members of the Organisation of African Unity (OAU), namely those that are party to the African Charter on Human and Peoples' Rights, is potentially subject to (confidential) scrutiny by the Commission set up under that Charter. The radical changes in Eastern Europe are epitomised by the human rights procedures now in place under the Conference on Security and Cooperation in Europe (CSCE).[17]

Although still meeting with some resistance, the practice initiated by US President Jimmy Carter and, at first nervously and then more systematically, emulated by other Western countries, of interceding bilaterally on cases and situations of apparent human rights violations, has developed into the stuff of routine' international discourse. This has been reinforced by actions of the European Community through its machinery of European Political Cooperation (EPC).

It is now, therefore, difficult as a matter of law to sustain the thesis that human rights matters are still not matters of international concern.

Developments in the doctrine of (non-)intervention regarding human rights

The doctrine of non-intervention encompasses more than mere non-intervention on human rights grounds (assuming such intervention to have been prohibited at least in the early post-Charter era). It was based on the notion that the internal political, economic and social structure and practices of a state were no other state's formal business. Thus, the use of force to affect any such matter was the extreme example of impermissible intervention against the 'political independence' of the state. Similarly, states could not interfere in 'civil strife' in another state.[18] There remained, and remains, some doubt as to whether assisting a government to maintain public order constituted a violation of the non-intervention principle, with the absence of external assistance to insurrectionary groups.

There is some current state practice that could perhaps be invoked to justify an embryonic exception to this broadly conceived non-intervention rule. This relates to states where the total fabric of government has collapsed, leading to situations characterised by anarchy, violence and non-protection of national or foreign rights. The principal exemplars would be the Arab League-authorised Syrian intervention in the Lebanon, the ill-fated OAU intervention in Chad and the intervention by the Economic Community of West African States (ECOWAS) in Liberia. It must be noted that these are all regional, not unilateral, interventions by organisations of which the target state is a member.

In this connection, the civil war in Yugoslavia merits attention. For, at one point, some members of the Western European Union (WEU) were contemplating similar intervention in that country. The WEU, comprising the militarily strongest members of the European Community (EC), was being portrayed as the 'military arm' of the EC. In the event, the WEU was persuaded, on practical rather than legal grounds, that armed intervention without the acquiescence of the warring parties would not be appropriate. Had the WEU gone ahead with such action, it could have raised questions about the legal propriety of a regional body, of which the target state was not a member, imposing its will. It might have been arguable that the support given by the CSCE for EC initiatives (Yugoslavia is a CSCE member) provided the necessary acquiescence or legitimation. Given that the CSCE is not a legal entity, that none of its principal instruments (Helsinki Final Act, Vienna Concluding Document, Document of the Moscow Meeting) envisages the relevant powers of intervention and that it qualifies dubiously as a regional arrangement or agency within the meaning of UN Charter Chapter VIII (which by article 43 requires Security Council authorisation for enforcement action), it would have been a strained argument. In the event, the problem eventually came before the Security Council with the support of Yugoslavia. The Security Council unanimously adopted resolution 713 (1991) on 25 September 1991, again with Yugoslav support as expressed by its foreign minister. The resolution expressed support for the initiatives undertaken by the EC member states 'with the support of' the CSCE member states. Its most far-reaching provision was the establishment of an arms embargo on Yugoslavia under Chapter VII of the Charter. Several Council members, including India, Zimbabwe and the potential veto-wielding China, made it clear that they were only prepared to discuss the problem, never mind approve the resolution, because Yugoslavia wanted it.[19] Even then, there were several pious and largely unsubstantiated incantations about the transborder consequences of continued fighting, for example, the generating of refugees. It is relevant that the resolution itself refers in its preamble to both the Yugoslav welcome for the convening of the meeting and 'the consequences for the countries of the region, in particular in the border areas of neighbouring countries'. It is also notable that the reference to Chapter VII is only contained in the paragraph imposing the arms embargo, implicitly denying Chapter VII 'cover' to its other provisions.

On the other hand, we are left with a resolution, dealing with a civil war with very limited direct transborder effects, which depicts the Security Council as 'concerned that the continuation of this situation constitutes a threat to international peace and security' (i.e.

not an express determination that such a threat existed). It also 'recalls' Chapter VIII (regional arrangements) of the Charter.

A similar example was presented in the case of Somalia's civil war between factions of the forces that overthrew the repressive government of President Mohammed Siad Barre. Here again the Security Council, by resolution 733 (1992), established a Chapter VII-based 'embargo on all deliveries of weapons and military equipment to Somalia until the Security Council decides otherwise'. The Council meeting was convened at Somalia's request, a fact noted in the first preambular paragraph of the resolution. Another preambular paragraph expressed the Council's concern (in the same language that it used for Yugoslavia) 'that the continuation of this situation constitutes . . . a threat to international peace and security'. By way of support for this, reference was made to the 'consequences on [sic] the stability and peace in the region' of 'the rapid deterioration of the situation . . . and the heavy loss of human life and widespread material damage resulting from the conflict in the country' and to an unidentified (presumably oral) report of the Secretary-General. There were indeed substantial refugee flows to neighbouring countries.

Clearly neither of these initiatives would have been possible without the support of recognised authorities of the Yugoslav and Somali governments. Whether in future such support will always be necessary is speculative. What if only one side in such a conflict favoured the action and the accredited diplomats favoured that side, or if the diplomats were silent, or the collapse of the country were such that there were no authorities capable of issuing acceptable credentials? Would the Security Council have to close its eyes to the situation? The probable answer now is 'yes', but the Yugoslav and Somali experiences could pave the way for a more flexible approach in future.

So, the evolution of a permitted exception to the non-intervention rule evidenced by these cases, where the intervention is aimed at restoring government, an essential element of full statehood, rather than determining the nature or policies of a particular government, can be envisaged. Indeed, it is not unconnected with the doctrine of humanitarian intervention to protect human rights: first, many of the worst situations in human rights terms are characterised by intense civil strife, with the authorities resorting to human rights violations as part of a counter-insurgency strategy; second, the relevance of the humanitarian motive to protect ordinary people from the depredations of those using force is potentially common to both types of intervention. But there are sufficient conceptual differences to suggest separate treatment of the two forms of intervention. The obvious one is that 'humanitarian intervention' (i.e. to protect human rights) normally posits the existence of a government with a substantial amount of power over a substantial population. It is likely to be able to offer organised military resistance to outside intervention. Yet, it may also be noted that a situation bearing the hallmarks of grave human rights violations 'justifying' external intervention could evolve into one of institutional collapse similarly 'justifying' such intervention. Here it should be noted only that the evolution of one exception to the non-intervention rule could have an impact on the evolution of the other. The same could also be thought of as applying in the case of the postulated idea of a right to outside intervention to provide necessary disaster relief to populations whose own governments cannot or do not provide it.[20]

As far as humanitarian intervention to protect human rights is concerned, we have already seen that even recent manifestations of armed intervention, arguably justifiable on human rights protection grounds if hardly actually so justified by the intervening states, have been generally overwhelmingly condemned by the organised community of states. This was even true of the Grenada intervention where a regional organisation was involved in the operation.

This does not necessarily mean that a regional organisation could not undertake or authorise an armed humanitarian intervention. Even while making clear its rejection of such unilateral intervention, the World Court in the *Nicaragua* case was at pains to underline the powers of the OAS to act. Of course, it did not spell out the limits of any such action.[21] Presumably that would partly depend on the powers of the organisation in question. It is nevertheless hard to see how it would happen without Security Council authorisation under article 43.

Could not the United Nations then engage in coercive action to protect human rights? As has already been seen, the United Nations has traditionally tended to consider human rights as a matter of domestic jurisdiction. The post-war discussion of Spain and the discussion of and adoption of resolutions on South Africa were exceptions that served to prove the rule. So were the discussions and resolutions on non-self-governing territories, given the artificial claim to domestic jurisdiction in respect of colonies. In any event, we have seen more recently that serious human rights situations as regards numerous other countries have also come to be discussable to the point of adopting resolutions. What the exceptions did signify, however, was that some human rights situations were of sufficient import as to cause them to be treated as affecting, or potentially affecting, international peace and security.

Indeed, this conception of the apartheid system in South Africa led the Security Council in 1977 to invoke Chapter VII of the UN

Charter to impose a mandatory embargo on military and nuclear collaboration with South Africa (resolution 418 (1977), 4 November 1977). Five days earlier the Council had expressed grave concern over 'reports of torture of political prisoners and the deaths of a number of detainees, as well as the mounting wave of repression against individuals, organisations and the news media' and the conviction that 'the violence and repression by the South African racist regime have greatly aggravated the situation and will certainly lead to violent conflict and racial conflagration with serious international repercussions' (resolution 417 (1977), 31 October 1977). The death that September of Black Consciousness Movement leader Steve Biko had been plainly relevant.

Especially remarkable about this initiative was that it had taken place after a spectacular deterioration in the *internal* human rights situation. Although its preamble referred to external acts and external effects of internal acts, it had not been incited by some recent South African military action against opponents in neighbouring countries. In other words, the final clause of Charter article 2(7) ('this principle shall not prejudice the application of enforcement measures under Chapter VII') had served to legitimate enforcement action aimed at redressing a human rights problem. That internal problem was, therefore, at least a threat to international peace and security. The fact that the action was not, and has never become, armed action is juridically almost beside the point. As an abstract proposition, if a human rights situation can amount to a threat to international peace and security, thus permitting the Council to take enforcement action to remedy the situation, there is nothing in article 2(7) restricting the enforcement action to measures short of the use of force.

Yet it was not until 1991 that the United Nations came close to acting on the basis of this concept. The political and military, as well as remaining powerful legal, inhibitions will be considered after we have considered Security Council resolution 688 (1991) of 5 April 1991.

Security Council resolution 688

The circumstances in which Iraqi President Saddam Hussein's military machine, comprehensively defeated by coalition forces in its attempt to annex Kuwait, reasserted its prowess by turning its guns on the armed and unarmed insurgent Kurdish and Shia populations, resulting in the mass refugee flows towards and into Turkey and Iran, together with the appalling attendant suffering, are described in detail in Chapter 3. It was these circumstances that were invoked by Turkey and France to justify the convening of the 2982nd Security Council meeting which took place on 5 April 1991. The meeting discussed a draft resolution submitted by Belgium and France, with the United Kingdom and the United States subsequently joining as co-sponsors. The text was adopted unamended at the meeting, to become resolution 688 (1991). It was the least widely supported of all the resolutions until then adopted by the Council in response to the Kuwait crisis. Ten members voted in favour, three voted against (Cuba, Yemen and Zimbabwe) and two abstained (China and India). Nine votes were required for adoption, including the 'concurring' votes of the five permanent members. Whether an abstention could be considered as concurring, a controversial question in the early years of the United Nations, is now not seriously disputed, and not at all by the permanent members themselves. So there can be no credible cavil at the formal validity of the resolution.

Nearly all the statements made by Council members at the meeting,[22] however, addressed the precise topic at issue in this chapter: would resolution 688 be *ultra vires* the Council by virtue of dealing with a matter pertaining to Iraq's domestic jurisdiction, rather than with a threat to international peace and security? Iraq and those voting against the resolution argued vigorously that the human rights and humanitarian concerns addressed by the draft resolution and invoked by its protagonists were beyond the purview of the Security Council and their very discussion was incompatible with Charter article 2(7), although they might be appropriate for consideration by other organs (that is, implicitly, organs not empowered to render binding decisions, much less to take enforcement action). Yemen, in particular, lamented the 'dangerous precedent' that adoption of the draft resolution would set. The Yemeni representative continued:

> We wonder what State, big or small, has no internal problems; what State will not at some point in time encounter internal difficulties and experience transborder problems? In our opinion, the text of the draft resolution is a first departure from the rule of maintaining a strict focus on the Council's responsibilities under the Charter.

For China, also, article 2(7) meant that 'the Security Council should not consider or take action on questions concerning the internal affairs of any State. As for the international aspects involved in the question . . . they should be settled through the appropriate channels.' This language could have justified a negative vote. India was more nuanced. Referring to the consultations that had preceded the presentation to the Council of the actual text of the draft resolution, the Indian representative noted:

Our endeavour was to focus the attention of the Council on the aspect of the threat or likely threat to peace and stability in the region rather than on the factors that have created the present situation. We believe that the Council should have concentrated on the aspect of peace and security, which is its proper mandate under the Charter, and left other aspects to other, more appropriate organs of the United Nations.

Those in favour of the resolution argued that the situation was, indeed, a threat or potential threat to international peace and security. While some underlined mainly the human rights aspects of the problem, with France considering them to amount to a 'crime against humanity', most pointed also to the mass refugee problem and its effect – the 'transboundary impact' in the words of the US representative – on the receiving states, especially Turkey and Iran. Some also referred to resultant 'destabilising' effects on the region in general. For Romania, also anxious not to create a precedent susceptible to later political abuse, this was a 'special case in the aftermath of the Gulf War'. It fell to the United Kingdom to make the point that article 2(7), 'an essential part of the Charter, does not apply to matters which, under the Charter, are not essentially domestic, and we have often seen human rights – for example in South Africa – defined in that category'.

There is virtually nothing in the statements of protagonists, antagonists or abstainers spelling out what language in resolution 688 raises the problems at stake. Indeed, the second preambular paragraph recalls article 2(7) and the third refers even to the existence of 'cross-border incursions' as part of the resolution's *considéranda*. (Turkey had referred to mortar shells landing on her side of the border and Iran had, in a letter to the Council,[23] referred to the shelling of an Iranian border town and the deaths of three border guards.) Moreover, nothing in the text requires or directly authorises any enforcement action. And statements by some supporting the resolution, describing the situation as a *potential* threat to international peace and security, may have been intended to imply the view that they considered this to be a Chapter VI question. What then was offensive about the resolution?

Problems doubtless began with the first operative paragraph whereby the Council:

> *Condemns* the repression of the Iraqi civilian population in many parts of Iraq, including most recently in Kurdish populated areas, the consequences of which threaten international peace and security in the region.

The accent is clearly on the internal repression, rather than on its external consequences. Effectively then, an internal human rights problem, from the geographic point of view, albeit with external consequences, is being considered a threat to international peace and security, the pre-condition for action under Chapter VII of the Charter, although nowhere in the resolution is Chapter VII expressly invoked. (But then, neither is Chapter VI.) Operative paragraph 2 builds on this. By it, the Council:

> *Demands* that Iraq, as a contribution to removing the threat to international peace and security in the region, immediately end this repression and expresses the hope in the same context that an open dialogue will take place to ensure that the human and political rights of all Iraqi citizens are respected.

Despite the absence of a reference to Chapter VII, the use of the verb 'demand' is peremptory, connotive more of decision-taking (Chapter VII) than recommendation-making (Chapter VI). Moreover, the demand applies to the ending of the (internal) repression. Indeed, it goes on to prescribe a means for ending it – open dialogue – with a reference to ultra-sensitive *political* rights.

The Council comes closest to pursuing an interventionist role in the third operative paragraph when it '*[i]nsists* that Iraq allow immediate access by international humanitarian organisations to all those in need of assistance in all parts of Iraq and to make available all necessary facilities for their operations'. This language can be understood as requiring Iraq to cede the normal right of a state to refuse access to the country to any foreign individual or organisation. On the other hand, it is not the practice of most humani tarian organisations, be they inter-governmental (e.g. the UN High Commissioner for Refugees) or non-governmental (e.g. the International Committee of the Red Cross) to enter countries and embark on relief operations without the agreement or, in any event, the acquiescence of the state in question.

There was no question of the resolution's requiring or authorising direct enforcement action at the time it was adopted. All coercive measures short of armed force envisaged in the Charter were already being deployed pursuant to the war, with a view to securing full implementation of the cease-fire resolution. While, on 4 April, President Bush had announced an aid airlift to Turkey, Operation Provide Comfort in its Iraqi dimension had not been developed, nor had the British safe havens proposal been launched. As described in Chapter 3, there was not yet the shared political will to take further military action among those who might be motivated and equipped to do so, much less within the Security Council as a whole.

At this stage, then, the significance of resolution 688 as a potential basis for underpinning a doctrine of collective humanitarian intervention was limited, though real. Like the investigation of the human rights situation in Chile undertaken by the Commission on Human Rights in 1975, this was the first time, other than in the case of South Africa, that the Security Council had described the internal human rights situation of a member state as constituting a threat to international peace and security. As such it had the *potential* for permitting the Security Council to take enforcement action and redress the situation. On the other hand, it had not expressly invoked Chapter VII, nor had it explicitly authorised any such action. Might it have implicitly authorised such action?

The safe havens operation was to provide the answer, at least for those undertaking the operation. The operation consisted of the establishment of enclaves, not called enclaves, to which the Kurdish refugees in Turkey could return in the confidence that they were protected from the depredations of the Iraqi military by the military of Western members of the coalition that had liberated Kuwait. The protecting forces established the safe havens despite the opposition of Iraq. Their governments described their action as being 'consistent with' resolution 688.

The only paragraph of the resolution addressed to UN member states other than Iraq is operative paragraph 6, by which the Council '*[a]ppeals* to all Member States and to all humanitarian organizations to contribute to these humanitarian relief efforts'. The efforts in question are presumably those referred to in operative paragraph 3 quoted above, as well as those requested of the Secretary-General under operative paragraph 5. This requested him 'to address urgently the critical needs of the refugees and displaced Iraqi population'. In fact, the safe havens operation was in support of bilateral relief efforts. Arguably, however, the declared intention to hand over the relief effort to the United Nations, eventually achieved, meant that the action could be understood as a contribution to 'these humanitarian relief efforts'. President Bush announced the military protection operation on 16 April while Eric Suy, the personal representative of the Secretary-General, and Prince Sadruddin Aga Khan were in Baghdad negotiating the agreement of 18 April by which the United Nations would establish 'Humanitarian Centres' (UNHUCS). It did not help the case that the Secretary-General made it clear that in his view a new Security Council resolution or Iraqi agreement would be needed for the military operation to be an official UN operation. On the other hand, resolution 678 under which the war had been fought had not been a blue beret affair; the Secretariat could well feel it needed a more explicit mandate to commit the organisation as a whole to action than should member states. He did authorise the first deployment of UN guards, without a new Security Council resolution, but equally without Iraqi objection. The first deployment of unarmed guards took place on 19 May and by 20 May they were lightly armed. Iraq eventually formally agreed to deployments in a 23 May annex to the 18 April agreement.

No Security Council member who voted for resolution 688 is known to have challenged the allied view that the operation was 'consistent with' resolution 688. The action may well be thought to have made possible the conclusion of the 18 April agreement between the United Nations and Iraq and its 23 May annex relating to UN security guards. Equally, allied reluctance to seek a further resolution can best be explained by the expected difficulties in obtaining one, at least without a formidable expenditure of capital, political or other.

The safe havens operation was aimed at removing neither the source of the repression, the Saddam Hussein government, nor the repression itself by some other means. It was used to make possible a relief operation necessary to bring the Kurds down from the mountains and, implicitly, to permit an *agreed* relief arrangement to be undertaken by the United Nations in various parts of Iraq, with a modest UN security component. The words of resolution 688 would have had to take some exiguous strain to allow a more ambitious military objective. Nevertheless, to the extent that the operation, with its limited aims, was 'covered' by it, the resolution represents what could be a first step towards a possible doctrine of collective military intervention to protect human rights.

As is often the case, special political circumstances made possible the adoption of the resolution. Apart from the mould-breaking developments in Eastern Europe and the former USSR (even before the August 1991 failed coup), without which even the UN-authorised military action to liberate Kuwait would not have been possible, there were unique case-specific factors at play. The most significant was the aforementioned military action itself and the events provoking it, which led to Iraq being accorded pariah status. There was also the sense of responsibility engendered by the expectations unleashed by the Iraqi defeat that induced the affected populations to rise up against Saddam. Consciousness of the weak UN response to Iraq's 1988 gassing of thousands of people, notably in Halabja, may have been relevant, as may the failure over the previous few years of the United Nations' human rights bodies seriously to take up the human rights situation in Iraq, despite insistent, well-documented complaints from non-governmental organisations describing as consistent a pattern of gross violations of human rights as could be imagined.[24] The willingness of the West to deploy the full range of its diplomatic resources to achieve its objectives was unusual (Iraq, by contrast, had never in the past flinched from doing whatever was necessary to secure its immunity from UN censure). Of crucial importance was the massive refugee problem inflicted not on the refugees, but on Iran and Turkey.

One perceptive and acute commentator, contemplating whether Chapter VII could be invoked to authorise coercive action for humanitarian purposes in a future case of this kind has opined that the Security Council 'is almost certain to premise its decision on a finding that the situation constitutes a threat to international peace and security in view of its transborder implications'.[25] We now turn to consider this and other possibly relevant factors.

Conditions affecting the legitimacy of possible UN intervention to protect human rights

Clearly not every human rights problem, even if it may now be characterised as being a matter of legitimate international concern, can readily be described as a threat, or even a potential threat, to international peace and security. There remains the question of whether the situation must have transboundary implications and what these might be. The human rights violations must clearly be grave and systematic, an aspect which will be discussed below when we consider the principles of necessity and proportionality. These principles will also serve to help assess the appropriateness of the nature and intensity of any intervention undertaken on human rights grounds.

Transboundary implications

There can be no doubt that the refugee problem created by the post-Gulf War situation in Iraq made it easier for some Security Council members to vote for resolution 688. It may even have been that without that problem, sufficient votes would not have been forthcoming. Does that mean that as a matter of 'law', direct transborder consequences, such as a refugee problem, are required for coercive action undertaken or authorised by the Security Council? The idea cannot be ruled out. Clearly a considerable number of states take that view. An argument may also be made that it would be conceptually dubious to interpret as threats to international peace and security matters which have no direct consequences beyond the frontiers of the state concerned. Fears about the potential for abuse of an alternative system without an objective threshold for coercive action are rife: would not any internationally unpopular regime be at risk of international action, thus calling into question the reality of the Charter protection of the *domaine réservé* from external intrusion? Furthermore, once the United Nations can intervene on human rights grounds, would that not weaken inhibitions on individual states or groups of states from 'taking the law into their own hands' should the United Nations be unable to act because of fluctuating majorities or capricious vetoes? Indeed, does not all this put at risk the very structure of an international system aimed at eliminating transnational conflict?

The response might be as follows. In an increasingly interdependent world, no state can require the rest of the world to stand aside, perhaps wringing its hands and adopting resolutions of censure, while its government kills and maims significant segments of its population, usually for the purposes of maintaining a power that had never had, or which had later lost, any shred of indigenous legitimacy. For this to be the norm would be to bring the world public order system into disrepute, thus undermining the support it needs. Meanwhile, if it were possible for the United Nations, the organisation of the world community, to act, this could decrease the incidence of unilateral, politically self-interested interventions. A growing number of influential governments take the view that there is a threshold beyond which inaction is impermissible. (This point seems to have been acknowledged by the former Secretary-General Pérez de Cuéllar in his 22 April 1991 speech cited in the Preface. Referring to article 2(7), he inquired 'whether certain other texts . . . in particular the Universal Declaration of Human Rights, do not implicitly call into question this inviolable notion of sovereignty'. While asserting that 'the principles of sovereignty cannot be radically challenged without international chaos quickly ensuing', he acknowledged that 'we have probably reached a stage in the ethical and psychological evolution of Western civilization in which the massive and deliberate violation of human rights will no longer be tolerated'. It was necessary 'to forge a new concept, one which marries law and morality'.[26] He pursued the point in his 1991 Annual Report on the Work of the Organization in the passage quoted by Paul Fifoot at the beginning of Chapter 5.) In addition it would be artificial, if not unconscionable, for the happenstance of geography to determine the international reaction to the fate of a particular population. Yet this would be the case if it were to be insisted that transborder effects be a condition for action: an island state could probably avoid generating a major refugee flow to other countries. In any event, it would merely put a premium on a military strategy by the state in question aimed at preventing refugees from crossing adjacent frontiers, thus potentially *increasing* the suffering of the victim population.

In Chapter 5 Paul Fifoot describes the extent to which external factors were relevant to the passage of resolutions under Chapter VI and VII of the Charter on Rhodesia and South Africa. They were clearly peripheral in the former case, somewhat more present in the latter. The South African case, dealing as it does with an independent UN member state, may be the more instructive. The external aspects of its policies related largely to its actions against the South African refugee populations in neighbouring states, elements of which were avowedly conducting a guerilla war against their government. Since the states of refuge had permitted themselves to be used as bases, it was possible for South Africa to argue that the incursions with their neighbours' frontiers were more self-defensive than aggressive. The fact that the UN ignored the argument simply reflected the basic reality that the world was not prepared to allow the shameful apartheid system to continue. In a sense, then, the external factors related not so much to the external behaviour of the South African government as to the reaction of neighbouring states to the internal conditions in South Africa. Even if the world was prepared to accord priority to eradicating this particular evil, it cannot be expected to accept in perpetuity that no other evils are capable of deserving similar attention. Alternatively, if the political will to take action is there, then there is evidence that very little in the way of direct external effect may be required for a determination of a threat to international peace and security. The Yugoslav and Somali examples referred to earlier suggest the same point in the context of internal strife leading to the collapse of central authority (albeit with the recognised official spokespersons requesting the action).

If direct transboundary effects are not required, or may be more required in theory than in practice, it does not follow that no restraints are required. On the contrary, if we cannot rely on readily identifiable criteria such as the creation of major refugee flows, then we must look hard at other factors to ensure that abnormal measures are only undertaken in response to an abnormal problem. It is submitted that traditional international law offers certain fundamental principles that can and must guide us here. These are the principles of necessity and proportionality.

Necessity and proportionality

When, during the 1837 Canadian Rebellion, the British set fire to an American boat that had been aiding the rebels and sent it over Niagara Falls, they agreed with the US Secretary of State's formulation of what elements were required to invoke legitimate self-defence: there must be a 'necessity of self-defence, instant, overwhelming, leaving no choice of means, and no moment for deliber-ation'.[27] This is commonly taken as the *locus classicus* statement of the relevant criteria for self-defence and, by extension, for other uses of force. The principle of necessity dictates that no measures short of armed force should be available to achieve the lawful objective. The principle of proportionality means that the level of force used should be commensurate with the harm it is aimed at preventing or redress-ing. These principles are primordially apposite to an assessment of the legitimacy of any humanitarian intervention. From them flow several key factors.

Thus, the principle of necessity dictates that nothing short of the application of armed force would be sufficient to stop the human rights violations in question. This means that, except where delay would permit massive, irreparable harm, all measures short of armed force should be exploited before resort to such force. Such measures may include measures of investigation, offers of conciliation or mediation, adoption of resolutions expressing concern, condemna-tion, etc., measures limiting political, economic and military rela-tions up to and including mandatory embargoes, and offers of peacekeeping. It is rare that a situation assumes the gravity and scope that would be necessary to justify an armed intervention out of the blue. Frequently, lower levels of repression precede the appear-ance of widespread atrocities. It is at the earlier stages that the lesser measures could be capable of halting a deterioration of the situation. In the case of Iraq, for example, it is fair to speculate whether Iraq would have gone as far as invading Kuwait, never mind unleashing all-out war on parts of its own population, if the United Nations had been more vigorous in dealing with its previous transgressions, both international (the invasion of Iran) and internal (widespread murder, 'disappearances' and torture; gas-bombing of Halabja and other places).

The principle of proportionality ensures that the gravity and extent of the violations be on a level commensurate with the reason-ably calculable loss of life, destruction of property, expenditure of resources and shock to the international body politic inherent in the violation of a state's frontiers. This presumably means that a central feature of the situation will be widespread violation of the right to life. Indeed, the violations may well need to amount to systematic crimes under international law such as crimes against humanity (see e.g. the UK reference to the Geneva Conventions and the German reference to the 'danger of genocide' in the Security Council debate on resolution 688).[28] It also means – regrettably but inevitably – that force will only be able to be used against states that do not wield a veto in the Security Council or whose capacity for military resistance does not permit them to make the costs, particularly in loss of life, so high as to equal or exceed the harm being inflicted internally. There will be acutely difficult questions of political assessment, in addition to the cost–benefit balancing exercise suggested here. For however inappropriate it may be from a human rights point of view, the world tends to be more understanding and indulgent of the transgressions of a democratically elected government faced with an armed insurrection than of a self-imposed tyranny stamping out threats, real or perceived, to its authority, even where those threats involve resort to violence. This is partly explicable in terms of the increasing value being accorded to the right to participate in government. It is probably more attributable to the sense that a democratically elected government has more legitimacy than one not so established and, furthermore, more legitimacy than any armed insurgency, spurning the ballot box, could have. This doubtless leads to a reluctance to bring serious pressure to bear on a democratic government violating human rights, however grievously or extensively. The foreseeable effect of the pressure could tip the balance of forces in favour of insurgents with less legitimacy and, given their rejection of the democratic process, no greater promise of respect for other human rights.

The same principle of proportionality also has implications for the selection of coercive measures short of armed force, such as economic or military embargoes. Here, however, it is even more difficult to apply. What nature and intensity of human rights violations would justify resort to such measures? The very fact that, even in the absence of direct transborder consequences, they have to be treated as amounting to a threat to international peace and security suggests that they must be serious and extensive. Threats to life and limb on a systematic basis could perhaps be sufficient. But could, say, widespread administrative internment? If so, would it be relevant whether the deprivation of freedom were aimed at repressing peaceful political dissenters or armed secessionists? By the same token, even non-coercive measures such as discussion, fact-finding, conciliation and mediation, at least as far as the Security Council is concerned, would only be justified in the case of a *potential* threat to international peace and security (under Chapter VI of the Charter). But perhaps other UN organs would not be so constrained.

Coercive measures would also be required by the principle of proportionality to be of an intensity such as not to outweigh the benefits they are aimed at securing. For example, any military action would need to comply scrupulously with international humanitarian law applicable in armed conflict (Geneva Conventions and Additional Protocols; Hague Rules) and in any event be the minimum necessary to secure those at risk. Is replacement of the offending regime, for example by one chosen on the basis of universal adult suffrage and political competition, a legitimate or even necessary political or military objective? Other coercive measures, such as an economic embargo would have to balance efficacy with the humanitarian needs of the population as a whole; children dying of malnutrition or diseases that would be treated by drugs obtainable but for the embargo are not an appealing advertisement for the cause of human rights.

In sum, it is possible to conceive of our problem in the form of a diagram in which one line ascends from relatively low levels of human rights violations to massive violations, while another ascends in the opposite direction from a low level of international intrusion (e.g. mildly worded expression of concern) to armed intervention.

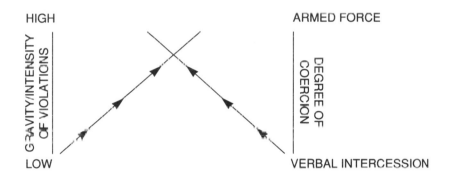

The point of intersection between the two lines is high on each scale. And so it must be if any doctrine of collective armed intervention to protect human rights is to be capable of acquiring the widespread degree of acceptance that will be necessary for it to have genuine legal legitimacy.

Conclusion

Until the advent of the United Nations, human rights were largely within the domestic jurisdiction of states and not a matter of international concern, in the sense that international law did not challenge government's treatment of their citizens. Even after the United Nations came into being there was no early agreement that such treatment could be formally challenged within or outside the organisation, other than by treaty-based machinery. In any event, coercive intervention was generally considered inadmissible, and even since the adoption of the UN Charter such intervention is generally seen as a use of force violating the independence and territorial integrity of states, as for a time was mere formal consideration of states' human rights practices. UN practice has since evolved to permit consideration of, and adoption of resolutions on, such practices, at least where the practices are grave or systematic. This is probably because the practices are no longer seen as essentially within states' domestic jurisdiction, nor is such action considered improper intervention. There remains the question of the legality of coercive measures or 'enforcement action'.

Such measures or action seem to be possible in cases where the representatives of the recognised authorities agree, which will tend to be situations where government itself collapses or its writ no longer runs over the whole territory (e.g. Yugoslavia and Somalia). Without that agreement there is no consensus on the matter.

There is some evidence that the United Nations could undertake or authorise the use of coercive measures. The main example is that of South Africa, involving measures short of armed force. The safe havens operation in northern Iraq, to the extent that it was 'covered' by Security Council resolution 688, is a fragile straw in the wind for future action.

If the wind is breathing in the direction of collective humanitarian intervention, it may be difficult to keep it blowing in the absence of a threat to international peace and security manifested by palpable transborder consequences. While such consequences ought not to be seen as decisive (if the events on board a ship are serious enough, they may disturb the peace of a nearby port), many governments will be reluctant at this stage to presume a threat to international peace and security without official acquiescence which governments violating human rights cannot be expected to give.[29]

In any event, any such evolution of UN practice must respect the principles of necessity and proportionality. This will require coercive measures to be the minimum necessary to redress the situation and not of such a nature as to cause more harm than that at which they are aimed. Recourse to armed force will only ever be justifiable in the case of massive human rights violations involving widespread loss of life and limb.

Notes

1. See 'Military and Paramilitary Activities in and against Nicaragua (*Nicaragua* v. *United States of America*), Merits, Judgment', *ICJ Reports 1986*, p.14, paras 187–211.
2. Vienna Convention on the Law of Treaties 1969, 1155 UNTS 331, article 31.
3. In *Soering* v. *United Kingdom* (1989), Eur. Court HR, (1990) 11 HRLJ 335, the European Court of Human Rights opined that although article 2(1) of the

European Convention on Human Rights provided for the death penalty as an exception to the right to life, '[s]ubsequent practice in national penal policy, in the form of a generalised abolition of capital punishment, could be taken as establishing the agreement of the Contracting States to abrogate the exception provided for under Article 2(1)' (para. 103).

4. See Fernando R. Téson, *Humanitarian Intervention: An Inquiry into Law and Morality*, pp.54–56. Transnational Publishers, Dobbs Ferry, NY (1988).
5. See Ruth B. Russell and Jeannette E. Muther, *A History of the United Nations Charter*, pp.780–1. Brookings Institution, Washington DC (1958).
6. See Howard Tolley Jr, *The UN Commission on Human Rights*, pp.16–19, 51–3. Westview Press, Boulder and London (1987).
7. See Rosalyn Higgins, *The Development of International Law through the Political Organs of the United Nations*, Part II. Oxford University Press, London, New York, Toronto (1963).
8. See Cecilia Medina Quiroga, *The Battle of Human Rights – Gross Systematic Violations and the Inter-American System*, pp.71ff. Martinus Nijhoff, Dordrecht, Boston, London (1988).
9. The term is borrowed from the language of the Geneva Conventions, 12 August 1949, on the protection of victims of war: Convention I, article 63; Convention II, article 62; Convention III, article 142; Convention IV, article 158. The term 'laws of humanity' is replaced by 'principles of humanity' in Additional Protocol I, article 1(2) and Additional Protocol II, preambular para. 4, both 1977.
10. See Thomas M. Franck and Nigel S. Rodley, 'After Bangladesh: The Law of Humanitarian Intervention by Military Force', *American Journal of International Law*, 67, pp.275–300 at pp.279–95.
11. The principal advocates of this position (a 'substantial minority of writers') are listed in Téson, *Humanitarian Intervention* (note 4 above), p.129, note 7, and include Téson himself. Another has edited a volume containing positions for and against the doctrine: Richard B. Lillich (ed.), *Humanitarian Intervention and the United Nations*, University Press of Virginia, Charlotteville (1973).
12. The principal advocates of this position are listed in Téson, *Humanitarian Intervention* (note 4 above), p.129, note 5. The most extensive recent work defending this position is Natalino Ronzitti, *Rescuing Nationals Abroad and Intervention on Grounds of Humanity*, Martinus Nijhoff, Dordrecht and Boston (1985). The present author falls into this group (see note 10 above and note 13 below).
13. Nigel S. Rodley, 'Human Rights and Humanitarian Intervention: The Case Law of the World Court', *International and Comparative Law Quarterly*, 38, 321–333 at 327–33; see *Nicaragua* case (note 1 above), paras 267–8.
14. ECOSOC res. 1235 (XLII), 6 June 1967; see Tolley, *The UN Commission on Human Rights* (note 6 above), Chapter 4.
15. ECOSOC res. 1503 (XLVIII), 27 May 1970; see *ibid.*
16. Nigel S. Rodley, 'United Nations Action Procedures Against "Disappearances", Summary or Arbitrary Executions, and Torture', *Human Rights Quarterly*, 8, pp.700–730 (1986); David Weissbrodt, 'The Three "Theme" Special Rapporteurs of the UN Commission on Human Rights', (1986) *American Journal of International Law*, 80, pp.685–699; Menno Kamminga, 'The Thematic Procedures of the UN Commission on Human Rights', *Netherlands International Law Review*, 34, pp.299–323 (1987); Commentary, 'The UN Commission on Human Rights and the New Working Group on Arbitrary Detention', *The Review* (International Commission of Jurists) 46, p.23 (June 1991).
17. See the 1989 Concluding Document of the Vienna Meeting, reproduced in *International Legal Materials*, 28, pp.527–566 and the 1991 Document of the

Moscow Meeting reproduced in *International Legal Materials*, vol 30. pp. 1670–16910.

18. Declaration on Principles of International Law Concerning Friendly Relations and Cooperation Among States in Accordance with the Charter of the United Nations, GA res. 2625 (XXV), 24 October 1970, cited with approval by the International Court of Justice in the *Nicaragua* case (note 1 above), at paras 188ff. Para. 192 in particular quotes the Declaration's enjoining of interference in civil strife.

19. UN doc. S/PV. 3009, 25 September 1991.

20. However, GA res. 46/182 of 19 December 1991, Strengthening of the Coordination of Humanitarian Emergency Assistance of the United Nations, contains the following 'guiding principle':
'3. The sovereignty, territorial integrity and national unity of States must be fully respected in accordance with the Charter of the United Nations. In this context, humanitarian assistance should be provided with the consent of the affected country and in principle on the basis of an appeal by the affected country.' This was assuredly included to palliate the sensitivities of Third World countries. However, the use of the word 'should' may leave a margin of manoeuvre where the affected state wantonly refuses assistance required by its population; see, e.g. the previous guiding principle: '2. Humanitarian assistance *must* be provided in accordance with the principles of humanity, neutrality and impartiality' (emphasis added).

21. After the overthrow of Haitian President Jean-Bertrand Aristide, an *ad hoc* meeting of OAS ministers of foreign affairs recommended 'action to bring about the diplomatic isolation of those who hold power illegally in Haiti' (para. 5) and that all states 'suspend their economic, financial, and commercial ties with Haiti and any aid and technical cooperation except that provided for strictly humanitarian purposes' (para. 6). See OAS doc. MRE/RES. 1/91, reproduced in UN doc. A/46/231, 3 October 1991, Appendix. In a presidential statement, the UN Security Council 'unequivocally condemned' the coup.

22. UN doc. S/PV. 2982, 5 April 1991.

23. UN doc. S/22436, 3 April 1991.

24. See International Commission of Jurists, *The Review* (note 16 above), p.25.

25. Oscar Schachter, 'United Nations Law in the Gulf Conflict', *American Journal of International Law*, 85, pp.452–473 at 469, (1991).

26. Secretary-General's address at the University of Bordeaux, UN Press Release SG/SM/4560, 24 April 1991.

27. *The Caroline* case, *British and Foreign State Papers*, 29, pp.1137–8; BFSP, 30, pp.195–6; quoted in D.J. Harris, *Cases and Materials on International Law* (4th edn), p.848. Sweet and Maxwell, London (1991). The World Court in *Nicaragua* (note 1 above) described as 'well established in customary international law' the rule 'whereby self-defence would warrant only measures which are proportional to the armed attack and necessary to respond to it' (para. 176).

28. UN doc. S/PV 2982, 5 April 1991.

29. See, for instance, the text of the 31 January 1992 statement issued by the Security Council summit, which only makes passing references to human rights (Reuters dispatch 01–0027: BC-UN-SUMMIT TEXT: 'Text of Final Declaration of UN Summit', 31 January 1992). Much heralded Western plans to make human rights the centrepiece of the declaration had to be abandoned in the face of opposition from China: Leonard Doyle, 'UN Summit set to "ignore human rights"', *The Independent*, 24 January 1992. China was probably not alone.

CHAPTER 3

'Safe havens' for Kurds in post-war Iraq

LAWRENCE FREEDMAN AND DAVID BOREN*

In the weeks after the conclusion of the Gulf War an uprising by Kurds in northern Iraq was suppressed by forces loyal to the government of Saddam Hussein. This led to the flight of the Kurdish population towards Iraq's borders with Turkey and Iran. To a significant but lesser extent Shi'ite rebels in the south fled towards the territory bordering Kuwait which had been occupied by coalition forces in the closing days of the war. The flight soon turned into a human tragedy on a massive scale. The crisis generated tremendous pressure on Western governments to intervene, particularly due to concern that the allied victory over Iraq had indirectly brought about the crisis. They sought to deal with the crisis as a standard relief operation but for a variety of practical and political reasons this proved to be inadequate. After a degree of transatlantic debate, they therefore decided to establish protected areas within Iraq to enable the Kurds to return in safety to their homes, where a relief effort could be more readily organised.

In so doing they created an important precedent for humanitarian intervention. The 'safe havens' were organised with full awareness of the fact that this constituted an 'interference in the internal affairs' of Iraq, but were justified by the failure of Iraq to conduct its internal affairs in an acceptable manner. For those governments involved the key problem was not the construction of a rationale for the policy but confining the effects of that policy. They did not wish to take on a long-term commitment of this nature, especially if it risked entanglement in a civil war, and so were anxious for more durable solutions to the Kurdish problem – either through an internal political settlement or, failing that, the assumption by the United Nations of responsibility for the welfare of the Kurdish people.

This tension in Western policy was aggravated by the regional

43

character of the Kurdish problem. The question of the situation of the Kurds in terms of humanitarian considerations was complicated by the political challenge they were seen to pose to central government in Turkey as well as Iraq. The management of the crisis during 1991 was shaped from the start by the government in Ankara which was at all times anxious to avoid giving any boost to demands for Kurdish separatism within Turkey.

Intervention undertaken for largely humanitarian reasons, as was the case in this instance, can never be politically innocent. The degree of Western protection accorded the Iraqi Kurds was relevant in the Iraqi government's negotiations both with the United Nations (as an alternative source of humanitarian assistance) and with Kurdish leaders who were seeking to achieve a longer-term political settlement. It became especially evident with the Iraqi–Kurdish negotiations that Saddam Hussein's readiness to make concessions was directly related to the degree of tangible Western support for the Kurds.

This chapter charts the origins of the crisis and the development of the Western response. It identifies the imperatives that shaped Western policy and the problems of implementing it. Because this policy was recognised at the time to be setting a precedent for humanitarian intervention in the future it is important to establish clearly the nature of the precedent and the issues that may well be raised by any operation of this kind. However, it is also important to bear in mind the very particular nature of the crisis. It came after Iraq had been severely battered in war and subjected to UN economic sanctions which the Iraqi leader was anxious to see lifted, even if this meant honouring Western demands.

Origins

Although, at some 20 million strong, Kurds represent the fourth largest ethnic group in the Middle East, they lack a state of their own. Instead they are split amongst Turkey (10 million), Iran (6 million), Iraq (3 million) and Syria (1 million). In all of these countries they have been politically disadvantaged and have challenged central authority, often at great cost to themselves. Following the collapse of the Ottoman Empire there were some moves to give them statehood, but they were not a popular cause and the attempt failed. In addition, they have not only been divided between states but divided amongst themselves on both religious and tribal bases.[1]

After the coup of 1958, Kurds in Iraq at first appeared to make substantial gains in their political rights; but they soon saw their distinctive identity suppressed in the name of a more pronounced

Arabist philosophy. As a result a rebellion began, led by Mustafa Barzani. This provoked a severe pounding of Kurdish villages but the suppression failed to subdue the Kurds, a failure that hastened the downfall of the regime of General Kassem. In the ensuing negotiations with the new Ba'ath regime Barzani demanded but was not granted full autonomy and so fighting resumed. For the rest of the decade this pattern was repeated with Iraqi offensives and negotiations failing in turn. Eventually in 1970 a peace treaty was signed but it could not hold because neither side was prepared to concede on the principles of autonomy and profit from the oil produced in the Kurdistan area. In the following years the Iraqi government continued with its efforts to suppress the Kurdish language and culture and persecute its political leaders. The Kurds' political and military resistance was sustained by Iran with Western support until 1975 when this was withdrawn following the Algiers accord between Iran and Iraq. A split then developed in the Kurdish leadership between the Kurdish Democratic Party led by Barzani's son, Masoud, and the Patriotic Union of Kurdistan (PUK) led by Jalal Talabani.

During the Iran–Iraq War Kurds in both countries demonstrated what was considered to be disloyalty by their governments. As the war with Iran drew to a close in 1988 Saddam Hussein turned his fire on the Kurds. There was evidence of the use of chemical weapons on a substantial scale. Many Kurds fled to Turkey where they were made to feel extremely unwelcome.

In March 1991, following Saddam Hussein's comprehensive defeat at the hands of coalition forces, and the dislocation in Baghdad resulting from air strikes against power supplies and communications, those opposing the Ba'ath regime were provided with a unique opportunity. With the regime at its weakest point there seemed every reason to believe that it would not be able to cope with a concerted challenge by its opponents. Moreover, there was reason to suspect, although there were no guarantees, that an uprising would get at least covert support from the coalition countries which had made no secret of their distaste for the regime and their desire to see Saddam replaced.

Yet even while the war was underway Saddam never forgot the threats to his rule from within. Substantial forces were not committed to the battle and others were extracted from the combat zone. Initially Kurdish *pesh merga* guerillas made rapid advances in removing the Iraqi Army, secret police and Ba'ath Party from most of Iraqi Kurdistan while Shias in the south, along with army deserters, threatened several major cities, including Basra. However, after defeating the southern rebellion the Iraqi government began repressing the Kurds and Shia Muslims. The brutality of the repression caused hundreds of thousands of Iraqis to flee their homes, thereby creating the huge refugee problem.

The failure of coalition forces to support the rebellion came as a surprise to those who had interpreted statements by Western leaders during the build-up to the war and the war itself as calling for an uprising. Of these the most notorious was that by President George Bush on 15 February 1991:

> . . . there's another way for the bloodshed to stop, and that is for the Iraqi military and the Iraqi people to take matters into their own hands to force Saddam Hussein the dictator to step aside and to comply with the United Nations resolutions and then rejoin the family of peace-loving nations.[2]

The administration also expected the Iraqi military to oust Saddam Hussein. Bush observed in late March: 'It seems unlikely he can survive . . . People are fed up with him. They see him for the brutal dictator that he is.'[3]

Coalition leaders, however, had always taken care to distinguish between a general desire to see Saddam Hussein toppled and having this as an explicit objective. American and British leaders had consistently denied any deliberate intent to change the regime. Repeated accusations that the removal of Saddam constituted President Bush's 'hidden agenda' resulted in a series of unequivocal statements to the effect that there was no such objective. As the British Prime Minister, John Major, put it early in the war, in a phrase picked up by President Bush, he would 'shed no tears' if Saddam fell but this was not a matter for the coalition.

The coalition had been determined to work within the terms of UN resolutions and these related to the liberation of Kuwait and the restoration of 'peace and security' to the area. This latter requirement might have been interpreted to allow for the removal of a man whose past policies had threatened regional peace and security, but was generally considered to be referring to removing Iraq's capacity to project military power, and especially weapons of mass destruction, beyond its borders along with a drive for peaceful settlements to other regional disputes.

With Iraq devastated, humiliated and bankrupt it was assumed that someone in the Iraqi political elite would recognise Saddam Hussein as a liability and that post-war recovery depended upon getting rid of him. The preferred mode of change was a coup. The British government was quite open about its preference for action from within the ruling Ba'ath Party or the military. The preference flowed naturally from a fear that a complete collapse of central authority in Baghdad would result in the country fragmenting with the ensuing chaos sucking in Iraq's neighbours.

But no gap was found between central authority in Iraq and Saddam Hussein himself. He had created the structures of power in the country and, recognising the potential challenge, in the aftermath of defeat he moved quickly to tighten rather than loosen his grip. The private thoughts of those close enough to Saddam to depose him might have been full of plots, but everything in their experience warned that he was a past master in thwarting them and dealing ruthlessly with the perpetrators.

The alternative – and widely anticipated – method of getting rid of Saddam would have been through a direct assault on Baghdad. This would have contradicted the promise to go no further than permitted under UN resolutions, confirmed accusations of neo-colonialism, involved a costly and potentially difficult military occupation of Iraq and created a responsibility for the political structure of a country in turmoil. These factors also restricted the immediate possibilities for direct support to the post-war rebellion.

A consensus within the Security Council on direct military action against the Iraqi occupation of Kuwait depended on the cooperation of China and the Soviet Union. Both these countries had long championed the principle of non-interference in internal affairs, as they believed that it helped protect them from Western attempts to change their political structure. Neighbours of Iraq were nervous with regard to the potential consequences of its dismemberment. Turkey and Iran would give no support to any notion of an independent Kurdish state. The Saudi monarchy, fearful of Iranian-supported radical Islamic movements, was loath to see Iran's influence enhanced by strengthened Shias in southern Iraq on its northern border.

In forging a domestic consensus to support the action taken against Iraq, President Bush had sought a strategy that would minimise American casualties and the risk of becoming entangled in a Vietnam-style quagmire.[4] The coalition forces had not prepared to take Baghdad. The administration had also accepted the view that Iraqi territorial integrity and a strong central state was essential to Middle East stability.[5] These factors, coupled with the need to take into consideration the views of other states in the region, and a strong interest in pursuing a multinational policy, limited Washington's scope for a determined push against Saddam Hussein.

Yet despite all these pragmatic considerations, the fate of the Kurdish uprising raised basic questions of obligation. Was it not the case that, while not actually promising support, coalition leaders had encouraged the overthrow of Saddam Hussein? Did not the US administration's decision to end the war when it did, leaving much of the Republican Guard intact, mean that while the external threat posed by Saddam was reduced the internal threat was left intact? To such questions President Bush responded:

> Do I think that the United States should bear guilt because of suggesting that the Iraqi people take matters into their own hands, with the implication being given that the United States would be there to support them militarily? That was not true. We never implied that.[6]

None the less Saddam must have been surprised not only by the abrupt way in which the war ended, but also by the lack of direct support for the rebels and the reduction in direct pressure.

The United States refused contact with the rebels even at the height of their rebellion when they controlled much of northern Iraq, including Kirkuk, and, together with the Shias rebelling in the south, posed a threat even in Baghdad where hit-and-run attacks were being conducted. Nor was US assistance forthcoming when Iraq deployed overwhelming superiority against the rebels. The United States did shoot down two Iraqi fixed-wing aircraft used against the rebels but mainly because those had been banned in the cease-fire agreement and posed a threat to allied forces. However, they refused to shoot down Iraqi army helicopters unless these too threatened allied forces. Only when the Kurds had become refugees was the United States prepared to assist them.

Operation Provide Comfort

By the start of April it was apparent that the rebellion had failed and that, in its stead, there was now a massive refugee problem. Soon there was the horror of 400,000 Kurdish refugees starving and freezing in extreme terrain and weather. The deaths totalled as many as 1,000 a day, mainly children and old people. Though the tragedy was brought home by pictures from Turkey, the number of Kurdish refugees in Iran was actually greater, amounting to as many as 1 million early in the crisis and up to 1.5 million at its height. Nor was the crisis limited to northern Iraq. As many as 71,000 Shia refugees fled to southern Iran with another 30,000 seeking refuge with allied forces in the demilitarised zone.[7]

The United States had anticipated a refugee problem following the war and had even pre-positioned supplies in Turkey to cope with it but these proved inadequate because, according to US National Security Advisor Brent Scowcroft, 'We did not expect the severity of the attacks on the Kurds'.[8] Early US predictions of refugee numbers were around 20,000. A January report for the UN High Commissioner for Refugees on post-war requirements for humanitarian assistance came closer to the mark but still fell short. It concluded there would be about 400,000 refugees and estimated that adequate aid would cost $175 million. Not only had this estimate proved too low but the United Nations had received only $35 million. By the end of April, when as many as 2 million people were seeking refuge the United Nations was requesting $236 million. Inadequate resources continued to hamper the United Nations' role.

The problem was further aggravated by the reluctance of the Turkish government to accept a substantial influx of refugees. For Turkey the refugee crisis came at an awkward time. It considered its natural place to be part of the West, yet with the end of the Cold War its strategic role had declined. In addition the European Community would not accept Turkey as a prospective member. To demonstrate a commitment to Western values President Turgut Özal signed the CSCE's Paris Charter in November 1990, thereby extending minority rights. Turkey's full support for the coalition from the start of the Gulf crisis, despite the economic sacrifices entailed, had done much to improve relations with the West and it was now anxious to capitalise on this. The crisis had enabled it to demonstrate that it still occupied a prominent strategic position, and it now expected to play a major regional role in the aftermath of the war.

As part of this it was prepared to liberalise its attitudes towards those already in Turkey. This followed earlier commitments to reform, designed to ward off separatist demands. In March 1991, when the rebellion still appeared to have some chance of success, Özal met emissaries of two Iraqi Kurdish groups.[9] The ban on speaking Kurdish was lifted in April 1991 with the passage of a law allowing 'languages and dialects other than Turkish' to be spoken. However, the scale of the crisis now threatened further liberalisation.

Ankara was fearful of Kurdish instability crossing the border from Iraq. During the Iran–Iraq War Turkish forces had twice crossed the border to attack Kurdish insurgents, with Iraqi permission. In 1988 the government had reluctantly provided some refuge to 60,000 150,000 Kurds threatened with repression in Iraq, and denied Iraqi requests for permission to pursue the Kurds across the Turkish border. But this influx of Iraqi Kurds had reinforced the separatist movement in Turkey. The Marxist Kurdish Workers' Party (PKK) headed by Abdullah Ocalan had been conducting periodic attacks on the Turkish army and officials since 1984. So now the Turkish army, to whom the central government had largely delegated responsibility for dealing with the Kurds, prevented the refugees from penetrating the countryside, which is one reason they remained exposed on the mountains. The Turkish army also prepared to defend itself against the starving refugees before distributing supplies in order to ensure 'orderly distribution'.[10]

The sense that, once again, the Kurds had been left to their fate when they might have had good reason to expect material support touched the international conscience. The scenes of the flight across the mountains were heart-rending. Their impact was accentuated by the presence of large numbers of Western reporters and television cameras. The war had meant that news organisations were still well represented in the area. As a result, international responses to the crisis were strongly influenced by dramatic media coverage relayed live from the Turkish–Iraqi border.[11]

On 4 April the British Prime Minister, John Major, announced £20 million of immediate aid while President Bush authorised an airlift of supplies. The following day the UN Security Council passed resolution 688, condemning the repression of Iraqi civilians, calling the consequences a threat to international peace and security in the region, demanding that Iraq cease the repression immediately, and insisting on immediate access for international humanitarian organisations 'to all those in need of assistance in all parts of Iraq'.[12]

Practical problems of relief included the logistics of helping so many refugees in such inaccessible areas. The mountain areas where the refugees to Turkey had gathered had poor roads made virtually impassable by mud and rain. Both terrain and weather hindered the distribution of aid. According to Daniel Conway, Ankara representative of the UN High Commissioner for Refugees: 'the basic problem is logistics. They are in one of the most inaccessible areas of the world, high in the mountains, scattered, out of reach. The roads are just traps for trucks.'[13]

Even air distribution had drawbacks. On 18 April, 12 military relief flights – 9 American, 2 British and 1 French – dropped 57.6 tons of relief supplies to the refugees. The aid was parachuted in large crates and consisted mostly of water, blankets and food. However the descending crates proved a risk to the refugees, some of whom were killed as they were unable to avoid them due to overcrowded conditions, ankle-deep mud and the speed of their descent. The need to shift from using transport planes to helicopters delayed the arrival of aid as did poor flying conditions.

On 13 April the Turkish government announced that its army would move refugees down from the mountains to more accessible and sanitary camps 35 miles further inside Turkish borders. These movements began on 15 April.[14] The scale of the air distribution was enormous. The US State Department estimated that about 600 tons of supplies were needed daily to meet requirements.[15] As a result of problems with distribution by aircraft, the United States relied increasingly on helicopter drops and truck deliveries. The aid finally began to have an effect, with the death-rate dropping from 400–1,000 a day to about 60 a day towards the end of April. By 23 April the number of air drops had reached 875 with the amount of relief supplies dropped near the Turkish–Iraqi border totalling 5,915 tons.

The problem on the Iranian border was if anything worse. Iran already had more refugees than any other country in the world. The nearly 1 million Iraqi Kurds who arrived in 1991 were joining some 600,000 still in Iran following past expulsions, as well as nearly 2.2 million Afghans who had sought refuge following the 1979 Soviet invasion of Afghanistan. Unlike Turkey, Iran did not prevent the new refugees entering the country at all. However, delays at the Iranian border to enable Iranian soldiers to search the fleeing Kurds resulted in increasing numbers of deaths. Iran was also reluctant to take in more refugees than it could handle at any one time. As a result, lines of Iraqis 50–80 kilometres long stretched back from the Iranian border. Gradually, the Iranians moved the refugees to camps.

Iran found it difficult to cope due to shortages of the necessary supplies. By Sunday 14 April Iran had spent as much as $57 million on the refugees, according to Western aid officials, far in excess of the contributions of any other country. A week later Iran appealed to the international community to help it aid the refugees. Foreign Minister Ali Akbar Velayati said: 'We expect those who have played the main role in creating this crisis to play a greater part in helping the refugees, which seems to be the minimum they can do.'[16]

The aid relationship was complicated by the uncertain state of relations between Iran and the West. Although the role played by Iran during the war was generally felt to have been helpful to the coalition, Teheran remained worried about Western intentions in the region. For the Americans and British, policy towards Iran focused on the potential influence of Teheran over those holding Western hostages in Beirut. Despite Iraqi accusations to the contrary, the Western response was therefore not to make aid conditional on efforts to release the hostages, but to expect some effort following aid.[17] The United States discussed what it could provide for Iran from their list of necessities and the first US relief supplies were scheduled to arrive on 27 April.[18]

The UN High Commissioner for Refugees attempted to coordinate Western aid by visiting Teheran. Nevertheless aid was especially slow to arrive in Iran and throughout the crisis the focus remained on Kurds along the Turkish border. Interior Minister Abdullah Nouri complained: 'Despite widespread propaganda, foreign countries have provided the refugees with little help. The world ought to be ashamed of its insignificant assistance to the Iraqi refugees.'[19]

Safe Havens

The logic of the longer-term response to the crisis was dictated by Turkey. Ankara wanted the Kurdish refugees removed from Turkish soil but not into a separate Kurdish state. The only alternative was some guarantee of safety for the Kurds within Iraqi borders. Thus President Özal declared on 7 April that 'We have to get [the Kurds] better land under UN control and to put those people in the Iraqi territory and take care of them.'[20] Western governments were initially reluctant to follow this logic. The possibility of some sort of safe haven was mentioned by US Secretary of Defense Dick Cheney on Sunday morning television as early as 31 March, but it was not taken up by other US officials. Gradually, however, the principle of non-interference became conditional.

For the United States, this process began with Secretary of State James Baker's tour of south-east Turkey shortly after the relief effort began. While his comments concentrated on the humanitarian aspects he could not ignore the political implications of any attempt to alleviate the Kurdish tragedy. Having 'witnessed the suffering and desperation of the Iraqi people, experiences of cruelty and human anguish that defy description', Baker went on to say that 'these people must be free from the threats, persecution and harassment that they have been subjected to by that brutal regime in Baghdad'. Initially, though, it was the relief effort that was to be protected rather than its clients. Baker observed that 'any threats of inter-ference or actual interference with the international relief efforts' might require the attention of the UN Security Council. At the same time Baker reiterated that the United States would not 'go down the slippery slope of being sucked into a civil war'.[21] The Kurds them-selves could only hope that Saddam Hussein would recognise that economic sanctions would be sustained so long as he continued to repress the Kurds.

By this time European governments, less constrained by fears of entanglement, were already considering more direct support for the Kurds. The French initiated calls for a bolder response to the Kurdish crisis.[22] The first concrete proposal to guarantee the safety of the Kurds was put forward by John Major to the Luxembourg summit meeting of the European Community (EC) on 8 April.[23] There Major proposed the creation of UN-protected Kurdish enclaves of northern Iraq. The summit had been called at the instigation of France to discuss what had been generally felt to be a weak Community performance during the Gulf War. Rather than get bogged down in an acrimonious post-mortem, Community leaders were pleased to be able to take an initiative in an area where the United States was dithering.[24] In addition to endorsing Britain's safe haven plan, EC leaders pledged refugee aid of $185 million. As one European official remarked at the time: 'The Kurds saved the summit so we must save the Kurds.'

Given its past policy, the United States was initially lukewarm to this idea. White House spokesman Marlin Fitzwater said that the proposal had 'some merits in terms of a possible solution or a possible partial solution . . . it is at least worthy of consideration'.[25] It advertised its own determination at least to protect the relief effort. Fitzwater reported that the US:

> warned Iraq this weekend, through its representatives at the United Nations, and through its embassy here in Washington, not to interfere with humanitarian relief efforts underway in Iraq. We informed Iraq that the United States, the United Nations, and other coalition officials would be operating in those areas to distribute humanitarian assistance to the Kurdish population. We expect these officials to be allowed to operate safely and without military threat from Iraq. Without going into specific operational instructions, we do not anticipate military threat from Iraqi air or ground forces. We continue to pursue this matter with UN officials. The refugee tragedy must be alleviated.

He added that the Iraqis had 'ceased military activities in that area for the last couple of days'.[26]

In order to prevent further Iraqi retribution and to stem the flow of refugees, Washington had instructed the Iraqi government not to send military forces north of the 36th parallel. Choosing the 36th parallel, north of the oil town of Kirkuk claimed by Kurdish separatists, reduced the likelihood that this policy would encourage Kurdish separatism.

Despite congressional pressure as well as the new position of the European Community to extend protection beyond the relief effort to the Kurds themselves,[27] President Bush was initially reluctant. In a speech on 13 April he still insisted that he did 'not want one single soldier or airman shoved into a civil war in Iraq that's been going on for ages', but he would 'not tolerate any interference in this massive international relief effort'.[28] Yet the second requirement did involve sending troops, even though their mission was restricted. Thus, following Bush's speech the United States began to establish camps inside northern Iraq. Five American ships carrying supplies were despatched to Turkey, thousands of US troops flew into southern Turkey, and hundreds of US military lorries and dozens of transport planes arrived to establish a 'food bridge' between the refugees. Turkish and Iranian permissions were requested and received.[29] Similar permission was not requested from Iraq. This intervention in Iraq was to last only until the international community became organised: the ultimate goal was to turn humanitarian relief over to international bodies – once there was 'a system in place that can meet [refugee] needs'.[30]

It inevitably proved difficult to confine the intervention to the protection of relief workers. If the Kurds were to be persuaded to come down from the mountains they too would need to feel secure. There was therefore a further elaboration of US policy. George Bush announced on 16 April that US troops would enter northern Iraq to establish refugee camps. He had effectively embraced the 'safe havens' concept.

> Following consultations with Prime Minister Major, President Mitterrand, President Özal of Turkey, Chancellor Kohl and this morning, UN Secretary General Pérez de Cuéllar, I am announcing an expanded, a greatly expanded and more ambitious relief effort. This approach is quite simple: if we cannot get adequate food, medicine, clothing, and shelter to the Kurds living in the mountains along the Turkish–Iraq border, we must encourage the Kurds to move to areas in northern Iraq where the geography facilitates, rather than frustrates, such a large-scale relief effort.
>
> Consistent with United Nations Security Council resolution 688 and working closely with the United Nations and other international organisations and our European partners, I have directed the US military to begin immediately to establish several encampments in northern Iraq where relief supplies for these refugees will be made available in large quantities and distributed in an orderly manner . . . adequate security will be provided at these temporary sites by US, British and French air and ground forces, again consistent with United Nations Security Council Resolution 688 . . . I want to underscore that all we are doing is motivated by humanitarian concerns. We continue to expect the government of Iraq not to interfere in any way with this latest relief effort. The prohibition against any Iraqi fixed- or rotary-wing aircraft flying north of the 36th parallel thus remains in effect.

Bush stressed the continuity in policy:

All along, I have said that the United States is not going to intervene militarily in Iraq's internal affairs and risk being drawn into a Vietnam-style quagmire. This remains the case . . . Some might argue that this is an intervention into the internal affairs of Iraq, but I think the humanitarian concern, the refugee concern is so overwhelming that there will be a lot of understanding about this.

In stressing his desire that this be only a temporary move, Bush emphasised that:

We intend to turn over the administration of and security for these sites as soon as possible to the United Nations, just as we are fulfilling our commitment to withdraw our troops and hand over responsibility to UN forces along Iraq's southern border, the border with Kuwait.[31]

Implementation

The coordination of allied relief efforts began almost immediately when James Baker, en route to the Middle East, met with the 12 European foreign ministers in an emergency session. In a joint news conference with Luxembourg foreign minister Jacques Poos (president of the Council of Ministers), Baker stressed the temporary nature of the initiative. At a more practical level it was agreed to create a single coordinating organ to overcome difficulties in distributing the aid. While foreign ministers discussed coordinating the plan, military leaders of France, the United Kingdom and the United States met in Stuttgart, the US Military Headquarters in Europe.

A relief infrastructure was built up by establishing forward humanitarian relief centres in Diyarbakir and Silopi in Turkey. Diyarbakir was to be the principal base for US and British C-130s and French C-160s, while helicopter and truck convoy deliveries would originate from Silopi. The Incirlik air base was an intermediate support base for arriving US C-5 and C-141 aircraft as well as for supplies trucked in and transported by rail from the Turkish ports of Mersin and Iskenderun. Potential camp sites had already been identified from the air.

Security for the camps included United States and allied ground and air forces, with increased numbers of combat air patrols in the area. In Turkey a stand-by force was prepared to deploy into Iraq in the event of Iraqi interference with the relief effort. The activity of US ground forces in Iraq was described by Fitzwater: 'Generally, we're talking about troops that would move in and out for short periods of times, hours, to help with camps or moving people around or food or water, those kind of things.'[32] According to Lieutenant General Marty Brandtner, director of operations for the Joint Chiefs of Staff, military teams could operate as far south as Mosul, 100 kilometres inside Iraq, to set up a supply hub. President Bush made it clear that although the numbers of US troops involved would be relatively small, they would have all the support they needed: 'We'll be able to protect . . . not only our own people, but . . . the people that we're setting out to protect, which is these refugees.'[33]

The plan called for six 'zones of protection', each capable of handling 60,000 refugees. The rationale for placing the centres in Iraq was that the terrain was more suitable and the sites closer to the refugees' homes. Once the campsites were selected, leaflets and loud-speakers communicated the news to the refugees on either side of the Turkish border, who were then transported in military lorries 'or whatever other mode of transportation is needed'.[34]

The plan involved a significant armed presence on Iraqi territory: 5,000 American troops with more available in the event of conflict. As the US 1st Infantry Division completed its withdrawal from the south, European Command troops moved into the north.[35] The British sent one brigade of Royal Marines, most of 3 Commando Brigade – about 2,000 men – to operate in Iraq from bases in Turkey.[36] The French also sent around a thousand troops and Dutch forces were also involved.

In order to limit the implications of this action, it was necessary to be sure that it could not be interpreted as support for Kurdish political objectives vis-à-vis Turkey as well as Iraq.

Baghdad had denounced the safe haven concept as a conspiracy, almost as soon as it had been proposed. According to Iraqi Prime Minister Saadoun Hammadi:

> The proposal to set up a zone under United Nations supervision inside Iraq to deal with the so-called refugee problem is a suspicious proposal that Iraq categorically rejects and will resist with all means . . . creating and inflating this problem is deliberate and is part of the chain of plots against Iraq's sovereignty.[37]

Now Iraq denounced the American plan as 'a continuation of the policy of intervention in Iraq's internal affairs'.[38]

Turkish views were especially important because implementation of the plan depended on its continued cooperation as the base for allied operations. The Turkish government naturally welcomed the safe haven plan, which would considerably ease its difficult political position. Initial air drops had been near the Turkish–Iraqi border, thus encouraging the refugees in their flight to Turkey, but air distribution under the safe haven scheme would continue further south into Iraq where demands were greatest, so that the Kurds would not be encouraged to come all the way to the border for relief. The US announcement in support of the safe havens plan took some of the pressure off the Turkish government which shifted towards worrying about the possibility that the safe havens could lead to a permanent Kurdish presence just south of the Turkish border.[39]

Although John Major had initially envisioned an 'enclave', British Foreign Office concern that the term implied a breach of Iraq's sovereignty led the proposed safety zones subsequently to be downgraded to 'safe havens,' which Major later said 'is perhaps a way I would prefer to put it rather than an enclave'.[40]

In addition, as British Defence secretary Tom King explained on 18 April, the Kurds would not be allowed to use the camps as bases for guerilla activity. The White House expressed the hope that the Kurds would not use the presence of allied troops as a cover to mount attacks against Iraqi forces:

> This is a humanitarian effort and we don't believe that the Kurdish guerrillas that are still operating in the northern sector would endanger the lives of their own fellow countrymen, fellow citizens, by exposing them to this kind of threat [through continued Kurdish attacks against Iraqi armed forces]. We are hoping that based on the mandate of 688, that all sides would abide by this humanitarian aspect, the Iraqi government as well as Kurdish rebels that may be operating in the sector.[41]

In practice it was extremely difficult to keep the implementation of the concept within strict limits. Its logic was to establish Western military authority over a substantial area of Iraq.[42] This became apparent as the new security arrangements were enforced. On 19 April Lieutenant General John Shalikashvili, the US commander in charge of the task force, met Iraqi officers near the town of Zakho in order to 'stop any possibility of inadvertent clashes between coalition forces and Iraq'. According to one officer present, Shalikashvili 'really specified that he wanted Iraqi ground forces to pull back. The General was not bending. He emphatically told them what to do.' The Iraqis noted the demands without necessarily agreeing to them.[43]

It was not enough that only Iraqi ground forces pulled back: if the Kurds were to feel safe when coming down from the mountains then there could be no Iraqi paramilitary presence either. On 21 April, as many as 200 Iraqi Ba'ath party police entered the town of Zakho, only hours after the Iraqi military had agreed to remain out of the area. This threatened to undermine efforts to convince the Kurds that it was safe to leave the mountains, just as French and British soldiers joined the US Marines operating in Iraq and 'working around' Iraqi troops.

As more Iraqi and coalition forces simultaneously arrived in Zakho the allies tired of 'working around' the problem and issued a 48-hour deadline for Iraqi troop withdrawal. Major General Jay Garner, the local allied commander, told Brigadier General Nushwan Danoun that the Iraqi 'police' breached Iraq's agreement to withdraw from the security zone and that if necessary the allies would use force to remove them.[44] After confirming the threat, Cheney was confident:

> I do not expect that we're going to find ourselves here engaged in conflict with Iraq. Certainly, there's no need for that . . . There should be no doubt in their minds about what the outcome would be. We have sufficient force in the area so that there's no question but that we would prevail.[45]

Iraq responded swiftly to the ultimatum. On 25 April Abdul Amir al-Anbari, Iraq's ambassador to the United Nations, declared that only 50 policemen remained in Zakho. The United States accepted this number and put in hand plans to register each policeman by name and to issue each one with an identity card. The swift Iraqi departure also reduced the risk of divergence in British and American policy towards the Iraqi police. The US military had intervened to delay British patrols which were intended to culminate, if necessary, in the forcible expulsion of the Iraqi forces.

On 26 April the Kurdish refugees began the trek to the safe havens. Now the actions of the Kurdish guerillas slowed progress. The previous day there had been a Kurdish attack on a UN convoy in northern Iraq. On 28 April it was reported that PKK guerillas at Qasrok were preventing their people from entering the allied refugee centres on the grounds that it was still too dangerous. Following allied requests, they desisted.

The expansive logic of the safe havens concept next manifested itself when it came to establishing the boundaries of the zones. The original concept envisaged quite modest areas but the logic of the scheme was to take up virtually all of Iraqi Kurdistan. If the idea was to encourage the refugees to return to their homes then their homes would need protection.

The military did this of their own volition when, without getting approval, they nearly doubled the size of the security zone. It was expanded to 30 kilometres east of Zakho. The troops encountered no resistance in extending the zone, even though it included some of Saddam Hussein's palaces where Republican Guard units were living. Hundreds of Iraqi soldiers were pushed out of the area as US troops moved within one mile of Dahuk, 30 miles inside the Iraqi border but north of the 36th parallel. The security zone now extended about 40 kilometres east from Zakho to Sirsensk, including all territory 'within 30 kilometres of this line, and to the south, the zone extends to a ridge line north of the city of Dahuk'. As Dahuk is the capital and a main communication hub of northwest Iraq, this was a significant expansion of the zone.

Estimated numbers of refugees in Turkey were down to 321,000 by 6 May, with 'another 200–300,000 displaced people receiving relief in Iraq north of the 36th parallel'. More than 4,000 refugees had entered the temporary relief camp. Fixed-wing airdrops had been suspended indefinitely, with camps being resupplied by helicopter and truck deliveries.[46]

This success in establishing safe havens left open two critical long-term questions: the possibility of handing over responsibility for the operation to the United Nations and the possibility of a Kurdish agreement with Iraq that would reduce the requirement for any international support.

The UN role

From the start there had been a presumption that the allies were taking emergency action to set up a relief system that would as a matter of course be taken over by the United Nations within months.

However, resistance was growing within the Secretary-General's office to what seemed to be a Western attempt to co-opt the United Nations to its own policy initiatives, irrespective of the views of the generality of the international community or the precise wording of the Charter. Thus Secretary-General Pérez de Cuéllar rejected an American, British and French request to place their troops in Iraq under UN command and give them blue helmets without the additional approval of the Security Council. On 17 April he observed that the deployment of foreign troops in Iraq posed political problems, although 'from the moral and humanitarian point of view' there was 'no difficulty'.[47] The allies were reluctant to seek a further Security Council resolution expanding the UN role while the United Nations Secretariat was itself reluctant to assume that authority without a resolution.

The Secretariat had been organising its own participation in the relief effort along a different path. Eric Suy and Prince Sadruddin Aga Khan of the United Nations had been working in Baghdad to obtain access to the Iraqi Kurds. Faced with a choice between a UN-sponsored effort and one sponsored directly by the West, Iraq opted for the United Nations. On 15 April it signalled to the United Nations that it would allow aid workers to enter the country to assist the Kurdish population. Prince Sadruddin's plan covered all of Iraq, including the southern cities of Basra, Karbala and Najaf, which made Baghdad's agreement essential.

On 18 April Iraq and the United Nations agreed a 21-point memorandum of understanding on establishing humanitarian centres in Iraq to care for all refugees and displaced persons. Baghdad approved UN promotion of 'the voluntary return home' of refugees and efforts to stem the outflow. Iraq pledged its full support and agreed to cooperate with the UN presence, primarily because they had authority over its character. UN centres could be established and run by UN civilians and other non-governmental organisations. The officials at UN camps, totalling 100 in all, would be civilians, including some from the International Committee of the Red Cross, regional Red Crescent Societies and the Iraqi Red Crescent Society. The idea was that they would be as capable as Western soldiers of creating a sense of safety that would encourage Kurds to come down from the mountains and to return to their villages.

This presented a problem for the allies as they had anticipated that the United Nations would take over their camps. Yet now the United Nations was operating on a parallel track. The full implications of this were not fully appreciated at first. On 19 April Marlin Fitzwater stated that:

> The UN is preparing to take over the camps and to run them. They are getting the necessary assurances from Iraq. Our troops are in there now surveying sites and getting ready to build the camps. Everybody is doing as much as they can as fast as they can to get the food in.

Fitzwater even described the camps being established and the ones the United Nations had negotiated with Iraq as 'essentially the same'. It was assumed that the agreement between Iraq and Prince Sadruddin simply informed Baghdad that camps were being established and

> that US, British and French personnel and military forces will be involved in helping to run them and get them established. Iraq essentially has agreed to all of that and not to interrupt those in any way.[48]

But Iraq had not agreed to cooperate with any plan involving military forces. UN officials were preparing to work at their own camps – not those of the allies.

The United States claimed that any additional camps set up were 'complementary rather than redundant'. If the United Nations became established in Iraq, then as a matter of course it would be able to assume responsibility for allied camps. Ironically this too was the Iraqi preference. If it had to have a foreign presence on its soil it much preferred this to be civilian UN workers rather than Western soldiers. By 24 April, therefore, both the allies and Baghdad were impatient for the United Nations to take control of the safe havens and they wanted greater coordination.

The continuing obstacle to an adequate UN presence was insufficient funds. According to the UN High Commissioner for Refugees, Sadako Ogata:

> UNHCR is not able to mount massive relief operations on credit. At a time when governments are urging the United Nations to take over and coordinate an emergency aid programme of such dimensions, it is vital that adequate resources be put at our disposal . . . If further special allocations are not made immediately, the entire humanitarian effort will be in dire jeopardy.[49]

On 11 April the United Nations appealed for $400 million but by the start of May only $185 million had been received.[50] Perez de Cuéllar told the Security Council on 29 April:

> Regrettably, until now, the response to the appeals [for funds] that have been launched has been very modest, especially for activities inside Iraq. If the United Nations is to implement this operation, as requested by its member states, and to alleviate the human suffering as well as contribute to stabilize a volatile situation, it is essential that it be given the necessary financial resources to do so immediately.

Despite inadequate funds to take on the task being urged on it the United Nations sent two convoys to Iraq along with UN personnel to establish facilities for distributing relief and to begin discussions with allied forces about the United Nations assuming responsibility for the allied camps. The goal, said Pérez de Cuéllar, was 'to assume responsibility for both the humanitarian centers and the camps as soon as possible – in accordance with the wishes of all parties concerned'.[51]

Three UN officials first visited the allied camp at Zakho on 28 April. A week later they had taken over responsibility for the food distribution system. By 13 May the United Nations was sending a food convoy to Dahuk, hoping that it would attract refugees closer to their homes, but they continued to show reluctance. The problem was that while both the allies and the Iraqis preferred a UN operation, it could not succeed unless the Kurdish people themselves were convinced that provisions were being made for their long-term security.

In an attempt to solve this security problem John Major, in a letter to the Secretary-General, proposed the authorisation of a UN police force; this would not necessarily require another Security Council resolution. This course of action seemed unlikely to succeed, however, due to Chinese concerns over the precedent for Tibet. John Major wrote: 'To give the Kurds the sense of security they need will require a UN presence on the ground and I believe that the idea of a UN civilian police presence is one we should develop.'[52]

There were obvious problems with this idea as few countries would contribute in the absence of a further UN resolution. The outcome of the proposal thus depended largely on its reception by the Secretary-General. After proposing the idea in private to the five permanent members of the Security Council on 23 April, the British government gained EC approval and then made the idea public. Pérez de Cuéllar was willing to consider a police force – though not a peacekeeping force – without further Security Council approval.

On 11 May Pérez de Cuéllar announced that he had received 'a very clear rejection from the Iraqi government. They do not want a United Nations police presence.' The key sticking point in the Secretary-General's negotiations with Iraq was whether UN policemen would carry arms. In the end the allies compromised on this point in the hope that it would still provide the necessary reassurance to the Kurds. President Bush announced on 16 May that he was prepared to seek a Security Council resolution authorising the United Nations to undertake the policing despite his belief that existing resolutions already granted that authority: 'We're contemplating going to the United Nations on that to get further authority.'[53]

The test for the new approach came in mid-May. Despite having agreed to withdraw from Dahuk, the Iraqi government was gathering forces in surrounding hills. Iraqi Special Forces were systematically plundering and destroying the city as well as arresting suspected Kurdish rebels. On 19 May, without any prior announcement, 10 unarmed UN security guards entered Dahuk to protect international relief workers. They carried only handcuffs. It was planned to expand the contingent to 50 or 60 within 10 days and arm them with light sidearms following Security Council approval.

The United Nations subsequently got Iraq to agree to the UN

police force in an annex to the original memorandum of understanding signed by Prince Sadruddin.[54] According to this agreement the handguns carried by the guards were 'personal weapons'. By 20 May the 10 security guards in Dahuk were wearing pistols, though they still had no power of arrest. Of the total 500 guards allowed to operate in Iraq no more than 150 could operate in any of the five regional centres. The agreement, signed in Baghdad on 23 May, did not provide the security of Major's original plan. Only 500 UN security guards with little authority were to replace allied troops which totalled 21,700 at the peak of deployment. British concerns included the safety of those Kurds who had offered their help to allied forces and were particularly vulnerable to Iraqi persecution.

After lengthy negotiations with the Iraqis, US troops visited Dahuk to survey the city's services and to reassure the refugees that it was safe to go there. They were described as neither occupying the city nor extending the security zone but merely entering to restore basic services. After further negotiations, on 22 May the Iraqis agreed to withdraw their military and police forces from Dahuk altogether. The Iraqis continued to control armed checkpoints outside the city to ensure that no armed Kurds entered, but they pledged to withdraw their troops and secret police 10 kilometres to the south.

A Kurdish settlement

Humanitarian relief could not be divorced from fundamental political questions such as Kurdish autonomy since the goal of the relief programme was to get the refugees back home. The safe havens announcement was welcomed by the Kurds but they were anxious from the start about the temporary nature of the deployment. They wanted indefinite protection, at least so long as Saddam Hussein remained in power. Izzedine Barawi, a KDP spokesman, saw the plan as 'an initial step', but argued for 'a permanent solution for the Kurdish problem', including reviving the 1970 agreement with Baghdad granting the Kurds autonomy and positions in the central government.[55]

President Bush recognised that the allied policy would not result in a permanent solution:

> I want to stress that this new effort, despite its scale and scope, is not intended as a permanent solution to the plight of the Iraqi Kurds. To the contrary, it is an interim solution designed to meet an immediate, penetrating humanitarian need. Our long-term objective remains the same: for Iraqi Kurds and, indeed,

for all Iraqi refugees, wherever they are, to return home and to live in peace, free from repression, free to live their lives.[56]

However, by the allies stepping in on their behalf, if only as a temporary measure, the Kurds' overall political position within Iraq was strengthened. Saddam Hussein was obliged to show greater flexibility. The Ba'ath Party was losing legitimacy, the army had been weakened and there was little chance that sanctions would be lifted while Baghdad remained in conflict with the Kurds. Kurdish guerillas had been defeated in Kirkuk, Arbil, Dahuk and Zakho, but a long, low-intensity fight was still faced in the mountainous regions. By neutralising his Kurdish foes and by appearing to liberalise Iraqi society, Saddam reasoned that he could split his domestic critics and impress international opinion. He thus quickly agreed to negotiations over Kurdish autonomy to which he declared acceptance in principle. He was quoted by the Iraqi news agency as saying in a meeting in Arbil, the administrative capital of the Kurdish autonomous region: 'What is past is past, and we are starting again.' This was, however, qualified by reference to 'The killers, the violators of people's honor and those who stole the assets of the state and the people and have not returned them – we do not give guarantees to those people'.[57]

The Kurds had strong incentives to negotiate. Their people were in wretched circumstances and their best chance of maintaining control of the northern areas which they still possessed was a permanent cease-fire.[58] Kurdish guerillas attempting to defend territory in the north were no longer protecting the Kurdish community which had fled across the borders. Nevertheless, the Kurds demonstrated the flexibility to end the deadlock. Jalal Talabani said at a press conference:

> We tried to overthrow the regime and could not. They tried to crush us and they failed. So we have both agreed that we must use political and peaceful means to end the conflict.[59]

Even so the willingness of the Kurdish leaders – Jalal Talabani of the PUK, Sami Abdul Rahman of the People's Democratic Party, Rasoul Mamend of the Socialist Party of Kurdistan, and Nechirvan Barzani of the KDP – to negotiate with the Iraqi government over Kurdish autonomy caused a rift between the Kurds and other groups represented in the opposition alliance.

The negotiations opened on 23 April in an atmosphere of mutual distrust.[60] Despite this they appeared to make rapid progress. A spokesman for the Kurdistan Front announced: 'We have come to the conclusion that a military uprising is not the solution. There has to be a political solution guaranteed by outside forces, namely the United Nations.'[61]

As a sign of good faith Baghdad extended the amnesty offered to Kurds two weeks earlier to include Iraqi Shias. Saddam Hussein also expressed a willingness to consider Kurdish autonomy, free elections in Iraq and a free press. The Kurds recognised that the concessions were due to Saddam's weakness and doubted that they would last if he grew stronger.[62] In this sense, the humanitarian relief effort helped. It provided security for the Kurds while they negotiated and kept the pressure on Saddam.

On 24 April Jalal Talabani announced that the Kurds had agreed in principle with Saddam Hussein on the establishment of Kurdish autonomy in Iraq: 'The agreement affirmed the principle of democracy in Iraq, press freedoms and allowing all Kurds to return to towns and villages.' Significantly, the Iraqi Information Minister, Hamid Youssef Hummadi, attended Talabani's announcement. Nonetheless, nothing was binding until Masoud Barzani signed the agreement. Foreign reactions to the announcement of the agreement in principle were favourable though cautious.[63]

Two key issues were left unresolved and they continued to dog the negotiations: the expansion of the 1970 autonomous region to include Kirkuk and the prospect for international guarantees to ensure that any agreement was honoured. One reason why the 1970 Agreement had collapsed was the failure to conduct a census in Kirkuk which would have shown a Kurdish majority there. Since then the government had actively shifted Arabs to the area in order to change the cultural balance. Saddam Hussein therefore insisted that Kirkuk, whose oil fields, unlike those in the south, were neither occupied nor damaged, would not be included in the new agreement.

Saddam also resisted efforts to secure international guarantees, which he saw as interference in internal affairs. Flexibility on this point was unlikely since international pressure was the principal reason for his willingness to compromise. On the other hand, past experience with Saddam led the Kurds to place considerable importance on the need for international guarantees.

The United States was still taking a generally cautious line on the future shape of Iraq. It backed away from encouraging Western-style democracy, which 'might be more destabilizing than stabilizing'. Instead, it declared that 'more democratization and broader participation' in government would be welcomed but should be allowed to proceed at its 'own pace'. If Saddam Hussein was talking to Kurdish representatives there seemed to be little reason why the United States could not also do so, although when these talks took place they focused less on politics than humanitarian aid.[64] US support for

Kurdish autonomy was nonetheless revealed in a US military document stating that the establishment of 'a permanent, secure autonomous Kurdish region as part of Iraqi reparations', was a basic US policy goal.[65]

While sympathetic to this position, the Kurdistan Front still hoped that the Security Council would guarantee the deal. The British Foreign Secretary, Douglas Hurd, hinted that this might be achieved through the continued use of sanctions which could be used to provide incentives for Iraq to abide by an agreement. Resolutions 687 and 688 instructed the sanctions committee to consider internal repression when discussing their continuation.[66] Little more than this was on offer, however. International unwillingness to provide a security guarantee and Iraqi unwillingness to tolerate one even if offered forced the Kurdish Front to abandon this demand in return for promises of greater democracy.

In mid-May Saddam Hussein met with a four-man Kurdish delegation headed by Masoud Barzani, the first such meeting since 24 April when Saddam had spoken to Jalal Talabani. Barzani emerged from his talks in Baghdad in a positive mood:

> We can say that we have covered an important distance on the road to finding a solution that serves the Kurdish problem and strengthens Iraqi unity . . . We call upon [the refugees] once again to return to their homes as many of them have done already.[67]

The 'important distance' consisted of an agreement in principle on a general amnesty for Kurdish guerrillas; returning all Kurds to their homes; rescinding emergency laws restricting Kurds; opening a university in Sulaymaniyah; rapid economic development of Kurdistan; and Kurdish participation in the Iraqi army and other state organisations in Kurdistan. The principal area of remaining disagreement was control of Kirkuk and the oil wealth there, but on 17 May Barzani declared that this was 'not a problem', saying, 'there is not full agreement in all areas but the difficult things we have passed . . . It is better for the Kurds to come back at least inside Iraq.'[68]

By this time the United Nations had already taken over management of the refugee camp in Dahuk, and United States withdrawal looked imminent. The United States offered free transport from refugee sites to many Iraqi towns but only a few hundred refugees accepted the offer. However favourable the refugees' response to a combination of allied protection along the way and the promise of a political solution, it was not sufficient. Many set up new camps just outside the allied relief centres. The refugee problem was being transferred rather than solved. They were prepared to enter Iraq, but unprepared to return home if that meant leaving allied protection.

Early departure by the United States risked removing the pressure on Saddam Hussein to compromise with the Kurdistan Front. This caused considerable concern among the Kurds. The statement by the Chairman of the US Joint Chiefs of Staff, Colin Powell, in early June that the United States favoured withdrawal 'sooner than we thought' undercut the Kurdistan Front's position in the negotiations with Baghdad. Disagreement between the Kurds and Saddam over Kirkuk persisted despite the Kurds' willingness to let Baghdad control the oil if they could administer the city and have a percentage of the wealth corresponding to their percentage of the Iraqi population as a whole (20 per cent). Jalal Talabani was now doubtful that there would be a final agreement: 'Perhaps at the end of the negotiations we will not be able to reach a final agreement.'[69]

The Kurds showed increasing fears as the departure of US troops approached. Armed clashes between the Kurdish *pesh merga* and Iraqi forces took place in Sulaymaniyah and Arbil, apparently triggered by army violence and attempts to round up military deserters and Kurdish guerillas. Neither Talabani nor Mahmoud Othman, leader of the Kurdish Socialist Party, were confident that negotiations with Baghdad would result in a satisfactory agreement. The two men were organising their forces in anticipation of a collapse of the talks. Other Iraqi opposition leaders called on the Kurds to end their talks with Saddam.[70]

Barzani was the main Kurdish leader who still believed in an agreed end to the crisis, though he, too, clearly linked it with the US presence in Iraq. He suggested a final agreement could be ready by the middle of June to enable the United States to withdraw. Divisions were now appearing. While Barzani was prepared to delay deciding on the Kirkuk issue, Jalal Talabani insisted that 'if there is no agreement on Kirkuk there will be no final agreement'. While Barzani expected a final agreement in a week, Talabani said 'I don't expect a final agreement'. Barzani was confident that Saddam Hussein would fulfil his pledges because of his current political weakness. Talabani remained sceptical.

Although Talabani denied a major rift he called for a full meeting of the Kurdish leadership. He believed they were on the verge of another Kurdish exodus. Talabani said 'I think if they [the allies] leave without achieving democracy in Iraq or before final agreement between the Kurds and the Iraqi government . . . people will again leave their towns for the mountains.'[71]

On 16 June Talabani met with Turgut Özal and Western diplomats in Ankara, where he was told that the allies had no firm schedule for withdrawal, despite the US departure from Dahuk. The pressure was now back on Saddam Hussein. As a result he offered the Kurds joint control of Kirkuk and discussions about its long-term future. The offer made it much more likely that the Kurdistan Front would accept the deal, although Talabani still had doubts. He described as 'unacceptable' Baghdad's demand that the Kurds support the Ba'ath revolution in return for military and political control of the provinces of Dahuk, Arbil and Sulaymaniyah, where Iraqi police and military would come under Kurdish control.[72]

Talabani therefore rejected the offer. The Ba'athists were arguing that Kurds in senior government posts would have to support the government, and also sever their links with foreign governments and aid agencies. Mahmoud Othman of the Kurdish Socialist Party, said: 'We can agree to peace but not to be partners with the Ba'athists. He wants to isolate the Kurds and their friends and wait until they are weak before moving against them.' Barzani backed the deal because he thought it was the best one he would be able to get and he counted on Saddam Hussein's political weakness to prevent him from reneging.[73]

Bolstered by renewed allied support the Kurds rejected Baghdad's proposal and moved to reassure other opposition groups that democracy would be a precondition for any agreement with Baghdad.[74]

Shias

Throughout this period a parallel debate was going on over the fate of the Shia rebels in the south. The United States had provided medical care, food, water and shelter material for approximately 40,000 refugees. Comparisons with the assistance accorded the Kurds led Arab countries to criticise what they perceived to be double standards. There were also the familiar comparisons being made between the concern for the Kurds and neglect of UN resolutions calling for the protection of Palestinians. Iraqi opposition members argued that if safety was provided for the Kurds then it should also be available for the Shias in the south.[75]

The Americans intended to transfer humanitarian responsibilities to the United Nations when the latter took over the demilitarised zone as stipulated in the cease-fire agreement. When that happened, according to President Bush, 'that will be very good assurance' that the Shias would not be attacked.[76] This gave little reassurance to the Shias who were desperate for permanent protection. Instead, as US European Command expanded the Kurdish relief effort, US Central Command continued to withdraw from southern Iraq. Assistance to

Iran and the Shias remained modest while Western policy on the Kurds moved quickly.

'The UN is not a police force and guaranteeing their safety is a very tall order,' said Prince Sadruddin Aga Khan, who had been asked by Pérez de Cuéllar to take responsibility for protecting and maintaining refugees and displaced persons in the areas of southern Iraq occupied by coalition forces.[77] The UN force sent to patrol the southern demilitarised zone numbered 1,440, but Pérez de Cuéllar did not believe that the United Nations was responsible for the safety of Iraqis there, merely for providing them with food, shelter and medicine. Eric Suy, who accompanied Sadruddin to Iraq to assess the basic needs of Iraqi civilians, concluded that the refugees in the south were worse off than those in the north and that they required 'enormous' aid. According to the Swiss Red Cross, since March as many as 30,000–40,000 southern Iraqi refugees passed through the Iranian town of Khorramshahr, where they had been placed in transit camps controlled by the Iranian Red Crescent.

The Shias' position was not helped by the refusal of Kuwait to allow them to enter Kuwaiti territory. Riyadh, however, did decide to allow up to 50,000 to enter Saudi Arabia. This followed both American pressure and recognition that Iran had accepted so many refugees. With American help the Saudis completed a camp near Rafha, just south of the Iraqi border, capable of accommodating at first 30,000 and eventually 50,000 refugees. In preparation for the final withdrawal from southern Iraq the US military had flown 500 refugees each day to the new camp. By 6 May, 12,300 Iraqi refugees had been transferred from southern Iraq to the Saudi refugee camp.

Nevertheless, Prince Sadruddin and the Iranian authorities warned that too little attention was being paid to the plight of those Iraqi Shias who had fled to the marshes in southern Iraq just as the United Nations declared the Iraqi–Kuwaiti border a demilitarised zone. By June it was reported that Iraqi forces had encircled 500,000 to 850,000 in the marshlands. The refugees were unable to flee into Iran because the only route passed Iraqi checkpoints on the Baghdad to Basra highway and Iraq was thought by Iran to be bombing them in preparation for further attack. Although Basra was one of the five regional humanitarian centres that the United Nations was allowed to operate, there was still no actual UN presence there. Both the United States and Prince Sadruddin doubted reports of Iraqi preparations for an assault on the Shias. According to Sadruddin, a mission to southern Iraq in the first week of June 'did not confirm the alarmist reports and did not witness any exceptional mass movements', while a UNICEF mission concluded that there were no more than 30,000 refugees in the marshes.[78] Whatever their numbers, the refugees were in a desperate position, dying of starvation and disease but afraid to flee further lest they be discovered by the Iraqi army.

As a result, and despite the doubts about both the scale of the refugee population and the likelihood of Iraqi repression, the UN coordinator in Iraq, Bernt Bernander, announced that new refugee centres would be established. In addition, Britain warned Iraq not to attack the Shia refugees. On 12 June the British Foreign Secretary Douglas Hurd telephoned the Iranian Foreign Minister Ali Akbar Velayati to discuss the situation. A British Foreign Office spokesman subsequently stated that 'Any action by the Iraqi government against the Shias would be in contravention of Security Council Resolution 688 . . . and would have very serious consequences.'[79]

By early July UN concerns were great enough to warrant consideration of whether to evacuate the trapped Shias. This was one topic discussed in Baghdad by an eight-man mission led by Prince Sadruddin. Reports indicated that the Iraqi government had both surrounded the marshes and was shelling campsites when they located them. Not surprisingly Baghdad proved uncooperative.

UN efforts to assist the Shias hiding in marshes now included transit centres similar to the refugee camps established in the north. The centres would not be refugee camps but would instead serve as collection points for food, medicine and other assistance, including transportation. Prince Sadruddin said the centres could not be in the marshlands themselves which were too vast and inaccessible and would therefore be set up near the main roads. However, he continued his efforts to convince the Iraqi government to allow them to be established on the edge of the marshlands, which the government appeared to have blockaded thereby preventing any food or supplies from reaching the more than 40,000 refugees in the marshes. Although the government denied the blockade it nevertheless punished Prince Sadruddin's visit to al-Hammar in the south with the suspension of all UN convoys to the area.

Rapid Reaction Force

The British government was more willing than that of the United States to provide guarantees for the Kurds and Shias. Both Britain and France disagreed with the US timetable for the withdrawal of US troops from the safe havens, which was initially put at 27 June. On 17 June, Douglas Hurd announced that British, French, Dutch and Italian foreign ministers had agreed not to withdraw from Iraq while there was still a risk to the Kurds:

We went into northern Iraq in order to persuade the Kurds to come down from the mountains – to save lives. We don't want the operation to end in a way that will merely re-create the same problem.[80]

The Americans did extend the moment of withdrawal from the end of June to 4 July, but Pentagon spokesman Bob Hall declared that it was in the Kurds' best interest for the United States to relinquish control of the relief effort to the United Nations and other international organisations:

> We've succeeded in creating a climate in which [the refugees] have gone back home. Now we're winding up that operation. We're turning it over completely to the international organizations.[81]

The disagreement between the Americans and Europeans was resolved in the form of a new proposal for a multinational rapid reaction brigade of ground forces stationed in Turkey to protect the Kurds in the event of reprisals from Baghdad. Operation Poised Hammer would benefit from US air support and depend on the extra credibility so created. European foreign ministers hoped that formation of the brigade would encourage Saddam Hussein to reach an agreement with the Kurds and avoid a new refugee crisis being provoked by withdrawal. At this point allied troops in northern Iraq numbered around 7,000: 3,600 US, 2,000 British and 1,500 French.

Douglas Hurd set down four conditions before withdrawal could take place: replacement of allied forces with UN forces; conclusion of an agreement between the Kurds and Baghdad; maintenance of sanctions until it was clear that Iraq would respect the agreement; and a clear warning to Iraq outlining retaliatory measures to be taken in the event of future repression of the Kurds. British officials reportedly suggested that these conditions should be registered at the United Nations to give them international status and were prepared to consider a new UN resolution to support the 'residual force'.[82]

The view that the Kurds were still vulnerable was shared by General John Galvin, Supreme Allied Commander Europe. He reportedly urged Washington to warn Baghdad that allied troops would be likely return to Iraq if Saddam Hussein undertook further repression of the Kurds. The State Department disagreed with this suggestion, defending the adequacy of previous statements such as that of Assistant Secretary of State John Kelly who told the House Foreign Affairs Subcommittee on Europe and the Middle East, 'if there were major action the US and other coalition forces would probably react to that one way or the other'.[83]

On 20 May Douglas Hurd and James Baker met, after which the

British Foreign Secretary claimed: 'We are in agreement on the elements which we believe need building up', which may have implied that there was not yet agreement on the timetable for withdrawal. However, US troops in northern Iraq were told that from midnight of 20 May their orders to withdraw had been cancelled for up to four more months. Baker had sympathy with Hurd's fear that a rapid withdrawal could precipitate a further crisis. However, he was having trouble with the Pentagon which was anxious to get American forces out as soon as possible.

With a slightly longer breathing space, Western countries now worked to create the optimal conditions for withdrawal. To bolster the plan for a UN police force, further funding was provided. In April the United Nations' request for $449 million in total had gained a response from the European Community of $134 million. Now, in June, the EC agreed to provide another £21.5 million as requested by the Secretary-General for the operation, and individual states renewed their offer to provide the manpower.[84]

Work also progressed on the residual allied force including 'the precise shape of it, where it would be located, who would be in charge, which nations would supply what to it'. US Defense Department spokesman Pete Williams confirmed that whatever the details finally agreed the force 'would clearly have combat power'. Before completing the withdrawal, he said, there will be 'clear markers laid down to the Iraqis on what we expect to see them do as they continue to abide by the UN resolutions and as they continue to cooperate with the humanitarian mission in Iraq'. He also said that the United States would be 'very upfront with the Kurds about what we are doing'. Marlin Fitzwater said that the force would complement the UN police force rather than replace it. The force would be 'a multinational rapid deployment force that could supplement UN forces in maintaining security in the area'.[85]

The agreement worked out in Washington by the US and UK defence secretaries, who had previously consulted the French defence minister, was for a brigade – about 5,000 troops – to be made available for use in northern Iraq. The force was to be composed of American, British, French and Dutch troops which would remain in the area with helicopter support after the other troops had withdrawn.[86]

The allies had intended to set up the rapid reaction force by the middle of July. The remaining allied troops in Iraq would then complete their withdrawal and regroup at a base five miles inside Turkey. The Turkish cabinet was expected to give its approval following a meeting on 10 July. However, detailed consultations between the allies and the Turkish government did not begin until

11 July. The government was apparently worried by opposition claims that the force to be based in Turkey – about 2,000 men split between the Silopi base and the US air base at Incirlik – could become involved in the local war between the Turkish army and the PKK, be used in non-Kurdish emergencies or delay normalisation of relations with Iraq. The Turkish government nevertheless approved allied plans.

The agreed plan was for a 'residual' allied force backed up by US aircraft carriers in the eastern Mediterranean. It was designed as a 'very visible warning' to Saddam Hussein not to attack the Iraqi Kurds who continued to fear him. The pull-out from Iraq on 15 July was accompanied by a warning to Saddam that the 'coalition retains a clear interest in peace within Iraq and is willing to respond militarily to Iraqi actions that disturb the peace'. The security zone was, in effect, to be left intact even with the coalition's withdrawal. The ban on fixed- and rotary-wing aircraft above the 36th parallel was extended indefinitely as were the interdictions on the Iraqi army, special police and military border guards. According to the Pentagon, to enforce the ban 'the coalition will undertake reconnaissance and other air operations above the 36th Parallel as needed'. When asked if Baghdad had responded, a Pentagon spokesman said 'This is not anything for them to respond to; this is something for them to be informed of'. Nevertheless 10 US officers remained in Zakhu after the allied withdrawal to coordinate with the Iraqi military and provide a fast channel for communications.[87]

The Pentagon described the force in the following way:

> The combined task force will maintain an appropriate level of air and ground forces in the region to see to it that the conditions which caused the Kurds and other refugees to flee from their homes do not recur, and to make certain that Iraq complies with the UN Security Council resolution that has to do with the refugees.

The US force was to include about 2,500 men from a helicopter-borne battalion and a reinforced infantry battalion with heavy weapons, as well as air support aboard an aircraft carrier in the eastern Mediterranean. The USS *Forrestal* was in that area with its escort vessels. Ground-based aircraft might also provide support. The British contribution to the rapid reaction force consisted mainly of a company of Royal Marines – about 120 men backed up by support troops. According to General Shalikashvili, the threat to use force to protect human rights in Iraq applied to the entire country, not simply northern Iraq: 'We're certainly not abandoning anyone,' he said.[88]

Aftermath

When in June there was an expectation of imminent American withdrawal, several thousand Kurdish refugees in Zakho demonstrated to protest. However, when the allied pull-out occurred, the Kurdish response was modest, with the Kurds furthest south expressing the greatest concern. Demonstrations in Zakho against the withdrawal were good-natured, well organised and expressed Kurdish gratitude for the help they had received. The Kurds were aware that the forces would be nearby but nevertheless worried about their future and the re-entry of Iraqi forces into the area. Within days of the allied departure Iraqi troops clashed with Kurdish guerillas, leaving up to 500 casualties.[89] In August, Turkey raided the bases of outlawed Turkish Kurdish guerillas now operating out of northern Iraq.

Masoud Barzani, in Baghdad for talks with the government, urged restraint and said that those opposed to further negotiations were seeking to use the incident to prevent them from going forward. As a result of the clashes the Kurds began to leave these areas in anticipation of continued fighting. After the *pesh merga* gained control the government continued to build up its forces in the area, but an agreement reached with guerilla commanders provided for equal forces of 500 men to police Sulaymaniyah. Estimates of the numbers of Kurds who had left their homes as a result of the fighting varied from 40,000 to 100,000. On 23 August Iraqi Kurds announced that the negotiations with Baghdad which had begun in April were over. Barzani and the other negotiators had returned to northern Iraq after 42 days of negotiations in Baghdad convinced that Saddam Hussein would make no more concessions.

The final draft agreement left the status of Kirkuk vague, but reportedly provides for the resettlement of Kurdish refugees recently and previously displaced. Barzani said: 'We have a final version of the agreement before us.' The Kurdistan Front was considering the possibility of ratification.[90]

Despite the continuing negotiations with the Kurdistan Front, the Iraqi military was amassing its forces in northern Iraq, around both Sulaymaniyah, which had been retaken by Kurdish rebels on 18 July, and Kirkuk. As tensions mounted the Kurdish population of Sulaymaniyah was becoming increasingly restless and a second Kurdish exodus became likely. Iraqi forces were thought to include five divisions in the area of Kirkuk and a number of helicopters operating north of the 36th parallel, where they had been forbidden by the allied forces.[91] Kurdish fears were exacerbated by the forcible removal of Kurds from their homes near Kirkuk in an escalation of Saddam's Arabisation of the area. These fears prompted Kurdish leaders yet again to seek assurances of support from allied governments, which were closely monitoring the situation.

Armed clashes, described by Prince Sadruddin Aga Khan as 'serious', began to occur. They appeared to be designed to test the strength of the *pesh merga* and the resolve of the allied coalition poised to intervene in Iraq. Virtually all of these clashes occurred in areas held by the PUK, the firmest of all Kurdish parties among the Kurdistan Front in rejecting the autonomy agreement. Either as a sign of weak morale or as an attempt to exploit divisions within the Kurdish leadership, Iraqi troops began to withdraw from around Sulaymaniyah, a predominantly KDP area.

The Kurds remained nervous about the commitment of the coalition. Nechirvan Barzani, the nephew of the KDP leader Masoud Barzani, acknowledged that 'Western involvement in April was just for humanitarian reasons. We have seen no political commitment.'[92] The review of Operation Provide Comfort due at the end of September raised the prospect of an allied withdrawal, thereby increasing the importance of continued support from Ankara. The Turkish government was reluctant to pledge greater unilateral support for the Kurds and had reservations about the presence of foreign ground troops in the run-up to a general election. Nonetheless it extended permission for allied ground forces to remain for another three months.[93]

The allies still began to withdraw their ground forces in late September. However, rather than retracting guarantees offered to the Kurds, the coalition reconfigured its rapid reaction force to make greater use of air power. Ground support aircraft such as the A-10 were replaced with F-111 fighter bombers and a new agreement with Turkey specifically allowed the aircraft earmarked for Operation Poised Hammer to remain in Turkey for another 90 days from 30 September. Strengthening allied air power in the region was accompanied by renewed pledges of support from NATO and Arab allies.

At the end of August, when they still felt they could count on allied support, instead of returning to negotiations in Baghdad the Kurdish leadership had asked the Iraqi government to clarify certain aspects of the autonomy agreement on offer. Soon after the announcement of allied intentions to withdraw, the discussions broke up without agreement. Fighting in northern Iraq worsened, particularly around Sulaymaniyah, causing more Kurdish civilians to head for the borders. In order to head off another refugee problem Kurdish and Iraqi military leaders signed a cease-fire agreement on 8 October. The terms of the cease-fire called for Iraqi forces to withdraw from positions occupied in the previous four days and for prisoners of war on both sides to be released. The second term was disputed by the

Kurds, however, who said political prisoners had to be included in the Iraqi release.

The cease-fire proved very difficult to implement. The day after it was signed the Iraqi army began shelling the Kurdish towns of Kifri, Kalar and Maydan, all below the 36th parallel and in important strategic positions for the defence of Kirkuk. The shelling heightened differences between the PUK and KDP over whether to accept the draft autonomy agreement offered by Baghdad. Jalal Talabani, speaking for the PUK, said the attacks signalled 'the end of negotiations'. In contrast, Masoud Barzani, leader of the KDP and chief negotiator for the Kurdistan Front, cited the coalition's decision not to intervene on the Kurds' behalf as evidence that the Kurds should take what was on offer rather than hold out for concessions unlikely to be forthcoming.[94]

The US Defense Department declared that 'by any definition, Operation Provide Comfort has been an outstanding success'.[95] Nonetheless there remained a sense that the Kurds had been given temporary assistance without any long-term solution having been found to their basic predicament. Although, according to Turkish figures, by 1 June there were only 12,000 refugees still waiting to be airlifted out of the border refugee camps, as late as the middle of July there remained around 1.5 million refugees near the Iranian border who were living in makeshift shelters and suffering from sickness, dehydration and malnutrition.

Turkey

Humanitarian intervention in Iraq placed political pressure on Turkey, where tension developed between its distinct policies towards Turkish and Iraqi Kurds. The basis for separate policies was the existence of serious divisions between Iraqi Kurds and the main Kurdish organisation in Turkey, the Marxist Turkish Kurdish Workers Party (PKK). While Iraqi Kurds sought an agreement with Baghdad granting Kurdish autonomy in northern Iraq, the PKK continued openly to campaign for an independent Kurdistan.[96] The PKK's method of campaigning was terrorist attacks against the Turkish army and government and against pro-government Kurds. The Turkish government, on whom the international effort to provide assistance to the Iraqi Kurds depended, found itself in an increasingly difficult position.

The PKK staged four coordinated attacks against towns in southeast Turkey, including Silopi, where there was a refugee camp for Iraqi Kurds. Attacks during the first weekend in July severely wounded several Turkish soldiers. The PKK was thought by some

Western diplomats to be aligned with Saddam Hussein to prevent the allied protection plan, but PKK leaders suspected Iraqi Kurdish leaders of selling out a Kurdish independent state to Saddam Hussein when they resumed talks with the Iraqi government on 6 July.[97]

Turkish President Turgut Özal was interested in talking to Iraqi Kurds as part of his liberalisation of Turkey's Kurdish policy but also as a hedge against the possibility that they would gain control of the northern Iraqi oil pipeline, an important source of Turkish revenue. Turkey's difficulty with the allied relief effort was that while it kept Iraqi Kurds from flooding into Turkey, it also provided the PKK with the opportunity for increased violence. Inasmuch as the relief effort helped the Iraqi Kurds in their negotiations with Baghdad, it also provided the PPK with an additional motive for violence since an autonomous region within Iraq would further weaken prospects for an independent Kurdistan.

In an attempt to preserve the support of the Turkish government, Iraqi Kurds maintained a dialogue with Ankara. On an early visit to Turkey, Jalal Talabani agreed secretly to restrict PKK activities in return for Turkish aid and continued international support. In subsequent meetings border security remained an important topic of discussion. One of Turkey's concerns was that the PKK had set up a sister party in Iraq, the Kurdish Freedom Party (PAK), to operate out of Kurdish refugee camps. As a result of Turkey's role in the Gulf War, Turgut Özal had considerable latitude to handle the Kurdish insurgency without risking official Western criticism. At a meeting with Talabani on July 25, Özal said:

> We will hit the nests of these terror groups in Lebanon, in Iraq . . . anyone involved in terror or supporting it will have no mercy from us . . . I spoke to the US President about it [at the weekend]; he said he was definitely behind us.[98]

On 5 August PKK guerillas attacked a Turkish army post near Sendinli. Nine soldiers and one village guard were killed and seven other soldiers were taken prisoner. In response, Turkish troops moved into northern Iraq to prevent PKK rebels from conducting cross-border raids. With F-4 and F-104 fighter bombers, helicopter gunships, and a commando regiment estimated at 2,000 men, the military established a three-mile buffer zone inside Iraq. The Turkish Prime Minister justified this step on the basis that there was a power vacuum in the area:

> There is no authority in north Iraq. We can't stay disinterested. We are establishing a three-mile zone. Turkish military aircraft

will attack anyone who comes into the area . . . Turkey is going to declare the zone to all the world.[99]

In the course of the operation Turkish forces flew more than 130 sorties against rebel strongholds, particularly those in areas near the joint Turkish, Iraqi and Iranian borders. It was in this area that Turkish forces concentrated, rather than attempting to enforce the security zone along the entire 150-kilometre border. According to a Turkish general staff statement read on state radio, 'In coordination with the operation, rebel hideouts have been raided and destroyed by commando teams backed up by armed helicopters'. However, a Kurdish Democratic Party spokesman said that the raids had been made against refugee centres and had killed 18 people, some of whom were women and children.[100] But the importance of Turkey in allied efforts to assist the Kurds placed obvious limits on what the allies were willing (or able) to do to underscore their demands.

Internationally, the response to Turkey's military action was hostile. In the West, Turkey's use of force against the Kurds was seen as inconsistent with allied efforts to protect them. From the Soviet Foreign Ministry the action elicited harsh criticism.[101] Domestic divisions over how to handle the Kurdish problem had more far-reaching consequences. In criticising the government's 12-year emergency rule of the Kurdish region the opposition Social Democrat Party (SHP) said that the government's security measures 'sometimes take on the dimensions of state terror'.[102] Turgut Özal's most serious political threat, however, came from the Turkish right wing who were unhappy with his policy of liberalisation toward the Kurds and who wholeheartedly approved of military action against the PKK. With a general election scheduled for autumn 1991 there was a chance that conservative sentiments could be translated into a new power configuration in Turkish politics, with the Motherland Party even losing control of the parliament.

The clashes between the Turkish government and Kurds escalated. An 11 October cross-border Kurdish attack on Begowa in which 11 soldiers were killed led to Turkish planes attacking rebel bases inside Iraq, reportedly dropping six napalm bombs on the village of Barnik.[103] The air attacks were followed by the advance into Iraq of 3,000 Turkish commandos to within nine miles of Cukurca. Kurdish leaders insisted that the areas being attacked were not guerilla bases and stressed that innocent civilians were being killed. According to Masoud Barzani, 'These are centres of civilian population and do not contain armed groups. We cannot remain idle watching these savage massacres.'

Following this statement Barzani appealed to the UN Security

Council to intervene to prevent further Turkish attacks. In a convergence of interest with the Kurds, Baghdad warned Turkey of 'grave consequences' if the operation and use of napalm continued. At the end of October it was reported that Baghdad was arming Turkish Kurds even while attacking those in Iraq.

At least three of the villages attacked by Turkey were within the allied security zone. A spokesman for allied forces in the region, Major Michael McKinney of the US army, said the allies were there to protect the Kurds from Iraq and not Turkey. Ironically, the Turkish raids caused Kurds to flee from the villages to which the allies, including Turkey, had helped them return. These villages may have been along a supply route through Syria from PKK bases in Lebanon. Many of the Kurdish guerillas were training in the Bekaa Valley and returning to Turkey to fight. Syria apparently assisted them in order to have bargaining power in negotiations with Turkey over water supplies.

There was an obvious political dimension to Turkey's reprisals against the Kurds in the week before the general election of 20 October. The governing Motherland Party feared that opposition gains would force them into a coalition or even into opposition. The conservative True Path Party (DYP) and the liberal SHP entered the pre-election phase in a strong position, largely due to inflation above 60 per cent. National security was also an important issue, however, with the government's Kurdish policy under fire from both left and right. Reprisal attacks in northern Iraq both highlighted the threat to Turkish security and suggested that the threat was external and thus, arguably, not the result of the government's more liberal policy towards the Kurdish community. The government's concerns were not unwarranted. The ruling Motherland Party was narrowly defeated by the DYP headed by Suleyman Demirel.[104] Whatever the outcome of the Kurdish crisis it contributed to bringing about a shift in Turkish politics.[105]

By the end of 1991, the traditional Kurdish arguments with both the Iraqi and the Turkish governments seemed no closer to being settled. Concerns over the safety of Kurdish refugees were heightened by the apparent inability of the United Nations effectively to distribute relief aid to the Kurds. There was growing criticism over the way the Kurdish relief effort had been handled. The British government, in particular, was concerned about the administration of the relief effort, which it saw as its own initiative. Britain's Minister for Overseas and International Development, Lynda Chalker, expressed to Prince Sadruddin Aga Khan Britain's 'grave concerns at the inability of the United Nations to utilise properly resources raised for the Iraqi people'.[106] In the wake of these criticisms Prince Sadruddin flew to Baghdad. The existing memorandum of understanding with the Iraqi government on UN involvement in Iraq expired on 31 December and Sadruddin wanted Baghdad's agreement to extend it by another 12 months. One month after imposing a tight economic blockade on Kurdish Iraq, Baghdad had shown some flexibility towards a political settlement, but it nevertheless wanted to keep international involvement to a minimum.

The Iraqi government used international humanitarian interest in the condition of the Iraqi people as a bargaining chip in negotiations with the United Nations. Baghdad refused to sell oil to enable the purchase of food and drugs because of the conditions imposed by the Security Council. These stipulated, among other things, that the money could only be spent for humanitarian purposes and that the proceeds would be placed under control of the United Nations, which would use 30 per cent of the money raised to finance Iraqi war reparations. In order to reduce the infringement on its sovereignty Baghdad sought to sell oil directly on the world market with the buyers paying 30 per cent of the total sale into an account under UN control. As long as the Iraqi people continued to suffer, pressure on the West to ease the economic sanctions against Iraq continued to grow.

The Iraqi government's own economic blockade on northern Iraq complicated the administration of Kirkuk and highlighted Kurdish dependence on Baghdad. Economic duress led Kurdish leaders to agree to withdraw Kurdish guerillas to defensive positions outside of Arbil and other northern cities in return for the lifting of the blockade. However, Iraqi troops attacked Kurdish guerillas who were blocking three major highways into Arbil. As a result the negotiations with Prince Sadruddin took place following an escalation of fighting in northern Iraq. The Kurds were prepared to make additional concessions to bring about the end of the blockade. On 25 December they sent a delegation to Baghdad for further negotiations. This time they were rewarded with concessions from Baghdad: the release of over 2,300 prisoners, including 400 Kurds, and the appointment of a Kurd as the Iraqi Minister for Health. Nevertheless, the blockade remained in place into the new year.

One reason for Kurdish concessions was concern that allied protection would end on 28 December. Extension of the agreement depended on Turkish approval, which remained highly controversial in Ankara. Eventually the government agreed to a six-month extension for allied use of Turkish air bases, but any renewal would have to be approved by parliament which, with Turkish–Kurdish tensions still acute, meant that the allied presence would effectively be concluded in the middle of 1992. In practice this meant that Saddam

Hussein had another six months to survive allied pressure, and a steadily more coherent internal opposition, after which he could hope that the threat of further military intervention would be removed and sanctions would start to fall apart.

Safe Havens as a Precedent

The basis for the safe havens policy adopted by the West in April 1991 had been a sense of obligation, reinforced by media coverage, to a minority in a wretched condition as a result of actions taken by a common enemy. As a group the Kurds had gained international sympathy, enhanced by a sense that they had been let down badly in the past. It was not just the scale of the human tragedy which turned this civil war into a case for external intervention; it was also the recognition that the resultant refugee crisis extended beyond Iraq's borders into Iran and Turkey. The potential for external intervention was made possible by the weakness of the Iraqi regime and the fact that international opinion was already mobilised against it. In resolution 688 there was the basis for a formal rationale to intervention.

The safe havens concept inevitably posed a direct challenge to the Iraqi state. It had to give up effective authority over contested territory, even if this territory did not pass directly into Kurdish control. Yet the challenge to the Iraqi state was limited by the allies' reluctance to accept responsibility for the conduct of political affairs within the territory they were effectively controlling. The limits imposed on the purposes of allied intervention as well as its duration meant that there was no long-term political settlement. Humanitarian intervention which fails to address the underlying dispute which has led to the crisis in the first place is liable to conclude without guarantees of no recurrence. As with any military operation such intervention requires a clear political objective and this must involve both a concept of a diplomatic settlement and active support for negotiations directed towards this end. The intervention succeeded in easing the immediate tragedy facing the Kurdish people but it did not prevent a recurrence, and it left relations between the Kurds and central government in Iraq and Turkey as uncertain as ever.

Despite this incomplete achievement, Western leaders self-consciously used this episode to begin to amend traditional notions of sovereignty and 'non-interference in internal affairs'. The allies initially tried to avoid setting precedents and so stretched their interpretation of sovereignty in international law. A turning point in British policy was signalled by Foreign Secretary Douglas Hurd when he said on 12 April that the division between internal and external policies of a nation is 'not absolute'.[107] In the US Congress, Lee Hamilton, Chairman of the House Foreign Affairs Committee, said:

> We are intervening in the sovereignty of Iraq, I think for good reason here, to help these Kurdish people. But how far that obligation goes and to what extent we're going to stay with it is not clear.[108]

French Foreign Minister Roland Dumas argued that the French concept of the 'duty to intervene' emerged from the Iraqi repression in a similar way to which the concept of 'crimes against humanity' emerged from the Holocaust. Moreover, in French law, he pointed out, it is a crime not to help someone who is in danger.[109] Prince Sadruddin subsequently stated:

> When you have a situation which threatens international peace and security, when a refugee problem becomes a massive exodus, it's no longer a problem for the country itself and provides a *locus standi* for international action. I am interested in this French idea of a *droit d'ingérence*, a right of intervention going beyond the Geneva Convention and providing the international community with some legitimacy.[110]

The US Ambassador to the United Nations, Thomas Pickering, observed that new ground had been broken:

> The response to the plight of the Kurds suggests a shift in world opinion towards a re-balancing of the claims of sovereignty and those of extreme humanitarian need. This is good news since it means we are moving closer to deterring genocide and aiding its victims. However, it also means we have much careful thinking to do about the nature of, and the limitations upon, intervention to carry out humanitarian assistance programs where States refuse, in pursuit of 'policies of repression', to give permission to such assistance.[111]

Most notably, at their July 1991 London summit, the Group of Seven, after citing the 'exceptional action' taken to support the Kurds, urged 'the UN and its affiliated agencies to be ready to consider similar action in the future if circumstances require it'. In practice, it will be if circumstances 'permit' as much as 'require'. This chapter has sought to demonstrate that it would be unwise to build too much on the safe havens case. It was an important precedent but the circumstances were exceptional and the long-term impact of the action was mixed. If, in order to maintain a sense of legitimacy, acts of intervention must not only be inspired by but also

confined to questions of humanitarian concern, then they will fail to
address the underlying political conditions which have stimulated
the concern in the first place.

Notes

* David Boren is a research assistant in the Department of War Studies, King's
College, London, where he is completing a PhD thesis on 'Britain's 1981 Defence
Review'.

1. Pauletta Otis, 'Political and Military Considerations of the Kurdish Case,
   1991: A Window of Opportunity?', *Small Wars and Insurgencies*, 1 (2) (April
   1991).
2. *International Herald Tribune*, 16 February 1991.
3. Quoted in Reuters, *International Herald Tribune*, 28 March 1991.
4. Forty-five per cent of Americans favoured aid to the rebels, but only half of
   these believed the US should use force on the Kurds' behalf. Richard Morin,
   International Herald Tribune, 6–7 April 1991.
5. Because both Kurdish and Shia Muslim leaders had associated themselves
   with the Iraqi opposition, formed in Damascus in December 1990, it was even
   more difficult to attend to the humanitarian needs of repressed Iraqis without
   appearing to interfere in Iraq's domestic affairs.
6. Bush News Conference, *USIA*, 16 April 1991.
7. Agency for International Development, *Iraq: Displaced Persons and Refugees*, 17
   April 1991.
8. Paul F. Horvitz, *International Herald Tribune*, 15 April 1991.
9. Jalal Talabani, head of the Patriotic Union of Kurdistan (PUK), and Masoud
   Barzani, head of the Kurdish Democratic Party (KDP). Alfred B. Prados,
   Kurdish Separatism in Iraq: Developments and Implications for the United States,
   Congressional Research Service Report 91–397 F, p. 5, 6 May 1991.
10. Phil Reeves, *The Independent*, 16 April 1991. Later, according to international
    aid workers, Turkish officials insisted that British and US troops sign papers
    saying that they had not witnessed any of the acts Turkish soldiers were
    accused of. Thirty foreign troops were asked to leave, possibly because they
    would not sign. Leonard Doyle, *The Independent*, 4 May 1991.
11. Nik Gowing, 'The Media Dimension 1: TV and the Kurds', *The World Today*,
    47 (7), pp.111–12 (July 1991).
12. Resolution 688 (1991), adopted by the Security Council at its 2982nd meeting
    on 5 April 1991.
13. Quoted in article by Hugh Pope, *The Independent*, 12 April 1991.
14. The emergency governor of south-east Turkey stated on Turkish television: 'In
    an initial stage starting from tomorrow we hope that about 20,000 Iraqis will
    be able to enjoy more comfortable conditions at the Silopi pilgrimage transit
    centre.'
15. In the first two days of Operation Provide Comfort 18 missions were flown,
    delivering over 172,000 pounds of supplies on 21 April alone. By 22 April a
    total of 4,164 tons of supplies had been delivered.
16. Velayati said that international aid to Iran had so far been limited to 108
    plane-loads which he described as 'by no means proportional to the refugee
    needs'. 'Iran refuses to have Kurdish safe havens near its borders', *Financial
    Times*, 22 April 1991.

17. The British response to Iranian aid requests was a message from the Foreign Office stating: 'We are going to help you with the problems you have. Please help us bring home those hostages who should never have been taken and kept for so long.' Quoted in article by Sarah Helm, *The Independent*, 19 April 1991.

18. This would be the first US aircraft publicly to land in Iran since the revolution in 1979. The only flights since the revolution were the aborted Desert One rescue mission and those connected with the Iran–Contra deal of 1986. German assistance was more welcome in Iran. Bonn announced on 23 April that it would send as many as 2,000 paratroops and engineers to help relief efforts.

19. Deliveries totalled only 50 tons by the middle of April, just a couple of per cent of that delivered through Turkey. By 4 May they had received only 6 tons of food – 5 grams per refugee – and some of that was rotten. Staff Dispatches, *International Herald Tribune*, 15 April and 4–5 May 1991.

20. Donald Macintyre, *The Independent on Sunday*, 14 April 1991.

21. On 9 April State Department spokesman Richard Boucher stated that: 'Resolution 688 provides authority to provide cross-border refugee services. If Iraq would refuse to cooperate with this international effort, we would be willing to look at other options, including further UN action.' White House press secretary Marlin Fitzwater announced the same day that: 'The world is reacting swiftly and with determination to counter Saddam Hussein's use of force against his own people. The international community has once again closed ranks and is insisting that Iraq end its repression and allow immediate and unimpeded access by international organizations to all in need throughout the country.' Both quoted in article by Davis Brashears and Edmund F. Scherr, *USIA*, 10 April 1991. For Baker's remarks see Staff Dispatches, *International Herald Tribune*, 9 April 1991.

22. President François Mitterrand accepted at the same time that 'we can't arbitrate by military means all conflicts in the world'. Quoted in article by Martin Fletcher and Bruce Clark, *The Times*, 15 March 1991.

23. Political pressure had been developing at home after the former Prime Minister, Margaret Thatcher, had observed after meeting Kurdish women on 3 April that, whatever 'the legal niceties', the Kurds needed 'not talk but practical action'. Major developed his plan very rapidly.

24. It was notable that, in contrast to its previous practice of close consultation with the United States, the British government had brought its safe haven proposal first to the European Community. This reflected British concern that the United States was acting too slowly. As this would have been unthinkable during the Thatcher years Britain's partners were anxious to provide encouragement. John Major and George Bush spoke on 4 April to discuss the passage of resolution 688 but they reportedly did not discuss the safe haven concept. On 8 April Douglas Hurd had spoken to James Baker and expressed concern about repression in Iraq. Baker had replied that the US would not interfere in internal Iraqi affairs, though he agreed the situation would have to be closely watched. François Mitterrand called the British proposal 'a major advance for the political dimension of the Community', in part because of the lack of prior British discussion with the United States.

25. Quoted in article by Martin Fletcher, *The Times*, 10 April 1991. US State Department deputy spokesman Richard Boucher said 'The idea of a safe haven, an enclave, a buffer zone, has been discussed in various ways at various times. It is something that we are discussing with our allies in New York.' Quoted in article by Davis Brashears and Edmund F. Scherr, *USIA* 10 April

1991; Rupert Cornwall, *The Independent*, 9 April 1991. Washington reportedly expressed irritation behind the scenes that John Major had pushed an unformed idea too far too fast.

26. Quoted in article by Dian Macdonald, *USIA*, 12 April 1991.

27. On 11 April the Senate passed resolution 99 recognising a US 'moral obligation to provide sustained humanitarian relief for Iraqi refugees' and calling upon the President 'immediately to press the United Nations Security Council to adopt effective measures to assist Iraqi refugees as set forth in Resolution 688 and to enforce . . . the demand in Resolution 688 that Iraq end its repression of the Iraqi civilian population'. Prados, *Kurdish Separatism in Iraq* (note 9 above) pp.30–31.

28. Speech by President Bush delivered at the Air University at Maxwell Air Force Base, 13 April 1991, *USIA*, 15 April 1991. Brent Scowcroft emphasised the same point: 'What we are saying is we will not countenance interference in refugee operations. We are not going to intervene, as we have before, in a civil war.' Paul F. Horvitz, *International Herald Tribune*, 15 April 1991.

29. Iran rejected the idea of safe havens on its border while approving of those near Turkey.

30. Defense Department spokesman Bob Hall quoted in article by Jacquelyn S. Porth, *USIA*, 17 April 1991.

31. Bush News Conference, 16 April 1991, *USIA*, 18 April 1991. The Bush administration's sensitivity about its role in the relief policy was revealed when it claimed full responsibility for the safe haven plan. Fitzwater declared, much to the irritation of the British press, that: 'This is the United States' proposal and President Bush presented it to the coalition in the last few days.' Sarah Helm, *The Independent*, 19 April 1991. This was after John Major had indicated pride in his own role when welcoming Bush's support for the safe havens plan. After saying that he was 'delighted that this proposal is now proceeding', Bush rejected as 'criticism that is often produced by people who make very little contribution themselves' the idea that he had been dithering while Saddam repressed the Kurds: 'this is the most wide-ranging proposal anybody has produced'. Craig Whitney, *International Herald Tribune*, 18 April 1991.

32. Staff Dispatches, *International Herald Tribune*, 17 April 1991.

33. Bush News Conference, 16 April 1991, *USIA*, 18 April 1991.

34. Defense Department spokesman Pete Williams quoted in an article by Paul F. Horvitz, *International Herald Tribune*, 18 April 1991.

35. To provide additional back-up protection for US forces the carrier *Theodore Roosevelt* and three other warships sailed through the Suez Canal on their way from the Red Sea to the eastern Mediterranean.

36. The force included specialists in engineering, water supply, communications, medicine and hygiene and was accompanied by Royal Navy Sea King helicopters.

37. Youssef M. Ibrahim, *International Herald Tribune*, 10 April 1991.

38. Iraqi Foreign Minister Ahmed Hussein Khodair. He did not, however, say that Iraq would resist the efforts with military force. Alan Cowell, *International Herald Tribune*, 18 April 1991. Deputy Prime Minister Tariq Aziz did say of allied camps: 'We refuse this. They have no right to send troops to our territory. This is interference in our internal affairs.' Again, he did not threaten resistance. Chuck Sudetic, *International Herald Tribune*, 19 April 1991.

39. Following a meeting with John Major, Turkish Prime Minister Yildirim Akbulut countered criticism of Turkey's aid efforts by those who were themselves unwilling to provide safe havens for refugees: 'We appeal to all countries

to take these refugees. We don't differentiate. Whoever is ready to take these people can . . . shelter them.' Immigration lawyers agreed that under international law most of the Kurds had the right to asylum on the basis of justified fears of persecution. Quoted in article by Sarah Helm, *The Independent*, 17 April 1991; see also Michael Simmons and Jane Howard, *The Guardian*, 16 April 1991.

40. Major quoted in article by Donald McIntyre, *The Independent on Sunday*, 14 April 1991. Later US Defense Secretary Dick Cheney also sought to clarify the distinction: 'I think the prime focus has to be on the humanitarian side of things. And we are not interested in creating enclaves, if you will, from which the Kurds can attack the Iraqis. We would clearly discourage that.' Quoted in Prados, *Kurdish Separatism in Iraq* (note 9 above), p.30. Pérez de Cuéllar also cautioned against the word 'enclave' because of its 'connotation which affects the sovereignty of Iraq'. 'Kurds' plight under discussion with Europeans', *USIA*, 18 April 1991.

41. White House Deputy Press Secretary Roman Popadiuk quoted in article by Dian McDonald, *USIA*, 18 April 1991.

42. The treatment of an Iraqi request to spray their grain crops with pesticide came to demonstrate the extent of US control over Iraqi territory. It was decided that 'The US government will not oppose the use of helicopters for pesticide application north of the 36th Parallel, provided the helicopters are operated by a third party contracted and paid for by the Iraqi government'. The US insisted that the UN Food and Agriculture Organization monitor the spraying on-site and that 'they should use only specified pesticides rather than one highly toxic compound which they have used in the past and which would be likely to have a harmful impact on nearby concentrations of people'. State Department Report, 25 April, *USIA*, 26 April 1991.

43. Edward Lucas, *The Independent*, 20 April 1991; Chuck Sudetic, *International Herald Tribune*, 19 April 1991; Foreign and Political Staff, *Financial Times*, 19 April 1991. Staff Sergeant Lee Tibbetts cited in Staff Dispatches, *International Herald Tribune*, 24 April 1991.

44. Phil Reeves, *The Independent*, 25 April 1991; Staff Dispatches, *International Herald Tribune*, 26 April 1991.

45. Davis Brashears, *USIA*, 26 April 1991. His British counterpart Tom King explained why the challenge had to be met: 'They have to go now. So great is the fear that, unless we can meet that concern and fear, we will have provided facilities which will not do the job for which they are planned.' Robert Mauthner and Mark Nicolson, *Financial Times*, 25 April 1991.

46. State Department report, 6 May, *USIA*, 8 May 1991.

47. Sarah Helm, *The Independent*, 18 April 1991.

48. White House report, 19 April, *USIA*, 22 April 1991.

49. Staff Dispatches, *International Herald Tribune*, 4–5 May 1991. Prince Sadruddin made a similar point. He accepted that the allies had been able to move much faster than could the United Nations: 'There is no way for the United Nations . . . to establish in a few days' time the sort of operational arrangements [required] . . . We are no match for hundreds of helicopters and thousands of troops.' At the same time, however, he was irritated by allied statements that the camps in their control would be turned over to the United Nations: 'You've got to be two to tango. This has to be discussed and sorted out. You can't be in the process of setting up a huge operation and then the UN being really constrained at this time with a lack of resources and funds and staff and personnel and just hand them over unilaterally.' In appealing for money

Sadruddin said if governments 'don't help in cash and kind it's going to be a difficult challenge to match what is being done bilaterally'. Robin Newmann, *USIA*, 22 April 1991; Frances Williams, *The Independent*, 20 April 1991.

50. Following the earlier appeal Germany had tripled its aid to the Kurds. Having opposed German military assistance overseas during Operation Desert Storm the German government was eager to participate in post-war humanitarian relief. Germany pledged approximately $200 million in addition to helicopter support while Japan pledged $100 million and sent four minesweepers to the Persian Gulf, to the satisfaction of the United States. For both countries this was a way of demonstrating a sense of international responsibility.

51. United Nations report, April 29, *USIA*, 30 April 1991.

52. For a text of the letter see 'Major presses UN on more aid for Kurds', *The Independent*, 2 May 1991.

53. Patrick Tyler, *International Herald Tribune*, 17 May 1991. At the same time Bush stated his belief that China should be granted most-favoured-nation trading status.

54. Previous UN guard deployments had been undertaken on the basis of the memorandum of understanding signed on 18 April.

55. Alan Cowell, *International Herald Tribune*, 18 April 1991.

56. Bush News Conference, *USIA*, 16 April 1991.

57. Compiled from Staff Dispatches, *International Herald Tribune*, 15 April 1991.

58. Saddam had used a cease-fire with the Kurds declared on 13 April to deploy large numbers of howitzers, tanks and armoured vehicles.

59. Marie Colvin, *Sunday Times*, 28 April 1991.

60. Kurds in Teheran held three hostages: Izzat Ibrahim, Deputy Chairman of Iraq's ruling Revolutionary Council, Hussein Kamal Hassan, the Minister of Industry, and the former Army Chief of Staff General Maher Rashid. They were to be held 'for as long as the negotiations go on'. 'Kurds distrust Saddam's "deal" over autonomy', *The Independent*, 23 April 1991. Saddam's hostages were at his negotiating table in Baghdad; one of the Kurdish representatives, Nechirvan Barzani, was the nephew of General Masoud Barzani, Commander-in-Chief of the Kurdish Forces.

61. Staff Dispatches, *International Herald Tribune*, 24 April 1991.

62. This scepticism was reinforced by Saddam's orders to the Iraqi army for the suppression of demonstrations; Iraqi troops were instructed to kill 95 per cent of the protestors 'leaving the remainder for interrogation'. Victor Mallet, *Financial Times*, 20–21 April 1991.

63. The British Foreign Office welcomed any steps that would facilitate the return of the refugees to Iraq. 'We have consistently made clear our support for autonomy for the Kurdish people within Iraq and respect for their political and human rights.' The US State Department described the pact as 'the product of a desperate situation. It remains terribly important to keep up the pressure.' The State Department said the United States would 'welcome any agreement' establishing democratic practices in Iraq. 'Iraq must cease human rights violations against the Kurds and accord the Kurds the full rights of citizenship. This would include full participation in the institutions of government and appropriate opportunities to express their religious, cultural and linguistic heritage. Looking at it from here we certainly hope that the talks in Baghdad are a step towards that direction.' State Department reports, 22 and 23 April, *USIA*, 25 April 1991.

64. Five Kurdish delegates met David Mack, Deputy Assistant Secretary of State for Near Eastern and South Asian Affairs. State Department deputy spokes-

man Richard Boucher said, 'As we've explained in the past, this series of meetings represents an opportunity to hear the perspectives of individuals on what is going on inside Iraq, and also for us to explain American policy and actions in the area.' According to Dr Mahmood Othman, the representative for the Kurdistan Socialist Party, the Kurdish delegates focused on the political situation in Iraq and their goal of autonomy, but the United States had focused mainly on humanitarian concerns. State Department report, 22 April, *USIA*, 23 April 1991.

65. Leonard Doyle, *The Independent*, 4 May 1991.

66. Speaking to the Foreign Affairs Select Committee, Hurd described Britain's Iraq policy as a staged process: 'The first step is to complete Operation Safe Haven. The second step is to build up the UN presence – protection as well as relief – so they can replace allied troops. The third step is that there should be an agreement inside Iraq in which the Kurds have confidence. We have taken a substantial part in one and two. I do not rule out taking part in stage three. It would obviously be a different part, because we are not contemplating military occupation of Iraq or any part of Iraq.' John Pienaar, *The Independent*, 9 May 1991.

67. 'Kurdish autonomy "moves closer"', *The Independent*, 13 May 1991.

68. 'Obstacles cleared in Iraqi–Kurdish talks', *Financial Times*, 18–19 May 1991; Staff Dispatches, *International Herald Tribune*, 18–19 and 20 May 1991.

69. Talabani acknowledged on 30 May that Baghdad refused to grant the Kurds any control over Kirkuk and some other northern cities and said that the Kurds continued to insist 'that all Kurdish towns and territory must be included in the autonomous Kurdistan'. According to Talabani, with regard to the coalition presence, 'It's one of the main reasons why Iraq is prepared to reach an agreement with us, to use it as a way to get the allied forces to withdraw. If they withdraw before reaching an agreement, it will weaken our position.' He was still interested in an international guarantee, though in diluted form: 'Perhaps we can link the agreement with Baghdad with Resolution 688 of the UN Security Council. In 688 there is a call for open dialogue between the Iraqi government and its opponents. The Security Council can endorse it, or take note of it or can say some words about it.' John Murray Brown, *Financial Times*, 3 June 1991.

70. Ayatollah Mohammed Taqi Mudaressi said: 'We call on our Kurdish brothers to return to the opposition ranks and stop negotiations with the Baghdad regime because it has become clear now that Saddam is not sincere in his offer to solve the Kurdish issue.' Staff Dispatches, *International Herald Tribune*, 31 May 1991.

71. Alan Cowell, *International Herald Tribune*, 8–9 June 1991; Hugh Pope, *The Independent*, 11 June 1991. Another major point of disagreement with Saddam was his attempt to force them to accept a constitution drafted by the Ba'ath Party. The Kurds insisted that it be drawn up by a freely elected parliament. Baghdad was apparently insisting that free elections would be held only in Kurdistan rather than in the country as a whole. But the Kurds worried that if the Shias were unable to become a political force there would be no effective opposition to the Ba'ath regime. Baghdad also continued to demand that the Kurds relinquish their heavy weapons. 'The Kurds', *Economist*, 8 June 1991; Annika Savil, *The Independent*, 22 June 1991.

72. According to Burham Jaf, a KDP spokesman in London, the agreement would mean all Kurds would be allowed to return from self-imposed exile and the 150,000 expelled to Iran in 1971 would also be allowed to return and reclaim

their possessions, including Kurds who lost their government posts for espousing Kurdish nationalism. Pensions would be granted to all the families of *pesh merga* killed or wounded by Iraqi troops. Furthermore, Kurdistan would have its own budget funded by Iraqi oil revenues. The towns and villages destroyed by Iraqi soldiers in the 1970s and 1980s would be rebuilt under an urgent reconstruction programme. Elections in Kurdistan would be held within three months and the new head of the Kurdistan Executive Council would hold a senior government post in Iraq, where free elections would be held within six months to a year. A multi-party system would be established with separate legal, executive and parliamentary functions. Freedom of the press would also be guaranteed. Patrick Cockburn, *The Independent*, 25 June 1991.

73. Hugh Pope and Patrick Cockburn, *The Independent*, 25 June 1991.
74. Hugh Pope, *The Independent*, 30 June 1991. A letter from the political bureau of the Iraqi Kurdistan Front to a joint meeting of London- and Damascus-based opposition 'action committees' informed them that Baghdad had not yet made any 'serious proposals' on democratisation. The action committees meeting in Damascus agreed to seek international support for the overthrow of Saddam. To that end they agreed to send a joint delegation to Kurdistan, requesting UN observers in all parts of Iraq to report on human rights violations and to become directly involved in the distribution of food and medicine. A secondary effect would be the employment of thousands of Iraqis for that purpose. The opposition also called for safe havens to be set up all over Iraq. Edward Mortimer, *Financial Times*, 4 July 1991.
75. One reason why the Shias were not given the same degree of protection as the Kurds was that Saudi Arabia did not want to see the strengthening of Iran, which was thought to have helped organise the Shia rebellion and which would benefit from any increase in Shia autonomy in Iraq.
76. Bush News Conference, 16 April 1991, *USIA*, 18 April 1991.
77. Quoted in Staff Dispatches, *International Herald Tribune*, 20–21 April 1991.
78. Staff Dispatches, *International Herald Tribune*, 13 June 1991; Sarah Helm and Chistopher Bellamy, *The Independent*, 15 June 1991.
79. Frances Williams, *The Independent*, 14 June 1991.
80. The message was reaffirmed by Luxembourg's Foreign Minister Jacques Poos, following an EC debate over reinforcement of the UN presence in Iraq and monitoring developments in Iraq: 'The Kurdish population is suffering severe feelings of insecurity. We have to do what we can to reassure them.' Lynda Chalker, the British Minister for Overseas Development, denied that the safe haven plan was in tatters and announced that phase three of the plan was underway: 'We are now in phase three of the operation to give relief to the Iraqi people, and that means integrating people back into their own communities in Iraq with protection.' Quoted in article by Sarah Lambert, Leonard Doyle and Stephen Goodwin, *The Independent*, 18 June 1991.
81. John Lichfield and John Pienaar, *The Independent*, 19 June 1991.
82. Robert Mauthner, *Financial Times*, 20 June 1991. These conditions were later repeated by John Major in the House of Commons. He called for a 'continuing deterrent military presence in the region' to reinforce allied warnings not to resume repression of the Kurds, which he said would 'meet the severest response'. Emma Tucker, *Financial Times*, 26 June 1991.
83. R. Jeffrey Smith, *International Herald Tribune*, 20 June 1991.
84. The French announced 'a European humanitarian operation under the European flag for the first time', Reuters, *International Herald Tribune*, 25 June 1991. The transfer of the relief effort to the UN posed possible problems to the

private voluntary organisations operating in Iraq without permission from the Iraqi government. US government assistance alone, through private voluntary organisations, totalled $15 million by 24 June. Most of the aid groups worked in Turkey, though Americares was an exception. However, they and European PVOs operating from Iran faced harassment from local Iranian authorities.

85. Defense Department report, 25 June, *USIA*, 26 June 1991; Reuters, *International Herald Tribune*, 25 June 1991.

86. The Iraqi military newspaper, *Al Qadisiya*, responded that the goal was 'reinforcing the illegal US military presence [in Iraq]', and would enable Washington, 'without so much as pseudo-international cover, to interfere in the internal affairs of the countries in the region'.

87. Bruce Carey, *USIA*, 15 July 1991. However, according to the allied commander, General Jay Garner, a small number of border police would be allowed into the security zone 'to perform a customs function'. Staff Dispatches, *International Herald Tribune*, 16 July 1991.

88. According to Defense Department spokesman Pete Williams: 'It looks like the combined task force will number about 5,000 military personnel from six nations, and will include an air force component headquartered at Incirlik, a support element based at Batman, and a combined forces ground element which will be at Silopi.' Nations participating in the force included the United States, Turkey, the United Kingdom, France, Italy and The Netherlands. Command of the force was assumed by US Air Force Major General L. Jamerson who was to be accompanied by the Turkish Air Force Chief of Logistics, Major General Doralim. 'These two commanders will consult and coordinate on all matters regarding the operation and will share all relevant information.' The role of the task force was 'to direct the deterrent operations of Operation Provide Comfort, including air operations, the reconnaissance, the surveillance efforts, and the ground force training'. Defense Department report, 25 July, *USIA*, 26 July 1991. The codename Poised Hammer was rejected as too bellicose and, lacking anything better, the allies stuck to Provide Comfort.

89. According to the Pentagon the clashes 'started as demonstrations by Kurds' against food distribution practices and other problems in northern Iraq. The Pentagon also maintained that the clashes occurred outside the security zone. They took place around Arbil and Sulaymaniyah, where the rebels had taken control.

90. Reuters, *The Guardian*, 23 August 1991.

91. The commander of these divisions was Interior Minister Ali Hassan al-Majid who, as commander of northern Iraq in 1988, had ordered the chemical attack on Halabja in that year.

92. Quoted in an article by Hugh Pope, *The Independent*, 21 September 1991.

93. The government had already agreed to extend its bilateral agreement with the US on defence and economic cooperation but that provided only for the Incirlik air base not the troops forming the ground element of the coalition rapid reaction force.

94. Andrew Hogg, *Sunday Times*, 13 October 1991. Not all of the violence was initiated by the Iraqis. On 7 October a Western journalist witnessed a Kurdish execution of 60 unarmed Iraqi prisoners of war. The KDP announced that it was conducting an inquiry into who had killed the POWs who had apparently been captured in hand-to-hand combat in Sulaymaniyah, but the event nevertheless damaged sympathy in the West for the Kurds. 'The Horrors of Sulaymaniyah', *Economist*, 12 October 1991.

95. Bruce Carey, *USIA*, 15 July 1991.
96. The PKK relies for its support on Turkish Kurds who number roughly half of the 20–25 million total Kurdish population.
97. The PKK had rebelled in 1984 and conducted periodic raids resulting in Turkish army casualties totalling 3,000.
98. Hugh Pope, *The Independent*, 26 July 1991.
99. Staff Dispatches, *International Herald Tribune*, 7 and 9 August 1991; J.M. Brown, *Financial Times*, 8 and 14 August 1991.
100. 'We totally reject Turkish claims that they are attacking PKK bases. These settlements are inhabited by displaced Kurds living in makeshift shelters.' Quoted in article by J.M. Brown, *Financial Times*, 8 August 1991. The KDP spokesman called on the Turkish government 'to end these atrocities and attacks on innocent Iraqi Kurdish refugees and we call upon the allied forces to intercede to prevent such attacks from recurring'. Staff Dispatches, *International Herald Tribune*, 8 August 1991.
101. 'Whatever the goals and causes motivating it, we do not think this kind of contact correspond[s] to the norms of tackling problems which are being currently asserted, the more so since the border of a sovereign state was violated.' The Soviet response to unilateral military action against a sovereign state was thus markedly different from its acquiescence in allied intervention. Statement by the Foreign Ministry's spokesman, *Izvestia*, 10 August 1991.
102. J.M. Brown, *Financial Times*, 19 August 1991.
103. According to the Kurdish Labour Party the raids killed three guerrillas and injured 35 bystanders, nine critically (of whom three were children and four were women).
104. On 22 October voting totals indicated that the parliament's 450 seats were allocated as follows: DYP 184; Motherland Party 112; SHP 84; Welfare Party (Islamic) 63; and the Democratic Left 7.
105. Demirel could form a coalition with any of the three leading parties. However, Turgut Özal's presidency posed an obstacle to an alliance with Motherland – ideologically the most compatible party. Demirel and SHP Leader Erdal Inonu had both campaigned on platforms calling for the ousting of Özal by changing the Constitution. Under the existing Constitution Özal's current term ends in 1996. The main reason for such antagonism towards Özal was his increasingly dominant role in government since his election as President in 1980. His Kurdish policy had been only one factor in criticism from other parties, but it had antagonised both the nationalistic DYP and the Liberal SIIP. As a result, Demirel's political options were further constrained due to the SHP's stance on the Kurdish issue. The SHP had increased its share of seats, in part, by representing the election as a referendum on Kurdish rights and in some parts of south-east Turkey had taken up to 70 per cent of the Kurdish vote as a result.
106. 'UK will express concern on Kurds', *The Independent*, 12 November 1991.
107. Sarah Helm *et al. The Independent*, 11 April 1991.
108. Quotes in Prados, *Kurdish Separatism in Iraq* (note 9 above), p.31. There was less support for a radical suggestion by Stephen Solarz, Chairman of the Asian and Pacific Affairs Subcommittee of the House Foreign Affairs Committee, that the US seek international support for a UN resolution calling for the removal of the Ba'ath government in Iraq and its replacement by a temporary UN administration. See David Rogers and Gerald F. Seib, *Wall Street Journal*, 19–20 April 1991.
109. Joseph Fitchett, *International Herald Tribune*, 13–14 April 1991; 'That slippery

slope', *Economist*, 13 April 1991; Edward Mortimer, *Financial Times*, 20–21 April 1991

110. Neal Ascherson, *The Independent on Sunday*, 5 May 1991. Sir Brian Urquhart, the recently retired Under-Secretary-General at the UN, also called for new laws to be established governing intervention against rogue regimes: 'We are constantly reminded of growing global interdependence. It is thus all the more strange that concern for human rights often tends to stop at borders.' Martin Walker, *The Guardian*, 18 April 1991.

111. Speech to US Council on Foreign Relations, 8 May 1991.

CHAPTER 4

Intervention in a fragmenting state: the case of Yugoslavia

JAMES GOW* AND LAWRENCE FREEDMAN

The Yugoslav unrest provided a critical test case for the new machinery of European security following the conclusion of the Cold War. In particular it allowed the European Community to assume a leading role in continental crisis management. Even those reluctant to see the Community in this role had to accept that the severity of the conflict demanded external interference of some sort and that no other institution appeared to be capable of providing it.

The crisis developed at a time when European politics still reflected the expansive mood following the November 1989 breach in the Berlin Wall. It presented a challenge to all those whose aspirations for the new Europe extended into processes of integration and cooperation in international institutions, such as the European Community (EC), the North Atlantic Treaty Organisation (NATO), the Western European Union (WEU) and the Conference on Security and Cooperation in Europe (CSCE), as well as the United Nations. The CSCE had just endowed itself with a mechanism for handling emergencies when fighting began in earnest in Yugoslavia. A meeting of the CSCE was called in Prague which Vaclav Havel, President of Czechoslovakia, called 'the first serious test of the newly formed security mechanism in Europe'.[1] It was, indeed, the first time that any of the network of institutions with an interest in European security had been faced with a local war.

It was the general risk and then the reality of violence which prompted intervention. In this sense there was a humanitarian impulse, but the concern extended beyond that to anxiety over regional economic dislocation, refugees and the involvement of neighbouring states. Some of the strongest expressions of concern resulted from the siege and bombardment of the historic port of Dubrovnik.

External intervention when it came was not simply in response to the plight of a persecuted minority. If anything it came in opposition to an attempt by a minority group – Serbs in Croatia – to achieve security through alliance with the Serbian republic and with support from the largely Serbian Yugoslav federal army. Had the concern been for minority rights, intervention would have come much earlier, when the Serbian government in Belgrade sought to deny the Albanians in Kosovo the autonomy to which they were entitled. This policy had the effect of aggravating fears in the other republics that Serbia was engaged in an unremitting drive for local hegemony. It was thus the failure to recognise the warning signs in the suppression of Albanian aspirations in Kosovo that left Europe unprepared to cope with the much more serious conflict that arose when Serbia was challenged by an altogether more substantial political entity.

At the time of writing the prospects for international efforts to end the Yugoslav civil war remain unclear. The fighting in Croatia was first halted, in general, on 3 January 1992, but the situation remains volatile. An overall settlement may still be some way off, but certain important foundations have been laid, including the diplomatic recognition of the republics of Slovenia and Croatia. The efforts of the European Community have kept alive the hope of an eventual settlement. Without such efforts, the human and material costs of the war could have been much worse.

Because the affair is not yet over it is difficult to draw lessons. However, this case study does seem to confirm the importance of political early warning and a readiness to act decisively while a conflict is still simmering, rather than waiting until it boils over, and also the need for a sustained diplomatic effort geared towards a political settlement as a necessary condition for any wider involvement.

The case also illustrates the importance of some coercive mechanism even while demonstrating the reluctance of European powers to get entangled in a messy civil war. If the coercive mechanisms are to be largely economic then their effectiveness depends on the vulnerability of the parties to sanctions of this nature and the readiness of all its trading partners to enforce them. This in turn may depend on some tendency towards military stalemate which provides the time for sanctions to take effect. The military situation on the ground is thus unavoidably critical in dispute settlement and if there is only a marginal ability to influence the situation then that will limit the ability to influence the overall development of the conflict. From this point of view, as the experience of handling the Yugoslav conflict demonstrates, there may be a general need to separate the functions of cease-fire mediation, which requires complete impartiality, and leadership of the quest for a political solution, which may require the exercise of influence. It seems that 'good offices' are no substitute for astute bullying if the participants have little inclination to be reasonable and if results are to be achieved.

For the international community, the crisis and conflict in Yugoslavia was a tangle of conflicting principles: territorial integrity, the right to national self-determination, the rights of minorities and the non-use of force. This matrix of conflicting principles was compounded by the complexity of detail in the Yugoslav case. That case will be summarised before an analysis is made of European intervention in Yugoslavia after the outbreak of war.

War in Yugoslavia

On 25 June 1991, two of Yugoslavia's six socialist federal republics, Slovenia and Croatia, declared independence from the federation. Of the two, Slovenia was the more ready for such a declaration, having spent six months making preparations after a plebiscite in December 1990 resulted in an 88 per cent vote for independence. Preparations paid off when Slovenia had to defend itself against the federal army in a limited 10-day 'war', but fighting was to be much more extensive later in Croatia.

There was no reason for the outbreak of conflict to catch anyone by surprise. The Slovenes had advertised their secessionist intentions for months, including identifying the end of June for the fateful act. Even Croatia, which only signalled its intentions and held a referendum late in the day (and once it had already become clear that Slovenia was serious), gave six weeks' warning. While specialists on Yugoslavia may have differed over the precise nature as well as the desirability of fragmentation, none doubted the severity of the crisis nor the intensity of the potential violence should a solution not be found.

For a proper understanding of the Yugoslav crisis, it is necessary to have a rudimentary understanding of the history of the country.[2] Yugoslavia was a more artificial amalgam than most countries, created at the end of the First World War because the Slavic peoples felt they ought to be able to live together and recreated at the end of the Second World War. Slovenia and Croatia were frustrated in their efforts to negotiate a different Yugoslavia. They had sought a restructuring of the country into a confederation of independent states, along the lines of the European Community. The idea of a loose association of states was backed by two other republics, Macedonia and Bosnia–Hercegovina. The remaining republics, Montenegro and, especially, Serbia, opposed this idea. Serbia instead proposed a new federation with greater central control than had previously been the case.

The confederal option was a way in which benefits such as a single market could be preserved while certain Yugoslav realities were formalised; in particular, this meant *de jure* confirmation of the *de facto* evolution of the six Yugoslav republics into independent entities. The federal system devised by Josip Broz Tito's communists after the Second World War to solve the nationalist problems which plagued Royal Yugoslavia between its formation in 1918 and its demise in 1941 provided the framework for embryonic states, particularly under the arrangements of the constitution adopted in 1974. This gave considerable powers to the republics. That power was reinforced by the mechanisms of the communist system: in Yugoslavia, all power was in the republics, each run by a communist party with specific local interests.

Tito had been the glue which held the country together. By the time communist rule ended in the Yugoslav republics, they were acting independently of each other and unable to cooperate for long enough at the federal level to carry out economic reform. The problems of achieving inter-republican agreement were accentuated by the electoral victories of governments of different ideological perspectives in all the republics, but each with a nationalist identity. The individual republics had thus been drifting apart both economically and politically for many years.

Tito had tried to guard against this by bequeathing to his successors an extraordinarily complex rotation system for the presidency drawn from a committee of the six republics plus the two autonomous provinces (both of which were located in Serbia and had forcibly come under Serbia's control since 1988). At the time the crisis broke there was no president because this body had failed in May 1991 to agree to the supposedly automatic accession of Stipe Mesić, a Croat, to take over from Borisav Jović, a Serb.

The central government was headed by Ante Marković (also a Croat) an economic reformer trying to make the best of a bad job. He was the person with whom other governments dealt and whom they wished to support. But in doing so they exaggerated his power for he had little sway over the individual republics, even when it came to securing contributions to the federal budget. Meanwhile industrial output was falling rapidly along with tourist revenue.

Although it was Serbia that claimed the greatest interest in continued federation, in many ways it was the hard-line communist leader Slobodan Milošević in Serbia who rendered this option unattractive. He cracked down ruthlessly on the Albanians in Kosovo and took away their autonomy, whipped up anti-Croat feeling amongst Serbs and appeared to the Slovenes to be promoting an economic policy based on using their productivity to subsidise his ambitions. For their part the Croatians did little to curb anti-Serbian sentiment and raised fears among the Serbian minority in Croatia that it could become vulnerable to a repetition of the vicious massacres perpetrated with Nazi support during the Second World War.

The Croatian government's decision to remove from his post the Serbian Chief of Police in the heavily Serb-populated area around Knin led to the radicalisation and mobilisation of the non-urban Serb communities in Croatia. This was increased by agitation from the Serbian government in Belgrade and by assistance from the federal army, elements of which aided local Serbs by allowing them weaponry and helping them to establish a 'Serbian Autonomous Region', the barricades around which made it effectively a no-go area. The army prevented the Croatian authorities from entering the region. From August 1990, the local Serbs, with federal army assistance, began to form paramilitary groups.

An essential feature in any understanding of the issues involved is the old Yugoslav defence system. The doctrine of General People's Defence in Yugoslavia developed a two-tier system of armed forces. One part was the Yugoslav People's Army, a highly-trained standing army based on conscription and run by the federal defence ministry. The other was a territorial defence force which would mobilise up to 85 per cent of the population into a resistance force; responsibility for this was given to the republics. Thus Yugoslavia had one technically advanced federal armed force and a series of less well equipped republican-based armed forces. These became the basis for the formation of republican proto-armies as Slovenia and Croatia sought full statehood.

The federal army, aware of the role the territorial forces might play, impounded virtually all of the weaponry designated for the Croatian force and about 40 per cent of that for use by Slovenia. The weaponry involved included artillery, anti-air and anti-tank rocket systems (and rockets). Croatia, for example, had 200 of each type of rocket system and 9,000–10,000 rockets for each. Both republics sought to replenish their denuded stocks by making purchases outside Yugoslavia.

The role of Western policy

The Yugoslav deadlock was strongly reinforced by Western policy. Led by the European Community, that policy gave its backing to the weak federal government in Belgrade and refused to admit the possibility of a reordering of Yugoslavia as Croatia and Slovenia, frustrated with the stalemate in inter-republican and federal politics, began to talk about independence. Croatia and Slovenia, having long argued for a confederation, in which they were supported by Bosnia and Macedonia, felt that there was no further point in trying to negotiate with the intransigent Serbian regime in Belgrade. Western policy, wittingly or unwittingly, backed Serbia, reinforced its intransigence and contributed to the diplomatic impasse. Because the West wanted what Serbia wanted, Serbia and the federal army had little incentive to be flexible. Slovenia and Croatia decided that the only way to break the stalemate was unilateral action. Western policy effectively served to legitimise the use of force against first Slovenia and then Croatia after the two declared their independence.

Slovenia was the most prosperous of the Yugoslav republics and had an affinity with Western Europe. It was a functioning democracy with a homogeneous population of 2 million, united behind independence. From the start, in shaping the Western response, however, the Slovenian case for independence was judged in terms of its relevance for the rest of Yugoslavia. A chain reaction was feared. Croatia was a less straightforward case because it was less well prepared and contained 600,000 Serbs amongst its 4.5 million population. The Croatian government itself was thought by some to have authoritarian tendencies, by others to be dithering and incompetent, and by all to have shown little development in terms of free market economics. If Yugoslavia broke up it was understood that awkward questions would be raised over the fate of Macedonia, in which both Bulgaria and Greece had an interest, while the population of the autonomous territory of Kosovo looked increasingly to closer association with next-door Albania which was making its own uncertain steps towards rejoining the community of nations.

Western leaders were also fearful that a successful Slovene break from Yugoslavia would encourage the Slovaks to break from the Czechs. Most of all they wished to give as little encouragement as possible to the disintegrative tendencies within the Soviet Union. At that time (before the failed August 1991 coup) fear of Soviet fragmentation was strengthened by continual reminders from Moscow that any encouragement would be judged an unfriendly act.

Beyond these immediate concerns was the general fear that any tampering with the territorial status quo would be a recipe for anarchy, that the principle of self-determination, celebrated while bringing the two Germanies together, could be taken too far. Nationalist leaders obsessed with independence might lose sight of questions of economic viability and could also make life uncomfortable for the minorities within the new borders who were obliged to secede with the majority and often felt far less secure as a result. Neighbouring states with old claims against bits of territory might promote secessionists in the hope of creating an opportunity for their own expansion. Perhaps also it was embarrassing for the European

Community to have an example close at hand of a failed experiment in federation. For those seeking closer integration within the Community, Yugoslavia was a poor advertisement, the obvious differences between the two notwithstanding.

The initial response from a Western country did reflect concern over minority rights. In November 1990, the US Congress, following its standard impulse on hearing of any abuse of human rights, passed the Nickels amendment ordering the cutting off of aid if Serbia did not end the repression in Kosovo by May 1991. The threat was only serious because, while the aid involved was a trivial amount, Congress also called for opposition to further support for Yugoslavia from the World Bank and the International Monetary Fund. In June 1991 the Americans threatened to invoke the Nickels amendment in order to bring pressure on the Serbs to clear the way for Mesić's accession to the presidency. This annoyed Yugoslavs generally because they felt they were being asked to suffer for Serbian misdemeanours and the Serbians because they considered Washington to be supporting Albanian secession. Marković managed to persuade Bush to call off the pressure on the grounds that the economic collapse that would be made more likely by the implementation of the threat would merely hasten civil war.

The European Community's approach was also based on economic carrots and sticks, although here they were more substantial than with the United States as 40 per cent of Yugoslavia's trade was with the Community. At the start of June 1991 the European Commission President Jacques Delors visited Belgrade and promised the Yugoslavs that, in the event of a constitutional settlement, progress could be made on an association agreement with the Community and direct or indirect financial support of between $4 and $5 billion would be made available. The basic principles were Yugoslav unity and democracy.

Unfortunately these principles were incompatible. The obvious preference for a solution based on Slovenia and Croatia being reassured through a Mesić presidency, in the hope that opposition to Milošević in Serbia would grow and Marković's reforms would begin to bear fruit, had to be balanced against the greater possibility that territorial unity would be enforced by Serbia mobilising the largely Serb-officered federal army.

The unwillingness to contemplate a restructuring of Yugoslavia reflected the challenge this would bring to established assumptions on both the importance of maintaining existing boundaries in Europe and the principle of non-interference. In June, a week before the crisis broke, the Council of the revamped CSCE met in Berlin recognising that Yugoslavia posed the first great test to that organisation.

The Yugoslav Foreign Minister, Budimir Lončar, described the country's steady internal collapse as a 'time bomb in the heart of Europe'.

The CSCE ministers expressed 'friendly concern' about Yugoslavia. The fact that they even managed to do that was hailed by some as a breakthrough of historic proportions, because until then it had been considered improper for the Conference to pronounce on the internal affairs of its member states. However, this breakthrough was only tolerated because the Yugoslav foreign minister did not object. The CSCE is debarred from taking decisions about a country without that country's consent. This makes it almost inevitable that the CSCE's only possible intervention in potentially dangerous situations developing within a particular country would be to reinforce its central government.

If Yugoslavia had declared its problem to be 'internal' and beyond the purview of the Conference nothing could have been said. This difficulty did not arise because the statement was wholly in line with the views of Yugoslavia's central government. The standard requirement of respect for democracy and the rights of minorities was stated, but most important was support for the 'unity and territorial integrity' of Yugoslavia.

This message was reinforced first by the US Secretary of State James Baker who visited Yugoslavia immediately after the CSCE meeting and then by the foreign ministers of the European Community who insisted that they wanted Yugoslavia to stay together and said that they would not deal with anyone claiming to represent the independent republics of Slovenia and Croatia.

European Crisis Management

As soon as the crisis broke at the end of June 1991 – with the federal army moving into Slovenia to assert federal authority – the European Community moved rapidly into crisis mode. The Community's zeal sprang in part from a quickly evolving sense that its attitude towards Yugoslavia prior to the declarations of independence had inadvertently contributed to the situation in which there was a resort to force: another policy approach might have made it possible to avert violence.

This sense of responsibility was outweighed, however, by the second mainspring of EC involvement: the impulse in some of the member states for a common foreign policy. In particular, the Community rushed in hoping to exorcise the ghost of EC indecision and inaction during the Gulf conflict. To this end, Italian Foreign Minister Gianni de Michelis told the press that Washington and

Moscow had been 'informed', not consulted, about the mission of the EC troika of foreign ministers.[3] De Michelis even suggested that the rapid despatch of the troika to Yugoslavia in the early stages of the conflict demonstrated that the Community already had, politically at least, a rapid reaction force.[4]

The diplomatic interest in Yugoslavia, in addition to a hope that self-determination might be exercised in a way which would not excite nationalist and territorial disputes elsewhere, included a concern to avoid total economic collapse in the region and to avoid refugee problems. Finally, the Community wanted to offer itself and its embrace for the various parties in the future, as part of the new, integrated Europe.

At a more abstract level, an impulse for European intervention was the European idea itself. On the one hand there were emotional reactions:

> If Europe means anything as a concept, the civil war in Yugoslavia must be stopped. It is intolerable that, 18 months after the collapse of communism in Eastern Europe, two republics with democratically elected governments should be crushed by a communist-led army that appears to have brushed aside the politicians in Belgrade to whom it owes loyalty.[5]

In addition, the Germans, having recently benefited from the principle of self-determination, were emotional supporters of others claiming this fundamental right (although they did not perceive that for Serbs Croatia's independence would mean the kind of split into two states that the Germans had been happy to repair for themselves). However, it was not only in Germany that a swell of popular opinion, mobilised by television images, placed pressure on EC governments to act in Yugoslavia.

Beyond all this, there were very practical reasons for EC involvement. Yugoslavia had represented the main trade route between the rest of the Community and Greece and there was therefore good reason to have peace restored. Furthermore, the Community had economic 'clout'. It was better placed than the United States, for example, because it was much more heavily involved financially in Yugoslavia. Whereas American aid amounted to only $5 million, the Community had large-scale aid and trade links: in addition to the EC's own links (£800 million aid over five years and a 40 per cent share of Yugoslavia's exports), it was also coordinating the Group of 24 industrial nations' aid programme of 3.6 billion ecu ($4.1 billion).[6] It therefore had a stick with which it could threaten Yugoslavia.

Finally, the EC-led intervention stemmed from the fact that, fortunately, the EC foreign ministers were all meeting together as the fighting began. This enabled a rapid response, including a decision to act and the formulation of a plan for dealing with Yugoslavia. As a result, the Community was quick off the mark in advancing its proposal within the CSCE framework because there was clearly a feeling that this was a European, not a transatlantic question. Just as the United States had little inclination to get closely and immediately involved in Yugoslavia, there was also reluctance in the Community to let the Americans be involved.

Although other international institutions, such as the CSCE, the Western European Union and the United Nations, were involved at various stages, it was the European Community which took the lead in the international handling of the Yugoslav conflict, even after the burden of arranging cease-fires and discussing peacekeeping troops had been passed from the Community to the United Nations. There were six phases of European intervention, although these overlapped: the despatch of a trio of EC foreign ministers to mediate; the EC proposal to the CSCE to assign monitors to Slovenia; the extension of the monitors' role to Croatia and the difficulties in securing a cease-fire there; discussions with the Western European Union about strengthening and supporting the monitors' work; the setting up of a peace conference in The Hague, coordinated by Lord Carrington, to mediate in the dispute and to seek a political agreement on the future of the Yugoslav republics; and the institution of a mechanism through which to grant diplomatic recognition to new states.

Phase 1: The Troika

The European Community, coincidentally gathering for its Luxembourg summit, despatched a mediation mission of three foreign ministers. The 'troika', made up of the past, present and future foreign ministers of the presidency of the European Council of Ministers, had become a familiar feature of a common European foreign policy. In June 1991 it comprised Gianni de Michelis (Italy), Jacques Poos (Luxembourg) and Hans van den Broek (Netherlands).[7] They took a three-point plan to Yugoslavia. This called for a resolution of the presidential crisis, the suspension of the implementation of the declarations of independence for a period of three months and the army's return to its barracks. This plan was borrowed from Ante Marković, who had obtained agreement to some of the details the previous week. The EC's 'success' lay in reinforcing this.

The immediate and overly triumphant return to Luxembourg following the first visit by the troika left the disputants to sort out the details. The prestige of a common foreign policy was put on the line without any guarantees that the brokered deal would be implemented. The session of the federal presidency on 29 June to appoint Stipe Mesić did not materialise and the federal army, instead of returning to barracks as the government had agreed, continued to act on its own in Slovenia – 'out of control'. The Mesić appointment failed to appear because Slovenia refused to attend the meeting, declaring that it was no longer part of Yugoslavia and so its representative, Janez Drnovšek, had resigned. The meeting was therefore none of its business.

Two days after having claimed to have cobbled together a deal the EC troika was back again. There was more night-time haggling and another, more cautious, expression of optimism. The basic deal was one which if pushed some weeks earlier might have made a difference. But the fighting had transformed the situation. The federal army's intervention confirmed Slovenia in its determination to free itself from the rest of Yugoslavia, while the success of the Slovene resistance had embarrassed and raised the stakes for the army while encouraging the Croatians. This was the opposite of the intended effect – any explanation for the army's precipitate action must include its belief that by picking on Slovenia (which it was assumed would probably not resist), Croatia would be deterred.

With the contending forces dispersed and lines of political control uncertain, a cease-fire agreed at the centre was inevitably difficult to implement. The terms of the cease-fire were critical for they would determine the balance of power during the three months of bargaining allowed for under the EC proposal. If, as the Slovenes demanded, the army had to abandon its equipment and give up the right to man borders then it would effectively concede any influence in the break-away republic.

In essence, the troika was trying to bully the Yugoslavs into ceasing fire. De Michelis appeared to be especially good in this role, arriving in Yugoslavia for the troika's second visit saying he was not interested in words, just signatures. The European Community and its member states backed up the troika's efforts to cajole the Yugoslavs into peace. An embargo on armaments and military equipment to the whole of Yugoslavia was imposed and there was an appeal to other countries to follow suit. The Community also decided to suspend the second and third financial protocols with Yugoslavia – that is, to block aid worth £700–800 million (although suspension was not effected because agreement was reached before this could happen).

The intervention succeeded in getting the Mesić appointment confirmed. However, the cease-fire agreement did not hold, in part because Slovene forces impeded the return of tanks to their garrisons where, it was feared, they could be repaired and refuelled for further attack. The federal army compounded this by launching its heaviest attacks to date, including aerial attacks, on the Slovenian capital Ljubljana.

Finally, on 7 July (with the backing of the CSCE) the troika succeeded in establishing peace in Slovenia. On the island of Brioni the EC mission got all the parties in the dispute to accept its plan. The Community had created the conditions for peaceful negotiations. Significantly, all parties agreed that a 'new situation' had arisen in Yugoslavia which required close monitoring and negotiation between the parties. Negotiations were to begin no later than 1 August and were to include all aspects of Yugoslavia's future, to be discussed without preconditions. The key question concerned border revenues – which were to be federal, but collected by Slovene officials and to be paid into a joint account to be controlled by the federal and republican finance ministers and one or two external controllers.

Although allegations persisted that both sides had breached the cease-fire agreement, in the main the agreement held. A function of its implementation was the 18 July decision of the federal authorities, including the defence ministry, to withdraw all federal army units from Slovenia within a three-month period.[8]

After Brioni, the phenomenon of the troika was less prominent, as the Dutch presidency of the Council of Ministers which had begun on 1 July became a leading element in galvanising EC efforts. It was the 'strong Dutch Presidency that made things happen'.[9] This included the organisation of a semi-military, yet open and flexible, monitoring operation, for the troika's final achievement at Brioni was to gain the agreement of all parties to the introduction of a monitoring mission. A preparatory mission of high officials was expected to arrive on 9 July 1991. This happened within the framework of the CSCE, although the Community was the driving force and leading element of CSCE activity.

Phase 2: The European Community, CSCE and Monitors in Slovenia

Under the Charter of Paris adopted in November 1990, the CSCE was given three organs: the Council of Ministers, the Committee of Senior Officials (CSO) and the Conflict Prevention Centre (CPC). At the first meeting of the Council on 19–20 June 1991, a mechanism for consultation and cooperation in emergencies was established. Under this regime, any member affected by a dispute could call a crisis meeting of the Council or the CSO, but this required support from 12 members. The CPC, on the other hand, could be convened at the demand of one member if its security was threatened. This is what happened in the case of Yugoslavia.

The CSCE mechanism for emergencies was invoked only two weeks after it had been agreed upon in Berlin. Although others, including the United States, wanted to leave the crisis for a meeting of the Council which had been called for 3 July, Austria requested a meeting of the CPC, arguing that it would act more quickly. The matter was, however, transferred to the CSO. This was largely because the EC foreign ministers who had been meeting at the time armed hostilities began (and who had, as a block, 12 of the 13 members whose support was necessary to call such a meeting), had quickly convened the CSO to discuss a proposal they had devised.[10]

Moving business to the CSO also emphasised the significance of the matter. Not only was the CSO the senior and more prestigious forum, but Germany also held its chair at the time. That the chair was held by such a major country clearly added weight and further prestige. Germany's chairing of the CSO coincided with its drive both for a common EC foreign and security policy and for EC involvement in Yugoslavia. The Community presented a draft resolution to the CSO session which began on 3 July in Prague. The CSO's first move at the meeting was to issue a joint appeal for an immediate cease-fire. It called for political control over all armed forces and demanded that the Yugoslav federal authorities fulfil their commitments under the CSCE Charter of Paris and the Helsinki Final Act which included the 'unequivocal renunciation of the use of force'.[11]

The EC plan was accepted virtually 'on the nod'. The facility with which it passed was not only because it was a good proposal, but also because of its timing: it was the only plan on offer in a situation requiring rapid response. In effect, this meant that the CSO (and therefore the CSCE) was passing the leading role to the European Community. The Community, of course, had shown itself eager to volunteer for the role by racing to present its draft resolution.

The possibility of veto by any member country, including the party at the centre of debate, hampered CSCE action. The text had to be agreeable to all 35 members, including Yugoslavia which would have to accept it for the plan to be put into action. Effective decision-making and the taking of practical steps could always be impeded by invoking the Helsinki principle of non-intervention in the internal affairs of a member state.

Because of this, it was only after 16 hours of talks that the CSO agreed to send a 'good offices' mission to Yugoslavia. Belgrade had objected to the term 'observers' which was finally dropped from the text which backed the EC's proposal to organise a mission to Yugoslavia. Nonetheless, such a mission would be sent to 'help stabilise a cease-fire' and to monitor the return of troops to barracks. The other major change was the Yugoslav objection to one of the proposed mission's roles: 'the establishment of a new constitutional order'.[12] This clearly contained too much of a threat to the existing federal institutions, particularly the army.[13] Although it would be a CSCE mission of good offices, the European Community and its member states were to prepare and to contribute to it.

The CSCE's acknowledgement of the European Community's leading role as mediator in the Yugoslav crisis was an indicator of its own weakness. The emergency mechanism had worked, albeit belatedly and uneasily. It was clear, however, that it was the Community which would lead international efforts to mediate the Yugoslavs' troubles. The CSCE handed the baton, in effect, to the Community. In so doing, it lent its authority to the EC mission. However, the EC mission had its own authority derived from its prompt response and its own 'clout'. It was clear that only a body of substance could begin to influence Yugoslav events.

The European Community effectively took responsibility for dealing with Yugoslavia on behalf of the CSCE. It took the only action it could within the CSCE rubric: envoy of a monitoring mission with consent from the Yugoslavs. The EC monitoring force was composed mainly of EC member countries, although the CSCE framework in which the Community acted was denoted by the participation of members from outside the Community.[14]

The Observer Mission (OM) was established with the objective of monitoring the situation in Yugoslavia, particularly in Slovenia. Its aim was to monitor 'implementation of the remaining elements' of the agreement reached between the Yugoslav parties with the involvement of the European Community.[15] The Mission was to start work as soon as possible and to last as long as deemed necessary by all parties; it would limit its activities geographically to Slovenia, with the possibility of extending them into Croatia – although the area of deployment was subject to review by agreement with all parties concerned.

The Observer Mission was to be composed of both military and civilian personnel and would number between 30 and 50. For speed it was proposed that recruits should be drawn initially from the Confidence and Security Building Measures talks in Vienna where expertise in the CSCE was available, although the possibility of supplementing these with personnel from other contexts was admitted. The Mission would establish a coordination centre within Yugoslavia. From this, smaller units of perhaps two observers would be deployed in different sectors; in each case these would be escorted by a liaison officer from each of the opposing parties at all times. Each unit would report to the Head of the Observer Mission who would submit a daily report through the Prague CSCE Secretariat to the CSO. The CSO was to evaluate the Mission and make decisions on its prolongation.

Members of the Observer Mission were to be given diplomatic immunity and freedom to travel within Yugoslavia and communicate with the Head of Mission and with embassies. It was made explicit that the Mission was not a peacekeeping force and would not therefore carry arms. OM officials were to be identifiable and distinguishable – this requirement led to their wearing white uniforms and being dubbed 'ice-cream men'.

Initially, the monitoring role was confined to Slovenia where hostilities had first occurred. In the main, the monitoring mission there worked successfully. This was because Slovenia presented a relatively easy mission for EC monitors. Both sides had agreed on withdrawal and had little further interest in prolonging hostilities. Although there were constant minor problems, with both sides eager to highlight difficulties, in the main the work of the Observer Mission in Slovenia became monotonous: an 8 a.m. start, chauffeur-driven to one or two meetings, small problems to resolve and, as one Greek participant commented, doing a 'psychoanalyst's job'.[16]

Phase 3: Monitors in Croatia

As peace was being established in Slovenia, fighting began to spread across Croatia. The conflict in Croatia had always seemed likely to be far bloodier and nastier than anything in Slovenia, because of the more complicated political and military situation there. Slovenia had been a clear-cut clash between, on the one hand, a republican force backed by political and popular will throughout the republic and, on the other hand, a federal army whose every hesitant and stumbling act made the illegitimacy of its operations ever more apparent. The role of the Observer Mission was fairly straightforward: to supervise the stand-down of both forces and the withdrawal of a federal army which reluctantly acknowledged that its continued presence in Slovenia was untenable.

In Croatia there was no simple divide between two parties who, as was the case in Slovenia, agreed on the course of events necessary and merely needed the assistance of third parties to help them achieve implementation of what they had agreed. Instead there were three main groups – the federal army, the Croatian defence forces and Serbian irregular paramilitary groups. All of these were increasingly factional and to some extent beyond the authority of their supposed political masters.

As the conflict in Slovenia eased, various Serb paramilitary groups began actions against Croatian defence and security forces – indeed, they had already attacked units of the Croatian interior ministry forces in May, killing 15 men.[17] While the Community was still focusing on the question of whether or not Yugoslavia should hold together, the Serbians had moved on. Having failed to cow Slovenia as a means of intimidating the Croatians, they had begun to tackle the Croatians directly. Their offensive had nothing to do with holding Yugoslavia together except for the warning that it contained for other republics that if they sought to leave the federation they would do so having relinquished those areas that Serbia regarded as its own.

A series of attacks throughout July and August saw Serb forces take military control of one-third of Croatia. These advances were supported by the federal army which provided artillery cover, logistical back-up, intelligence and aerial power, although it never led offensives. Officially, the army claimed to be separating the Serb and Croat forces.

The fighting in Croatia, whilst intense where it occurred, remained fairly low-key in this period. This was partly as a result of the ease with which the Serbian–federal army coalition was able to seize territory (which in turn was due to lack of preparation and poor tactical sense in the Croatian forces). Although there were some talks between the various Yugoslav leaderships on ways to secure peace and on the future of Yugoslavia – without EC involvement – there was no greater chance of agreement without outside mediation than there had been in the months leading up to the declarations of independence.

Despite the battles throughout Croatia, extension of the Observer Mission's role was not proposed until 23 July when the German Foreign Minister, Hans Dietrich Genscher, urged this move. On 25 July the European Community decided to try to extend the Mission's mandate to the war-ravaged republic. Four days later, the Community decided to increase the Observer Mission from 50 to 500 officials. This move was ratified at an emergency CSCE meeting in Prague on 8 August, convened by the EC foreign ministers who had drafted their proposal at a meeting on 6 August. At that meeting it was also stressed that international pressure had to be placed on all the Yugoslavs, but especially on the Serbs. Although various measures were reviewed, such as the imposition of sanctions and discussion of Yugoslavia at the meeting of the Western European Union the following day, no firm steps were taken.

In Prague, the federal Foreign Minister, Budimir Lončar, had approved the Community initiative, including the decision to increase the Observer Mission, although the CSCE decision to do so stressed that where they would be deployed was a matter for the federal government. In the end this mattered little as, despite Lončar's assent, the EC's peace move was vetoed by the Serbian government on 3 August. Slobodan Milošević did not relent until 2 September – and then only after intense pressure from within and without Yugoslavia. In particular, the European Community threatened to isolate Serbia, impose sanctions and, it was hinted, even investigate the possibility of granting recognition to Croatia. On this last aspect, Genscher was most forceful, indicating that Germany might consider a unilateral recognition of Croatia if Serbia and the army did not bring hostilities to a halt.

When Serbia did agree to sign under this pressure, it was with bad grace. Milošević grudgingly signed but refused to join the toast until Hans van den Broek (by now holding the chair of the EC Foreign Ministers' Council) virtually forced him to do so. Van den Broek announced that the European Community would send in its monitors as soon as the cease-fire came into effect. While the Observer Mission would supervise the cease-fire, it was also agreed that a peace conference would be convened, sponsored by the Community, at which five judges, three from Yugoslavia and two from the EC, would act as arbiters. It was intended that the peace conference should begin within two weeks (see below).

Implementation of the cease-fire agreement was strained as preparations began for the conference. The Observer Mission began to move into areas of Croatia following preparatory forays by the EC's special envoy, the Dutch Ambassador to Paris, Henri Wijnaendts, who had judged that the federal army was not acting as a buffer force, as it had continued to claim, but was openly siding with Serb forces. This informal coalition created problems for cease-fire agreements.

Both the Croatian and federal forces were signatories to the general agreement in which they declared that they would not fire unless fired upon. The Serb insurgents, however, were not signatories – Milošević was presumed to have signed on their behalf. He, however, had stressed that Serb leaders from Croatia should be participants in the negotiations and at the peace conference. Breaches of the cease-fire undoubtedly reflected the ambiguity in the position of the Serb insurgents which was exploited. Serb forces, albeit in alliance with the federal army, opened fire on Croatian positions; in so doing they were not breaking any agreement they had made. The Croatians returned fire – and in doing so were not breaking their word either.

The joint positions of the Serb–federal army alliance meant Croatian fire hit the army. The army would then open fire, having been fired upon first; like the other two forces, it would not have broken the agreement. Even when agreement was made with the putative political leader of the Serbs in eastern Slavonia, it was broken by units not under his authority and by others which, although acknowledging him, had reportedly heard nothing of any agreement.[18]

The stress upon the maintenance of the general cease-fire agreement was evident as bursts of fighting occurred in several parts of Croatia. The Observer Mission was able to make itself useful in several instances, acting as go-between to resolve local difficulties and misunderstandings. Wijnaendts himself was instrumental in negotiating a local cease-fire around Osijek, although he was made pellucidly aware of the inherent fragility of any agreement when the next day his hotel in the town was hit by mortar fire from the besieging Serb forces.

In other cases, the monitors proved themselves able to negotiate local agreements which had far more resilience than the general agreements. This was particularly true in the area around Knin, although stability here was helped by the fact that Serb–federal forces were in control of large swathes of territory. This helped the local OM officials to get the leader of the self-declared 'Serbian Autonomous Region' of Knin, Milan Babić, to give his word that his troops would not fire first.[19] Further local agreements were made at Gospić and Novska.

The monitors' strategy of building agreement from the ground up made sense and had some success, but proved too onerous. In general, the small number of monitors (75) relative to the task at hand and sustained breaches of the peace led to the conclusion that the Observer Mission in Croatia had failed. To have any effect, monitors needed to be at the front-line. There was, however, no front-line as such and there were so many battles that it was impossible always to be in the right place at the right time. Van den Broek blamed the failure on the fact that the Observer Mission had gone into Croatia at a time when violence had already become too widespread to get monitors into place successfully.[20] None the less, the monitors continued their work, especially the performance of another assignment – the provision of objective information. The monitors were valuable as independent witnesses to what was happening amid billows of propaganda. One particular instance was confirmation from the Mission's head in Zagreb, Simon Smits, that, according to the EC monitor in Dubrovnik, the old town there had been hit.[21]

The difficulties of the Observer Mission were obvious. Henri Wijnaendts himself had twice come under fire and monitors had been wounded. Increasingly there was talk of sending a European armed force into Croatia. Some thought of this as an intervention force to protect the Croats. Discussion was, however, about an armed peacekeeping force to support the monitors.

Phase 4: The Western European Union and an Armed Peacekeeping Force

There was another problem in maintaining the agreement. Croatian forces were tempted to break the agreement anyway. Hans Dietrich Genscher's statement that if fighting continued his country would consider giving Croatia recognition unilaterally was interpreted in many quarters as saying that Germany *would* give recognition if the fighting continued. This was an incentive to some Croatian forces to initiate actions which would prolong the conflict and hence, it was presumed (falsely), speed recognition by a major European country.

Genscher's unease forced him to make clear that such a tactic would not work, but he continued to voice the disquiet widely felt in his country. Whilst maintaining that unilateral recognition was not out of the question, however, he began to push for stronger EC action.

Although there was some suggestion that an armed European peacekeeping force be sent to Yugoslavia, there was never much prospect of this happening, for a variety of reasons. The first of these was the situation on the ground: where there was no peace there could be no question of sending a force to ensure it. A distinction had to be made between a peace-creating (or peace-making, or peace-enforcing) force and one for peacekeeping.

This distinction reflects the legal basis for sending any armed force. While Yugoslavia was recognised as a sovereign entity in international law, its permission would be necessary for the envoy of any armed force for any purpose. In the event of a change in Yugoslavia's status – either removal of recognition, or recognition of its republics, especially in this case Croatia – it would have become possible to argue a case for giving defensive assistance to Croatia. In this instance, the force's role would be to establish, not maintain, a cessation of hostilities.

In humanitarian terms, there might have been a moral impulse to stop the one-sided, bloody war. But there was no legal rubric for this. Parallels were made with the UN-sponsored intervention to protect Kurds in Iraq. In that case, however, specific UN resolutions on Iraq were broadly interpreted to 'allow' intervention within the boundaries of a sovereign state. A peace-enforcing force was appropriate to the situation in Yugoslavia and corresponded with a sentiment that it was necessary to 'do something' to stop the attacks on Croatia. However, this type of intervention was never what was really being debated, despite perceptions that this was what was in question.

The Croatian government clearly thought that such a force was necessary and that its purpose would be, effectively, to defend Croatia. Indeed, it is likely that such a force would have had this role as there seemed little question that it was the Croats who were in need of both a cease-fire and help. Diplomatically, however, this was not a realistic possibility.

The European Community had from the earliest stages in Slovenia clearly set its sights on a comprehensive settlement on the future of Yugoslavia. This meant that any outcome of the conflict had to be one agreed upon by all the parties including, notably, even Serbia. This was for good reason. Any outcome to which Serbia did not assent was a recipe for perpetual instability. Intervention on behalf of Croatia would have required recognising Croatian independence first.

The Community was against any such recognition because of the likelihood that it would drive the Serbian leadership further into its paranoia that there was a conspiracy (or a set of conspiracies) against Serbia. In particular, recognition would have lent support to views that there was a Vatican plot to destroy Yugoslavia, an Austrian ambition to recreate the Habsburg Empire and a German plan to build a Fourth Reich. Discussions with Serbia were already extremely awkward. Recognition and intervention at this stage would have made dialogue impossible and also therefore a political solution by agreement of all parties – the only kind of agreement likely to endure in the long-term.

What those encouraging an EC intervention force had in mind was a traditional UN-type operation in which the 'blue berets' would arrive to monitor a cease-fire line that was recognised by the belligerents. However here they lacked the prior agreement of both parties. Even if they had had it, there were obvious problems connected with sending observers or even armed troops into areas where the fighting men were under no obvious political control.

Moving into civil wars requires considerable local knowledge and a readiness to exert authority early on. But the Community and the Western European Union lacked a reliable means of intelligence-gathering and interpretation, nor were there agreed rules of engagement for troops on the ground. The experience of such ventures suggested that it was far easier to get in than to get out and that sooner rather than later the intervening force would be seen as favouring one side rather than another and would therefore be seen as a legitimate target for an aggrieved party. The British had enough experience in Northern Ireland of keeping the peace where there is a deep and unresolved political dispute to want to accept responsibility for one at the other end of Europe. It was always going to be extremely unlikely that either Serbia or the federal army would accept foreign troops, although it was not ruled out completely for the future. There was little prospect for the time being of a peace-keeping force being welcomed by Belgrade.

There was also the question of who would make up such a force and how large it should be. A military option was not readily available and therefore impractical. The European Community had no defence structures. The closest it had to any kind of defence institution was the Western European Union composed of nine of its member states. Although the French spoke of the Western European Union (WEU) as the 'military arm' of the Community ready to move in when ordered and send whatever forces were required to keep the peace in Yugoslavia, that was an aspiration, not a reality. The WEU lacked forces of its own and offered no command structure. It had only the most rudimentary experience of coordinating naval activity – on both occasions in the Gulf.[22] It could only serve as a useful cover for endeavours that would otherwise lack a multinational authority, but someone else would need to do the coordinating.

At this time Germany was in the chair of both the Western European Union and the CSCE. Germany was unlikely to be seen by the Serbs as a disinterested party anxious to help. Thus it would be coordinating an activity in which it could not get involved. Of the other eight WEU members, four had only very small armed forces – Luxembourg, The Netherlands, Belgium and Greece. Of the rest, Spain had no experience on which to draw; Italy was prepared, but was unlikely to be acceptable to Serbia; this left France and the United Kingdom.

France was keen to form and send a force – although it made clear that it was only prepared to do this when a cease-fire was holding on the ground and the conditions for peacekeeping existed. France was eager to see such a force formed by the Western European Union as the seed for the creation and elaboration of a 'European' defence force and, therefore, defence policy. The British had been designated head of NATO's rapid reaction force and it was suggested that this could be given authority by the WEU to act on its behalf. But this force, despite initial exercises, was still largely conceptual. The composition and logistics of any WEU force would have to be worked out from scratch, or borrowed informally from NATO.

Nonetheless, the Dutch proposed contracting the Western

European Union to investigate the possibility of gathering a force of 6,000 lightly armed troops to act as a peacekeeping force. The British objected to this, arguing that a much bigger force of 30,000–50,000 would be necessary. Indeed, a ground force for such an operation would have to be large, given the nature of the war in Yugoslavia and the terrain on which it was being fought. The terrain was mostly mountainous and the war was being fought between a variety of forces all over southern, central and eastern Croatia – although only in southern Croatia was the situation at all clear-cut. In the rest of the republic, the war was being fought on a patchwork pattern, with no obvious front-lines.

The absence of a front-line meant that there would be no single 'green line' to police as in other instances, such as Cyprus or Egypt. Operations would be 'village by village and street by street' making them extremely complex and hard to co-ordinate.[23] Most of all, this meant a large deployment was needed.

The United Kingdom was against the organisation of a 'European' armed force. However, it developed the requirements for such a force if only to demonstrate to its partners that this would be no small enterprise. The force suggested was far more substantial than that put forward by the Dutch. This was for two reasons. The first concerned the situation in Croatia (and, it was envisaged, perhaps later also in Bosnia). This required large numbers of troops to be spread all over the republic between the belligerents: one side would be controlling one mountain and another could be controlling the next; or one belligerent might be defending a village or a town and its opponent laying siege, while in the next village the parties might have reversed roles. Moreover, there was, the British argued, not unreasonably, a considerable threat that a force would have to defend itself as it tried to keep the peace. In the end, the legal and practical difficulties faced in sending an intervention force to Yugoslavia reflected the lack of political will when it came to getting involved in what could well be an extremely difficult and protracted military operation which, if it went wrong, could result in substantial casualties among the WEU forces.

The prospect that the Western European Union might send an armed force to Croatia was almost certainly the prompt for the Americans to call an emergency meeting of NATO. Any WEU force would have to rely on NATO for logistical support. This would implicate the United States, which although not against a European peacekeeping force, did not want to be a part of it and indicated its opposition to German involvement (which was unlikely anyway). However, US anxieties were removed by the WEU decision not to send a force, merely to instruct its Secretariat to investigate the possibilities for strengthening and supporting the Observer Mission.

The Secretariat came up with four options: to ratify officially the logistical support already being provided to the Observer Mission; to give the Mission an armed bodyguard for the 'escort and protection' of 4,000–6,000 troops; to create a lightly armed peacekeeping force of the same size; or to send a heavily armed force of 25,000–50,000 to maintain a truce should it be achieved.[24] The United Kingdom alone opposed all four measures, although it joined in the consensus that only the first step could be taken without agreement from all the Yugoslav factions.

It is also of interest to consider the question of air cover for the Observer Mission in Croatia. This of course would have required the agreement of all sides. Such cover might have been useful; it would certainly not have been vulnerable in the same way that troops on the ground would be. Yet emphasis was constantly placed on the great difficulties a ground force would face when policing the peace. Similarly, there was, apparently, no suggestion at this point of looking at the possibilities for naval involvement in any peacekeeping force, despite the role being played by the Yugoslav navy, nor was there consideration of naval back-up for the Mission (for example, in its efforts along the Croatian coast, particularly around Dubrovnik), although this was to appear in a limited way in November.

After the high tide of EC–WEU deliberations on a peacekeeping force at a meeting on 18 September, the question of a peacekeeping force, or of any other measures which might be taken, was passed on to the United Nations. Even a day before the meeting, some member countries, such as Germany and Portugal, were suggesting that peacekeeping forces should be arranged by the United Nations. After the WEU decision not to send a force to Yugoslavia, the French and Germans shifted the question to the United Nations which was due to commence its General Assembly in New York the following week. Even so the two disagreed on the purpose. The French merely sought a mandate for European action; the Germans were looking for full-scale UN intervention. Either way, there was little prospect at that time that the United Nations would be any more likely to send any kind of force than had the Europeans.

In spite of this, the Yugoslav delegation to the United Nations tried to block Security Council discussion on the issue. None the less, Canada and Austria called for the Security Council to be convened to discuss Yugoslavia. They argued for discussion under Chapter VII of the UN Charter (which had been used to justify intervention against Iraq the previous year). At the same time the Yugoslav federal President, Stipe Mesić, called for the United Nations to order a cease-fire and send in a peacekeeping force. The Austrian Foreign

Minister, Alois Mock, warned countries that not to get involved now would only mean embroilment later in a worse conflict.[25]

Attention in the United Nations focused on embargo measures, with regard to oil and arms. In the end, there was a decision to impose an arms embargo on all parties in the Yugoslav war. This broadened steps already taken by the British and other European governments after the first week of fighting in Slovenia at the beginning of July. Like those moves, it was a well-intentioned gesture that was unlikely to prevent fighting and, insofar as it had any effect at all, would simply compound the asymmetry of the two sides: whereas the Croatians were short of weapons which could only be obtained through capture or through international purchase, the federal army and the Serbs had access to the products of at least 78 per cent of the military industry which had made Yugoslavia 90 per cent self-sufficient in defence requirements.[26]

Although the United Nations was later to appoint former US Secretary of State Cyrus Vance as its special envoy for Yugoslavia, this represented the limits of UN involvement until the European Community prompted further activity towards the year's end. The subject of Yugoslavia had been raised at the United Nations in response to a general feeling that the European effort had achieved all that it could, but in practice the outcome of UN discussions was to return the initiative to Europe. The appointment of Vance, for example, gave an added dimension of backing to the work of the Community – especially of its special envoy, Lord Carrington, who had been asked to coordinate a peace conference.[27] Indeed, Carrington, whilst unable to secure a lasting cease-fire, was making notable progress given the intensity and complexity of the conflict on the one hand and the relatively limited means at his disposal on the other.

Phase 5: Carrington's Mission

The 2 September cease-fire which opened the way for the Observer Mission to go into Croatia also included agreement to begin talks on the future of Yugoslavia to be held in The Hague. Only a day later, it was announced that the conference would be convened on 7 September in The Hague under the chairmanship of Lord Carrington. Talks would be on the basis of three principles: no unilateral changes of borders; protection of the rights of all minorities; and full respect for all legitimate interests and aspirations.[28] The conference proceeded alongside the Observer Mission's entry into Croatia and various efforts to obtain a durable cease-fire.

Carrington was widely perceived as a fine candidate for the challenge ahead when he took up his role as the EC's representative and coordinator of the talks. As a former Secretary-General of NATO and the former British Foreign Minister credited with the 1980 settlement on Rhodesia/Zimbabwe, he had the diplomatic background to deal with the tortuous Yugoslav conflict. He was also widely regarded as having the personal qualities to be able to gain the trust of all parties.

The charmless task ahead was confirmed by the opening session of the conference. Although the conference had been called on condition that the cease-fire was maintained, it began amid renewed fighting in Yugoslavia and with verbal offensives from both the Serbian and Croatian Presidents. After the opening session, however, the conference became closed as Carrington began a series of private meetings with all the Yugoslav leaders and foreign ministers in an attempt to mediate.

Although Lord Carrington initially insisted that, for the conference to proceed, an end to hostilities was a prerequisite, he continued his work in spite of the seemingly unstoppable violence. At Igalo in Montenegro on 17 September he appeared to have waved a magic wand as he conjured signatures to a cease-fire agreement not only from Croatia's President Franjo Tudjman and the Serbian leader Slobodan Milošević, but also from the defence secretary, General Veljko Kadijević.[29] It was, however, too much to expect that one afternoon with Carrington was enough to bring peace. As became the norm with Yugoslav cease-fires, signatures proved insufficient to halt combat.

The joint statement was flawed. It recognised that leaders could only pledge that 'everyone within our control and under our political and military influence should cease fire immediately'[30] – that is, they could not (or were not prepared to) guarantee that fighting would stop. In this regard, the local mediation efforts of OM members would continue to be more constructive than any kind of general agreement among the leaders. The Igalo agreement was also weak because it required that all forces 'instantly and simultaneously' should 'withdraw from immediate contact and from actual or previous areas where hostilities have or are taking place'.[31] Of course, neither side was prepared in practice to do anything which would weaken its position without a guarantee that the opponent was reciprocating.[32] The lack of specificity involved virtually rendered the document null and void as soon it was signed. Later efforts at arranging cease-fires increased specificity, but did not diminish the growing perception that a lasting cease-fire was not a realistic possibility, as each agreement failed to be implemented, or broke down with mounting ferocity.

In these circumstances, Lord Carrington had to forget his early statements to the effect that there could be no peace talks without a cease-fire and proceed with the conference anyway. His evaluation was that 'by making progress – if we can make progress – we think it will be more likely that the cease-fire will hold and that we can get a solution that is acceptable to all the parties to the dispute'.[33] To this end the two expert groups that had been meeting intermittently on human rights issues and constitutional matters would be in session almost permanently.[34] A third group of experts later began work on economic affairs.

At the beginning of October, the European Community discussed the possibility of giving Yugoslavia 'diplomatic quarantine' – that is, effectively removing recognition from the country and its official representatives. Although this did not necessarily imply recognition of the republics, it was a clear signal of the way the wind was preparing to blow. A day after this was discussed, and after the Serbian–federal army forces had received setbacks for the first time, Carrington was able to produce the most significant breakthrough to date – and perhaps of the whole dispute. On 4 October, he secured Milošević's agreement to seek a political solution 'on the basis of the independence of those wishing it'.[35]

This solution would include a 'loose alliance of sovereign or independent republics' and 'adequate arrangements' for minorities and 'possibly special status for certain areas'. The key feature, however, was Milošević's acceptance that there could be no 'unilateral changes in borders'. Carrington, whilst recognising the amount of work and the difficulties which lay ahead, did not hesitate to recognise that this had been the major stumbling block and that it represented a major concession:

> This is the first time that Serbia has recognised the right of other republics to self-determination – subject to respect for minority rights. By discussing issues such as the autonomy and special status for minorities we are going to the heart of the political problem. I hope this will speed up the political process for a cease-fire.[36]

In securing the Serbian President's recognition of the territorial integrity of Croatia, Carrington had achieved a major breakthrough. It would be hard for Milošević to backtrack on this public agreement. That agreement provided the basis for the negotiators in The Hague and the EC officials to work towards a proposal for a political settlement.

The path ahead remained rocky, however. Within two days the

fighting intensified as the 90-day moratorium on the Slovenian and Croatian declarations approached its end on 8 October. Croatian President Tudjman, after a period of considerable pressure from his army of critics, ordered full mobilisation; the federal army responded with renewed vigour across Croatia, including bombardment of the historic port of Dubrovnik. The European Community, on the basis of reports from the Observer Mission, identified the army as the chief offender and reacted swiftly. It set a deadline of midnight on 7 October for a truce, after which Yugoslavia's trade agreement would be suspended, ending all trade,[37] and sanctions would be imposed. A supplement to these measures was a threat that 'those responsible for the unprecedented violence in Yugoslavia, with its ever increasing loss of life, should be held accountable under international law'.[38]

The midnight deadline was met and a truce came into effect for several days, although not before the federal air force had made an attack on the presidential palace in the Croatian capital of Zagreb. There were though, as ever, pockets where the fighting persisted. With the assistance of EC monitors, both the federal army's blockade of Croatia's ports and the Croatian National Guard's siege of federal barracks throughout Croatia (especially in the capital Zagreb) were lifted. The monitors were essential in enabling both sides to carry out their commitments, providing supervision and channels of mediation as the army began to leave its barracks in Zagreb (this process was halted half-way through as tension increased).

As clashes grew again, there was a strange hiccough in proceedings. Both Tudjman and Milošević were invited to talks with Soviet President Mikhail Gorbachev in Moscow on 15 October. Gorbachev got both men to agree to begin negotiations on peace within a month.[39] This, while desirable, was odd: both sides were already involved in such talks in The Hague. Whatever was said went unrevealed, but, after meeting with Russia's President Boris Yeltsin and having a further session with Gorbachev the following day, Milošević and Tudjman emerged with different demeanours. The Serbian president was obviously buoyant and satisfied, whereas his Croatian counterpart was clearly unhappy.

Afterwards, whilst on the ground the Serb coalition pressed on, the Serbian stance at The Hague hardened. On the basis of the discussions with all parties in The Hague, Lord Carrington and Hans van den Broek offered the Yugoslav republics a plan for political redevelopment. That plan was to rearrange Yugoslavia along the lines of the European Community itself.[40] Van den Broek stated categorically that border changes were 'not an option'.[41] This plan coincided with the various proposals advanced by Slovenia, Croatia, Bosnia–Hercegovina and Macedonia in the year leading up to the war. Significantly, a fifth republic, tiny Montenegro, also accepted the EC proposal.

Montenegro had been staunchly allied with Serbia throughout the years of crisis. Now, President Momir Bulatović told an emergency meeting of the republic's Parliament: 'We cannot adopt an in-between attitude. We can only accept or refuse.'[42] He added that refusal would mean international isolation and sanctions – something such a small republic could hardly afford. There was, however, considerable discontent among the Parliament's members.

With five out of six republican leaderships accepting the EC plan in principle, the only stumbling block was Milošević, who rejected it, although this rejection was not completely out of hand. Serbia's chief objection was the proposed position of the Serb communities outside Serbia. Having been classified as part of a 'nation' in the old Yugoslavia, these would now become 'national minorities'. Serbia's position was that these minorities should be 'sovereign'; this corresponded with the proposal of the Serbs in Croatia.[43] A further major stumbling block was the quid pro quo for Serb political autonomy in Croatia: restoration of autonomy for the Serbian provinces of Kosovo and Vojvodina, the removal of which had been Milošević's central political platform and only real achievement since coming to power in 1986. Suggesting this, he said, constituted interference in Serbia's internal affairs.

The Serbian President could not easily accept the proposal, given the pressure on him from powerful elements in the Belgrade Parliament and the position of the Croatian Serbs. His scope for rejection was, however, limited as the big guns of the United States and the Soviet Union were lined up behind the EC proposal, with threats of general international isolation and economic sanctions:[44] with five republics ready to head in one direction, it seemed there would be a shotgun divorce if Serbia did not relent.

In addition to Serbia's leadership, its partners in the war, the federal army, repulsed the EC plan. Defence Secretary Kadijević thought Lord Carrington's plan would prove catastrophic and renewed charges that the plan was, in effect, 'Germany very openly . . . attacking Yugoslavia for the third time this century'.[45] He also bewailed the reality that the plan would mean the end of the federal army. EC responses to this sob story were unsympathetic. The EC reaction was characterised by Carrington: 'The leadership of the federal army is acting in a totally unjustified fashion, bears a heavy responsibility and is accountable for what it is doing.'[46]

Milošević, along with the army leadership and Serb leaders from Bosnia and Croatia, drafted an alternative plan for a 'mini-Yugoslavia', to include Serbia, Montenegro and others who wanted to remain part of a Yugoslav federation – the enclaves in Croatia and Bosnia would become 'autonomous federal units'. In this plan, rearrangement of Yugoslavia would be according to referenda held on an 'ethnic, not a republican, basis.'[47]

The Serb coalition, however, was doing little to encourage support for its position. The continuing bombardments in eastern Slavonia and, especially, the high-profile assault on the historic port of Dubrovnik raised international impatience with Serbia and the federal army. That impatience manifested itself in an ultimatum: Serbia was given one week from 28 October to accept the EC plan. Otherwise, it would face comprehensive economic sanctions (although earlier statements that these would need to be backed by the United Nations were repeated). If Serbia did accept, the conference would continue with all six republics; if it did not, van den Broek warned, 'the community will continue its patient negotiations with the five republics who are willing. This would be in the perspective of their right to independence.'[48]

Moreover, the EC Commission had been given legal advice that it could act immediately to suspend its trade agreement with Yugoslavia and take punitive measures. The latter would include diplomatic quarantine of the federal Yugoslav state and Serbia. The European Community would then be in a position to 'take a series of positive measures to discriminate in favour of particular republics', said one official, even prior to formal diplomatic recognition.[49] Recognition itself would take a little longer but was now on the agenda. By the end of October, 13 countries were accepting Slovene passports, although asserting that this did not constitute recognition. The Italian Foreign Minister, Gianni de Michelis, said that the Community's aim was to wind up the peace conference by mid-December, by which time the 'treaty will be signed with the individual republics, and will represent official EC recognition of their independence'.[50]

The threat to Serbia was clearly beginning to tell. The leader of the Serb community around Knin in Croatia, Milan Babić, said that he had been coming under heavy pressure from Milošević to accept the EC plan. This was an indication of the divergent claims being made on the Serbian leadership: on the one hand, there was its mission to stand with the Serbs in Croatia, on the other, the growing strains within Serbia proper as economic difficulties added to growing disillusion with the war. Serbia continued to oppose the plan.

At the beginning of November, it appeared that EC efforts, backed by references to the CSCE and the United Nations, had produced the framework for, and encouraged evolution towards, a political settlement on Yugoslavia, albeit one which, after much deliberation, was still rejected by Serbia. That settlement would be a product of EC mediation, but perhaps more of EC strongarm threats. Indeed, on several occasions, the Community had made progress towards gaining cease-fire agreements or agreement on negotiations on the future of Yugoslavia, but only after exerting pressure on the less willing parties. The strong Dutch presidency of the EC Council of Ministers was extremely important in this regard.

The dynamics and complexity of the conflict meant that cease-fires were always going to be difficult. Indeed, Lord Carrington's strategy of constructing the framework for political resolution was probably wise. The existence of both Croatian and Serbian extremist groups, as well as a federal army whose operations, in spite of whatever Kadijević continued to say, were beyond political authority, meant that a political agreement would probably not mean a prompt end to fighting. Cease-fires were thus unlikely to be effective; political negotiations to remove the principal causes of the war would create the conditions for a wind-down of hostilities. It was possible, therefore, to perceive a contraflow in EC activity: at the same time as its efforts to stop bloodshed and destruction (inevitably) failed, Carrington was constantly putting the building blocks of a political compact in place at the Hague peace conference. In reality, peace could only be achieved on the basis of such an agreement.

Phase 6: A Division of Labour – Towards Truce and Recognition

Lord Carrington had done extremely well in the circumstances, but, alas, not well enough. The dual role played by the European Community of seeking to mediate both a cease-fire and a political settlement more or less ended with the so-near-yet-so-far failure at the end of October. At first, the Community appeared to be passing the baton to the United Nations as the three of its members on the UN Security Council began to push for measures to be taken by that body, including taking responsibility for dealing with cease-fire and peacekeeping discussions. This meant that by mid-November, it was Cyrus Vance, not Lord Carrington, who was taking the lead in negotiations to halt the fighting. Carrington and the Community, meanwhile, continued with the political groundwork.

The 'good cop–bad cop' teaming of the United Nations and the European Community, which evolved more or less by accident, was both more acceptable to Serbia and more practical in terms of the quest to deal with the politics of the dispute. Serbia found the United Nations a more agreeable partner in talks because it did not appear to be driven by German ambition – as did the Community in Serbian eyes – and it forced the United States to take a more obvious interest in the matter. The European Community was freed from the responsibilities of neutrality involved in mediation and able therefore to assert its influence where this could be used to encourage political dialogue. Thus the Serbian belief that it was a victim of German expansionism, as expressed through the Community, did not impinge on cease-fire discussions in the same way as it had previously. As a result, the Community could take stronger positions without prejudging efforts to stop the fighting. Indeed, it was able to exert pressure in terms of the political agenda in a way which created the conditions for the first really stable break in the seven months of fighting.

Cyrus Vance, with relative ease, negotiated a cease-fire three weeks into November and gained agreement, in principle, for the deployment of a 10,000-strong UN peacekeeping force – if the peace was maintained.[51] This was the fourteenth cease-fire agreement of the war in Croatia and it fared no better than the previous baker's dozen. Eventually, on 3 January, a cease-fire came into effect which, although continually and increasingly broken by small skirmishes, was still essentially in force a month later. That peace was, however, only achieved as a result of the Community's political exertions.

EC member states were becoming increasingly impatient, with Germany, in particular, pushing insistently for recognition of Slovenia and Croatia, making it clear that it would grant recognition before the year's end even if this meant breaking ranks with Community colleagues. The subject of Yugoslavia, however, was placed on the back burner until after the dishes on the Maastricht menu had been cooked and consumed on 10 December. This was clearly a move to prevent the main meal at the EC's Maastricht summit, the signing of treaties on greater European union, from being adulterated.

With Germany intending to recognise Slovenia and Croatia before Christmas, with Cyrus Vance apparently making no greater progress than his European predecessors and with the prospect of a negotiated political settlement which had seemed possible in November receding daily, the question of recognition came to the fore. Several Community members opposed this course for fear it would complicate the situation, not only in Croatia, but in other Yugoslav lands, particularly in Bosnia–Hercegovina. The Germans, with Italian backing, countered that, on the contrary, recognition would be the decisive step which would break the circle of violence and induce a more compromising Serbian attitude.

The German analysis was probably correct. Throughout the Yugoslav crisis, both before and after the outbreak of war, the unwillingness or inability of outsiders to intervene, added to the relative weakness of the republics interested in independence – even Slovenia – meant that the Serbian camp had no incentive to use means other than war. EC pressure had almost brought Milošević to a point of conciliation, but, in the end, the EC threats had been hollow and, once the Serbian President had realised this, the Serbian camp could continue its campaign with impunity. The threat of recognition was the ultimate political instrument available to the Community. It offered the possibility of a telling act which would radically alter the character of the conflict.

However, if the German analysis was correct with regard to halting the violence in Croatia, it was wrong in other respects. German concentration on the two north-western republics which had experienced war meant that the delicate positions of Bosnia–Hercegovina and Macedonia were overlooked. As the external world's stand before the end of June had more or less condemned Slovenia and Croatia to violence, the German position was in danger of repeating this with regard to the weaker would-be independent republics. The German policy, while right about stemming the Serb–federal army tide, offered little promise in other respects.

These considerations, added to general reluctance to agree to precipitate recognition, led the Community, supported by pleas from Lord Carrington, to persuade the Germans partially to delay recognition. This would permit it to happen in an ordered way, within a framework which gave Bosnia, Macedonia and, if it wished, Montenegro, the opportunity to seek recognition. After a long meeting into the early hours of 17 December, the EC foreign ministers discussed the question of recognition before emerging with a formula: an adjudicator would be appointed and applications invited from all the Yugoslav republics wishing to be recognised as independent; republics would be judged according to various criteria, including conditions for individual and minority rights and the rejection of territorial claims; the Council of Foreign Ministers would then implement the adjudicator's recommendations on 15 January.

At the same time, on 15–16 December, there was another 'victory for German diplomacy' at the United Nations,[52] where the Security Council authorised the sending of 15 military monitors to Yugoslavia to monitor the situation and assess the chances of gaining a cease-fire and the opportunity to deploy a peacekeeping force. Cyrus Vance, meanwhile, would continue the pursuit of a workable cease-fire agreement. This he achieved on 2 January, the fifteenth of its kind; unlike the best of the others, it was to last for more than a few days and be virtually complete.

There were two major reasons for the success of this particular cease-fire: the imminence of recognition, creating a situation in which, for the first time, Serbia's interests would unquestionably be best served at the negotiating table, and the fact that Vance, as a UN representative, offered a route to peace which avoided open concession to German influence. On other occasions the Serbian camp had evaded cease-fire accords because the Community had been unable to coerce more strongly for fear of increasing Serbian fears about Germany. For Serbia, an EC-arranged cease-fire, backed by political coercion, could be interpreted as capitulation to Germany. A UN-brokered cease-fire, on the other hand, was, for Serbs thinking in those terms, an escape from the feared embrace of Germany: accepting arrangements made by Vance became an alternative to capitulation to the Germans.

Milošević and the army leadership also demonstrated a reawakened interest in the EC peace conference. Indeed, as Lord Carrington noted after the conference had reconvened on 9 January following a month-long gap, Serbian enthusiasm for the conference was now far greater and the attitude of its leadership 'more constructive', having 'obviously taken note' of the shift towards recognition of Croatia by EC members.[53] If Croatia was to be recognised, then Serbia's only chance now to gain any benefit from that situation was at the peace table.

Despite a remarkably brazen attack on two EC helicopters by federal army MiGs, causing five deaths, the Community moved unruffled towards the 15 January deadline. That incident, representing perhaps a last spiteful poke at the Community and a warning to those who would sign-up for a UN peacekeeping force, was the only major infringement of the 3 January cease-fire. If the intention had been to deter peacekeepers, the Security Council decision the next day to send 50 observers showed that it had not worked. Following the incident, one of the main figures in the dispute, Federal Defence Secretary Kadijević resigned. Ironically, the replacement of this politically astute soldier with one far less so, the erstwhile Chief of Staff General Adžić, made the political situation easier, as Adžić's greater proximity to the Serbian leadership facilitated the army's 'withdrawal' from the old Yugoslavia which had had Kadijević's loyalty.

On 15 January, however, having achieved much in awkward circumstances in the seven months since the army clashed with Slovenia, the Community made a serious and dangerous mistake. This was similar to the mistake Germany almost made in December and concerned Bosnia and Macedonia in particular. Slovenia was recommended for recognition by the adjudicator, French lawyer Robert Badinter, without any problem. The only other republic to satisfy the EC conditions, Macedonia, was not, however, given recognition, while Croatia, which did not meet the conditions, was recognised by the 12 Community members, a number of other European states and Canada. Badinter felt that Croatia's legal provision for minorities was unsatisfactory; the EC foreign ministers granted recognition only after receiving assurances from President Tudjman that the matter would be rectified quickly.

Badinter had delayed dealing with the delicate case of Bosnia because the failure to hold a referendum there meant that the people's will had not been made clear; he recommended the holding of an internationally supervised referendum to clarify the matter. Macedonia, however, was a different matter. Badinter had no problems in this quarter, in spite of a curious clause inserted by the Greeks at the 16–17 December foreign ministers' meeting. This explicitly required a commitment

> to adopt constitutional and political guarantees assuring that it [the republic] has no territorial claim towards a neighbouring member State of the Community, and that it will not undertake propaganda hostile to that state, including the use of a name which implies territorial claims.[54]

Greece, however, persuaded its fellow Community member states not to recognise Macedonia. Its ostensible reason was that, despite duly made constitutional provisions that Macedonia had no territorial claims, a continued use of the 'historically Greek' name would imply expansionist claims on Greece. The ludicrous proposition that tiny Macedonia, with a population of little more than 2 million, an exhausted economy and without armed forces, represented a threat to a country which not only had its own armed forces, but also the added benefits of EC and NATO membership (with the latter including American bases), was not summarily rebuffed by Greece's Community partners, as it ought to have been. Instead it was entertained, initiating an unnecessary bout of Balkan tension and the first notes of an extremely perilous 'political pirouette which has already led to two regional wars this century'.[55]

Greece had two interests in opposing Macedonia's recognition. One, perhaps the more significant, was that Greece, a member, would not qualify under the Community's tests for the Yugoslav republics with regard to minorities. Not only does Greece have an ethnic Macedonian minority which it does not recognise beyond occasional admissions that they are 'Slavaphone Greeks', it also has Turkish and Albanian minorities which it labels 'Muslim Greeks'. Greece's real fear was that the existence of a Macedonian state might encourage its 'Slavaphone' community to seek collective rights.

In terms of Greece's second reason for opposing Macedonian independence, its fear that Macedonia would be prey to Bulgarian expansionism, the move was highly counter-productive. Greek obduracy only added to Macedonia's need to turn to Bulgaria – and beyond that, to Bulgaria's new friend, Turkey. Both countries are regarded by Greece as adversaries. The Greeks in reality got their calculations wrong: blocking recognition only drew attention to the Macedonian minority in Greece; and the surest way to have prevented Bulgaria's absorption of Macedonia either *de facto* or *de jure* – something both Serbia and Greece might be prepared to fight about – would have been to support its independence.

The EC's hesitancy in recognising Bosnia was understandable; over Macedonia it was much less so. In both cases, however, the Community's failure to recognise opened up issues which would have been better left untouched, particularly that of borders. There is a general international interest, beyond the Community, in protecting borders against unwilling change. The failure to recognise straightaway opened a debate which included the fate of Macedonia and of its Albanian minority – which had generally shown interest in independence, but which would resist absorption by either Serbia or Bulgaria. It also raised the question of Bosnia–Hercegovina, with a market immediately opening up with bidders for parts of that republic.

One of the prime bidders was Croatia, whose Foreign Minister Zvonimir Separović was ready to accept pieces of Hercegovina as early as 16 January, saying that concessions (over Krajina, presumably) could not be 'one-sided';[56] Croat leaders in Bosnia–Hercegovina openly began to talk of 'unification' with Croatia'.[57] It was not impossible that by the time the Bosnian independence referendum was held on 29 February and 1 March, that a *de facto* union would have occurred. In unwelcome harmony with this note was tension in the central Yugoslav republic, with exchanges of fire between Croatian local police and federal army reservists near Mostar.[58] Indeed, it appeared that there was going to be a downside to the recognition of Croatia.

Whereas the Serbian camp had at last been reined in through recognition, Croatia, freed from the need to behave in order to win its prize, was acting in an increasingly confident manner and seemed uninterested in the arrival of a peacekeeping force. If the Croatians were to be kept under any control it was necessary for UN peacekeepers to be present. The German Foreign Minister, Hans Dietrich Genscher, under pressure from his Community colleagues, was obliged to obtain promises from Tudjman that Croatian objections to plans for a peacekeeping force would be dropped.

However problematic, influence on a recognised Croatia would still be greater than influence on Serbia had been while Croatia remained unrecognised. This added to the chances that a UN force could be deployed, as did the concerted pressure applied by most parts of the Serbian camp on the recalcitrant Milan Babić to accept UN peacekeepers in Krajina. The methods used included attempts to dislodge him, encouraging regional opponents against him and, according to the Krajina leader, virtually being kidnapped by the federal army leadership which tried to make him agree under duress to the peacekeeping plans.[59] Finally, the suggestion that Serbia, whether under that name or as Yugoslavia, would be recognised as the legal successor state to the federal state of Yugoslavia was an incentive for Slobodan Milošević and his allies to be amenable in negotiations on peace, including a new-found understanding for the situation of the Albanians in Kosovo.

All this made it seem more likely than not that peacekeepers would be deployed by the spring in parts of Croatia. The sustained cease-fire which made such a deployment conceivable was in large part a result of the EC's intervention, in particular of the recognition granted to Croatia. At the same time, the European Community appeared to have made blunders over the recognition of Macedonia and Bosnia. By its failure to recognise these republics on 15 January, and by missing the chance to establish the borders of those republics, the Community, having used its position (albeit without complete cohesiveness) to resolve some Yugoslav issues, possibly opened the way for another volatile set.

Evaluation

The Yugoslav crisis indicated that for the EC countries joint diplomatic activity was becoming (or had become) a policy in itself. In this way, Britain and others were able to deter Germany from an inclination to give early recognition to independent Slovenia and Croatia by emphasising the importance for European integration of 'not breaking ranks'. On the other hand, Germany, in the end, was able to lead its partners towards recognition.

The Europeans also had a key role in creating the space in which negotiations between the Yugoslavs could take place, as there was no possibility of their being able to resolve their differences alone. Indeed, their inability to do so was a cause of the war. It was necessary to allow politics to reemerge as a precondition of seeking any political settlement. From this point of view, it was probably inevitable that sooner rather than later a decisive intervention, namely recognition, was necessary to break the political deadlock. Recognition was the key. Whilst it was correct to try for an overall settlement, once this had come so close to succeeding and yet failed, not to recognise would have been to make the perfect the enemy of the good.

In a sense, the European Community operated a twin-track policy: while Lord Carrington coordinated the peace conference in The Hague with the political leaders, monitors operated in Yugoslavia trying to deal with the belligerents on the ground. The former was seeking a political solution for the Yugoslav republics, while the latter were charged with defusing the military situation locally. In different ways, both were working towards the ending of hostile fire. An end to combat only became possible, however, once the Community had relinquished responsibility for obtaining a cease-fire. This freed it to use its weight politically to create the conditions in which a durable truce became attractive – on condition that Cyrus Vance and the United Nations were entrusted with the cease-fire details.

Early on in the war, a German newspaper commented on the Community's response: 'Hectic, clueless, muddled and contradictory – that's how the 12-nation European Community stumbled through its first major test since the end of the Cold War.'[60] That harsh judgement seems excessive – although the bungling over Macedonian and Bosnian independence demonstrates that there were certainly contradictions in its policy. Overall, however, in very difficult circumstances and with limited means at its disposal, the Community effort made great progress towards resolving the Yugoslav conflict. It managed this only through applying pressure on the various parties to the Yugoslav dispute. Its rewards were greatest whenever it browbeat reluctant political leaders.

In effect, the CSCE effort in Yugoslavia worked more through coercion than mediation; one of the most significant aspects of the European handling of the Yugoslav conflict being the operation of the European Community in conjunction with the CSCE. The latter authorised EC activity in Yugoslavia, but what it authorised was an EC initiative. The CSCE process happily delegated responsibility to a willing volunteer. This suggests that any future activation of the CSCE mechanism would rely on a similar pattern. With regard to this, it should be noted that the Community had two advantages: coordination of a block of 12 member states in order to activate the Committee of Senior Officials of the CSCE, and the absence of any counter-proposals.

Finally, the European Community was also the leading light in two other areas. On discussion of a peacekeeping force, the dual membership with the Western European Union of nine foreign ministers enabled discussion of such a force. The Community's limitations were also shown, however, when dealing with this issue. Nonetheless, the fact that this and the question of sanctions were both referred to the United Nations because of the need for broader backing in such matters should not prevent recognition that, even vis à vis the UN, the Community was the dominant actor. Although Cyrus Vance, as UN envoy, took over responsibility for cease-fire and peacekeeping discussions, he did so at the behest of the European Community. This was to the advantage of efforts both to end the fighting and to engineer a political solution. In the end, it was only the political action by the Community which shifted the Yugoslav balance sufficiently for a UN-brokered peace to be in the Serbian camp's interest.

For those subject to bombardment, the European response was obviously too little. For example, Luka Bebić, the Croatian defence minister at the time, judged, 'Europe has failed the exam and we are no longer ready to support her ostrich-like policy'.[61] From the perspective of achieving a concerted, albeit sometimes divided, limited and uneven, response, the Community did rather better, although the human cost in Yugoslavia makes 'success' an inappropriate term. If the gaffe over recognition for Macedonia and Bosnia were to prove rectifiable, then EC common foreign policy, while lacking coherence and self-assurance, would emerge from the crisis reasonably well, though not perhaps with 'flying colours'. Europe, perhaps thanks to the curious alchemy of German leadership, Italian support for it, British limitation of it, French ambition and, unquestionably, the calibre of the Dutch presidency, and in spite of the tensions this created (Greek mischief notwithstanding), probably got it as right as circumstances allowed. This alloy of common foreign policy was, however, inescapably less than gold.

Notes

* James Gow is research officer in the Centre for Defence Studies, King's College, University of London.

1. Quoted in *The Guardian*, 4 July 1991.
2. For the background to the crisis see James Gow, *Yugoslav Endgames: Civil Strife and Inter-State Conflict* (London: Brassey's for the Centre for Defence Studies, Defence Studies no. 5, 1991); Gow, 'Deconstructing Yugoslavia', *Survival*, (July–August 1991); Gow, *Legitimacy and the Military: The Yugoslav Crisis* Pinter Publishers, London (1992).
3. *The Guardian*, 1 July 1991.
4. *International Herald Tribune*, 1 July 1991.
5. Editorial Comment, *The Independent*, 4 July 1991.
6. *The Wall Street Journal*, 1 July 1991.
7. The British were happy to see the troika in action because it signalled that the

EC could function as one through inter-governmental action; there was no need to create new institutions.

8. Until the beginning of November, there were still 1,000 federal army troops with their equipment. This is because they had been unable to obtain permission for transit through Italy or Hungary and would otherwise have to go through the war zone in Croatia to reach their destination in Serbia.

9. A British member of the Observer Mission interviewed by one of the authors.

10. Britain was more reluctant than others to see the Council meet, believing that it would force member countries to state a firm policy – which action in itself might be unhelpful.

11. *The Guardian*, 4 July 1991.

12. *The Financial Times*, 8 July 1991.

13. For its part, the Soviet Union issued a unilateral declaration that the mission to Yugoslavia should not be taken as a precedent; although generally positive in its involvement, the Soviet Union still found it difficult wholeheartedly to endorse a text permitting a 'good offices' mission to intervene in a member country's internal political disputes.

14. It was also suggested that there should be representatives from Canada, Czechoslovakia, Poland and Sweden.

15. Annex II of 'The Brioni Declaration' signed by all parties in the Yugoslav crisis and the EC ministerial troika, 7 July 1991.

16. Quoted in *The European*, 13–15 September 1991.

17. See Gow, *Endgames*, (note 2 above), p.24.

18. Interview with monitor returned from Osijek area.

19. *The Times*, 12 September 1991.

20. *The Financial Times*, 14–15 September 1991.

21. *The Times*, 24 October 1991.

22. In 1987, the WEU provided the umbrella minesweeping operations at the time of the American reflagging of Kuwait oil tankers; in 1990 the WEU performed a similar, if very limited role, in coordinating its members' involvement in enforcing the UN blockade of Iraq.

23. British Foreign Secretary, Douglas Hurd, quoted in *The Guardian*, 20 September 1991.

24. *The Financial Times*, 1 October 1991.

25. *The Times*, 26 September 1991.

26. See James Gow, 'Arms Sales and Embargoes: The Yugoslav Example', *Bulletin of Arms Control*, 3 (August 1991). However, it later became clear that the federal army, too, had imported weaponry: Miloš Vasić, 'Putevi oružja: Nemačka veza', *Vreme*, 26 January 1992.

27. It was clear from the announcement of Vance's appointment that his role was not to take over, but to consult with those already active in seeking peace in Yugoslavia. Reuters, 8 October 1991.

28. *Borba*, 5 September 1991.

29. It was noteworthy that at this meeting the hard-line Chief of Staff of the federal army, General Blagoje Adžić, accompanied Kadijević, thereby adding his imprimatur to the agreement.

30. 'Statement by the Lord Carrington, the Presidents of the Republics of Croatia and Slovenia and the Minister of National Defence at Igalo on 17 September 1991.'

31. *Ibid*.

32. Jim Smith, 'Cease-fires and the Yugoslavian Conflict: Lessons Unlearned', Research Paper, Department Of War Studies, King's College, University of

London.
33. *The Financial Times*, 27 September 1991.
34. Delegations of experts were sent from each of the six Yugoslav republics. To these were added officials and legal experts of the EC and its member states.
35. *The Guardian*, 5 October 1991.
36. *Ibid.*
37. However, British Foreign Secretary Douglas Hurd noted that EC trade with Yugoslavia had become minimal and that any trade embargo would be ineffective without full UN backing. BBC radio interview, cited in 'Weekly Record of Events', *Report on Eastern Europe*, 18 October 1991.
38. Quoted in *The Independent*, 7 October 1991.
39. 'Sovmestnoe Kommunike Presidentov SSSR, Serbii i Horvatii-Obonobschenie', TASS, 15 October 1991.
40. *Politika*, 19 October 1991.
41. *The Independent*, 18 October 1991.
42. *Yugofax*, 6 (31 October 1991).
43. *Ibid.*
44. *The Financial Times*, 19 October 1991.
45. *The Guardian*, 23 October 1991.
46. *The Independent*, 26 October 1991.
47. *The Guardian*, 24 October 1991.
48. *The Guardian*, 29 October 1991.
49. Abel Matutes, Vice-President of the European Commission, quoted in *The Guardian*, 29 October 1991.
50. Quoted in *The Guardian*, 1 November 1991. The Dutch presidency of the EC quickly supplemented de Michelis' statement with the clarification that 'the EC itself does not recognise anyone'. Recognition was a matter for the individual member states, which separate states, of course, operated with a high degree of coordination.
51. *International Herald Tribune*, 25 November 1991.
52. 'Weekly Record of Events', *RFE/RL Research Report*, (2) (10 January 1992).
53. 'Weekly Record of Events', *RFE/RL Research Report*, (3) (17 January 1992).
54. Cited by Didier Kunz, 'La Macédoine, poudrière des Balkans', *Le Monde*, 28 January 1992.
55. Jonathan Eyal, 'EC blunders in Balkan power game', *The Guardian*, 20 January 1992.
56. Quoted in *The Guardian*, 17 January 1992.
57. *Frankfurter Allgemeine Zeitung*, 4 February 1992.
58. *Borba*, 3 February 1992.
59. *Ibid.*
60. *Süddeutsche Zeitung*, 2 July 1991.
61. Quoted in *The Times*, 17 September 1991.

This chapter was completed at the beginning of February 1992, before extensive violence emerged in Bosnia–Hercegovina. For analysis of this later phase of the Yugoslav troubles see James Gow and James D.D. Smith, *Peace-making, Peace-keeping: European Security and the Yugoslav Wars*, London Defence Studies No. 5, Brassey's for the Centre for Defence Studies, London, May 1992, pp.47–51.

CHAPTER 5

Functions and powers, and inventions: UN action in respect of human rights and humanitarian intervention

PAUL FIFOOT

Introduction

In his annual report for 1991 on the work of the United Nations, Javier Pérez de Cuéllar, the Secretary-General, wrote that

> the campaign for the protection of human rights has brought results mostly in conditions of relative normalcy and with responsive governments. In other conditions, when human wrongs are committed in systematic fashion and on a massive scale – instances are widely dispersed over time and place – the intergovernmental machinery of the United Nations has often been a helpless witness rather than an effective agent for checking their perpetuation . . . It is now increasingly felt that the principle of non-interference with the essential domestic jurisdiction of States cannot be regarded as a protective barrier behind which human rights can be massively or systematically violated with impunity . . . The case for not impinging on the sovereignty, territorial integrity and political independence of states is by itself indubitably strong. But it would only be weakened if it were to carry the implication that sovereignty, even in this day and age, includes the right of mass slaughter or of launching systematic campaigns of decimation or forced exodus of civilian populations in the name of controlling civil strife or insurrection.

He could well have also instanced (as he did in his 1988 Report) 'summary arrests and executions, disappearances of individuals, the systematic practice of torture and killing of unarmed demonstrators'.

133

Señor Pérez de Cuéllar is not making a new point. His predecessor wrote in a 1981 report *Present international conditions and human rights*:

> The principle of respect for the sovereignty and independence of States should be compatible with an international order flexible enough to provide ways and means of dealing with situations involving gross violations of human rights. Otherwise, the notion of an international order may be called in question when such violations occur without an adequate response from the international community.

International cooperation in this context was seriously inadequate. 'It could be asked whether the organs charged with the responsibility of fulfilling the Charter mandate in the field of human rights should not be so organised as to respond more adequately and effectively to human rights concerns.'[1]

These observations identify two aspects of the UN Charter which affect the ability of the international community to respond to gross violations of human rights and humanitarian problems whether as a result of deliberate oppression by a government or as a consequence of war (whether international or civil), famine, disease or flood, namely the issue of non-intervention in matters which are essentially within the domestic jurisdiction of a state and the existing organisation (i.e. the various organs and the distribution of functions and powers between them) of the United Nations. Both these aspects are of significance in the decision by an organ of the United Nations whether to act in any particular situation or set of circumstances. As regards the protection of human rights and humanitarian relief (as with other issues), and in the absence of the consent or acquiescence of the state concerned, the perception of the extent or limitations of the specific functions and powers of the relevant organ may be as restrictive as the assertion of the exclusive competence of domestic jurisdiction. Moreover, in examining (as is proposed in this chapter) what the organs of the United Nations may do or have done in the field of human rights (though less so as regards humanitarian relief), it is necessary to caution against treating what has been done in any one case as a precedent for what might be done in a later case. The organs principally concerned, the General Assembly and the Security Council, are political bodies which regard themselves as entitled to determine their own competence; their interpretation of article 2(7) and of their own functions and powers is not necessarily determined wholly by legal considerations, and their willingness to act in a particular situation does not indicate that they would be willing to act in a similar one. This is not only a consideration in the Security Council where, to take only one factor into account, the permanent members can play the veto as a joker in the interests of their own policies or that of their clients;[2] it is also a highly significant consideration in those organs of wider membership where there are not unfounded fears of the prospect of setting precedents of 'intervention' on a purely human rights issue, notwithstanding the general acceptance of intervention as regards South Africa. An examination of what has been done will, nevertheless, indicate what may be done in the future if there is a sufficient political will to act.

Before turning to an examination of what has been done by the organs of the United Nations, it would be as well to guard against false analogies and to note that, unlike the United Nations and its organs, some other institutions charged with the enforcement or supervision of human rights agreements are not inhibited by a domestic jurisdiction clause. This is not only the case with enforcement or regulatory machinery established by an instrument developed outside the UN framework, such as the Court and Commission established to ensure the observance of the commitments undertaken by the parties to the European Convention on Human Rights. It also applies to the Human Rights Committee established under, and for the purpose of monitoring the observance of, the International Covenant on Civil and Political Rights, an instrument drafted by the UN Commission for Human Rights and adopted by the General Assembly. There is no provision in that Covenant which reflects article 2(7) of the Charter. On the other hand, acceptance by UN member states of the jurisdiction of the regulatory machinery of that Covenant does not follow from their membership of the United Nations but depends on their specific consent to this particular regime by a separate accession to or ratification of the Covenant.[3] However, the substantive provisions of the Covenant, as distinct from the regulatory machinery, have a dual role. In addition to providing rules by which the Human Rights Committee will judge acceding or ratifying states, they provide human rights standards domestically for the United Nations itself and these standards will determine the approach of the Security Council, General Assembly or Human Rights Commission[4] when acting on any human rights issue under the exceedingly general provisions of articles 55 and 56 of the Charter. Unlike the Human Rights Committee, these other organs may need to have regard to article 2(7) if their consideration of a human rights question affects individual states.

Standard-setting

One of the purposes of the United Nations, as declared in article 1 of the Charter, is to 'achieve international co-operation in solving international problems of an . . . humanitarian character, and in promoting and encouraging respect for human rights . . .'. Member states pledge themselves to take joint and several action in cooperation with the United Nations to promote universal respect for, and observance of, human rights and fundamental freedoms and the Economic and Social Council is charged with making recommendations and draft conventions for those purposes.

In February 1946, as one of its first acts, the Economic and Social Council established the Human Rights Commission, the functions of which included the drafting of an international bill of rights and international declarations or conventions on civil liberties, the status of women, freedom of information and similar matters.[5] By 1948, the Commission had prepared a Universal Declaration of Human Rights, which was adopted by the General Assembly 'as a common standard of achievement for all peoples and nations' on 10 December 1948. This was only the start of a considerable output of standard-setting instruments. The principles in the Universal Declaration were expanded in the International Covenant on Economic, Social and Cultural Rights and the International Covenant on Civil and Political Rights, both of which were adopted and opened for signature, ratification or accession by the General Assembly in 1966. In addition, the United Nations, or conferences convened by the United Nations, have produced and adopted for ratification or accession by states conventions on genocide, apartheid, discrimination in many forms, torture, statelessness and refugees; a number of these conventions have their own enforcement or regulatory machinery.

The organs of the United Nations have also provided states with declarations, guidelines, standard minimum rules, codes of conduct and basic principles over an even wider area in the field of human rights. Although this activity is often referred to as legislation, none of these conventions or other instruments is of itself binding on a member state by reason of its membership of the United Nations. The formal power of the General Assembly, like that of the Economic and Social Council, is confined to recommending states to accept the instruments it has prepared, sponsored or adopted.

Self-determination of colonial and trust territories

A particular concern of the Charter which influenced its purpose of developing friendly relations among nations was respect for the principle of self-determination. The Charter includes specific provision for colonial and trust territories. The Declaration regarding Non-Self-Governing Territories in Chapter XI, reinforced as time went on by the statement of political rights in article 21 of the Universal

Declaration of Human Rights,[6] the 1960 Declaration on the Granting of Independence to Colonial Countries and Peoples,[7] and the common article 1(1) of the two International Covenants,[8] provided the basis for consideration of, and recommendations on, any 'colonial' issue by the General Assembly and the Special Committee established by the Assembly to monitor the 1960 Declaration.

The United Nations persisted in its aim of promoting 'the realization of the right of self-determination of the peoples of the Non-Self-Governing and Trust Territories'[9] notwithstanding objections by the colonial power on the grounds of domestic jurisdiction. Indeed, the very purpose of the trusteeship system, as set out in Chapter XII of the Charter, was to lead the territories placed under trusteeship to self-government or independence, and it had as one of its objects the encouragement of respect for human rights and fundamental freedoms. The Trusteeship Council was expressly empowered to intervene in the affairs of a trust territory, monitoring its administration by way of considering the administering authority's annual reports, examining petitions and making periodic visits.

Recommendations by the General Assembly

The concern of the General Assembly to pursue the human rights and humanitarian objectives of the Charter goes beyond its role in standard-setting and the promotion of the right of self-determination. The Assembly consists of all the member states of the United Nations. Its functions, as set out in article 10 of the Charter, are to:

> discuss any questions or any matters within the scope of the present Charter or relating to the powers and functions of any organs provided for in the present Charter, and except as provided in Article 12, [it] may make recommendations to the members of the United Nations or to the Security Council or both on any such questions or matters.

(The exception in article 12 provides that the Assembly shall not, unless requested to do so by the Security Council, make any recommendation with regard to any dispute or situation within the competence of the Security Council while the Council itself is considering it.)

The functions set out above are expanded in subsequent articles to provide for studies and recommendations promoting international cooperation. They not only expressly include 'assisting in the realisation of human rights and fundamental freedoms for all without distinction as to race, sex, language or religion',[10] but extend to 'situations resulting from a violation of the provisions of the present

Charter setting forth the Purposes and Principles of the United Nations'.[11] The Assembly has powers of an executive character regarding the financing and internal working of the United Nations.[12] There is, however, no extension of the powers of the Assembly as regards member states; these are confined to making recommendations.

The question of an infringement of human rights in independent states surfaced in the early years of the United Nations. In 1946 the Assembly took up the question of the treatment of Indians in South Africa and as time went on the issue of apartheid became a continuing item which together with Israeli practices and human rights in Palestine, has dominated the agenda of all relevant UN organs. But notwithstanding constant and considerable attention to South Africa and the occupied territories, violations in other countries have not been ignored. The Assembly has taken into consideration, and passed resolutions on, allegations of violations of civil, political, social, economic and cultural rights in a variety of states from Hungary (in 1956, where the Assembly's concern was that free elections should be held under UN auspices[13]) to Tibet (in 1959, where it called for respect for the fundamental human rights of the Tibetan people[14]), Kampuchea/Cambodia (condemning violations of human rights over many years), Guatemala (in 1982, where it expressed its concern at 'the serious violations of human rights . . . particularly those reports of widespread repression, killing and massive displacement of rural and indigenous populations'[15]) and El Salvador (in 1990, expressing its deep concern 'about the persistence of politically motivated violations of human rights . . . such as summary executions, torture, abductions and enforced disappearances'[16]). In addition to addressing violations of human rights, the General Assembly has also concerned itself with the humanitarian aspects of dispossession, refugee flows and human misery whether or not arising from war or civil strife, human oppression or natural causes, and has sought the assistance of the specialised agencies and member states in the provision of relief works.[17] In resolution 46/182 adopted on 19 December 1991, the Assembly adopted a series of guidelines intended to strengthen the coordination of emergency humanitarian assistance within the UN system which included provision for 'a high-level official emergency relief coordinator' directly responsible to the Secretary–General.

The more detailed examination of human rights violations now takes place in the Human Rights Commission which is authorised to examine information and study situations which reveal a consistent pattern of gross violations of human rights. The Commission examines allegations of violations either on the basis of a country approach or by a 'thematic' approach under which it considers instances of, for example, torture or disappeared persons in whichever country they occur. Since 1986, it has examined allegations of violations of human rights in South Africa, Namibia, the occupied territories in Palestine, Afghanistan, Kampuchea/Cambodia, Western Sahara, Iran, Chile, South Lebanon, El Salvador, Equatorial Guinea, Haiti, Albania, Romania, Cuba and Kuwait under Iraqi occupation, and has passed resolutions of varying severity embodying its conclusions. The Commission's Subcommission on Prevention of Discrimination and Protection of Minorities also receives petitions from individuals concerning 'a consistent pattern of gross and reliably attested violations of human rights' and reports them to the Commission.

This brief résumé of the activity of the Assembly and the Commission shows there is no longer any hesitation in principle in taking up human rights issues, including gross violations of human rights in individual states. The issue is not their assumption of the capacity to take such questions into consideration, but of a lack of ability to take effective action in respect of a violation or pattern of violation, however gross or persistent. The organs of the United Nations give a wide interpretation to the power to make recommendations. The Commission and the Assembly may, and do, make judgments, resolving that there has been a violation of human rights. They may express their 'concern' (Chile, 1986) or their 'grave concern' (Iran 1988); they may 'denounce' (Afghanistan, 1986), 'urge cooperation and response' (Iran, 1986), or 'deplore' a refusal to cooperate (Afghanistan, 1986); they may 'condemn' or 'reiterate' their condemnation of particular violations or a persistent occurrence of gross and flagrant violations (Kampuchea, 1988; South Africa, 1989; and Cambodia, 1990); they may 'condemn' or 'strongly condemn' the offending state or its authorities (South Africa and Israel, 1990 and Iraq in Kuwait, 1990 and 1991). They may demand that states change their policies or desist from certain action (South Africa as regards apartheid at various times) or urge them to respect their obligations under human rights instruments (Iran, 1986). Most recently in the case of the putsch against President Aristide of Haiti in September 1991, the Assembly 'Strongly condemns both the attempted illegal replacement of the constitutional President of Haiti and the use of violence, military coercion and the violations of human rights . . .' (resolution, 46/7 cf 11 October 1991). But neither of these organs has any coercive power. Even where the Assembly or the Commission appoints groups of experts, rapporteurs or commissions of inquiry, they can only act in the country concerned with the acquiescence of that country. Refusal is common: Hungary refused to admit a committee of investigation in 1956; a special committee to investigate Israeli practices affecting the human rights of the people in the occupied territories has been in existence since 1968, but Israel has refused to admit it. Indeed ECOSOC resolution 1503, which empowers the Subcommission on Prevention of Discrimination and Protection of Minorities to consider consistent patterns of gross violations, authorises the investigation of complaints 'only with the express consent of the State concerned . . . conducted in constant cooperation with that state and under conditions determined by agreement with it'.

An offending state may make strong efforts to avoid condemnation and regional, group, ethnic and religious affiliations may, against all the evidence, help it to do so as was the case with Iraq for several years until 1991 after its invasion of Kuwait; but, even if condemned, a resolution of the Commission or General Assembly calling for, or demanding, remedial action by the offending state has effect only to the extent that that state is willing to comply with it; it has no direct consequences for the offender who intends to ignore it. Despite numerous resolutions against South Africa and apartheid and demands for compliance, and in the absence of the necessary cooperation from the Security Council to expel it from the organisation, the only action against that state which the Assembly has been able to effect on its own has been to uphold a decision of the President of the Assembly on 12 November 1974 that the 'consistency with which the Assembly had refused to accept the credentials of the South African delegation [to the General Assembly] was tantamount to saying in explicit terms that the General Assembly refused to allow the delegation of South Africa to participate in its work'.[18] As a result, South Africa was effectively barred from the Assembly and subsequently from conferences held under UN auspices. Other international organisations also excluded South Africa from participating in their proceedings.

Lacking the power itself effectively to ensure a change of policy or practice in a state which it has condemned for violations of fundamental human rights, the General Assembly has, in the case of South Africa, sought to utilise its Charter power to make recommendations to member states in order to call upon them to adopt measures to put pressure on that country to change its policies and practices. Amongst other things, it has called upon states to

> end diplomatic relations with the South African Government; close ports to all South African flag vessels; prohibit ships from entering South African ports; boycott all South African goods and ban exports to South Africa; and refuse landing and pass-

age facilities to all aircraft belonging to the Government and companies registered under South African laws.[19]

Such recommendations by the Assembly are, however, not mandatory and states are free to comply with them or not as they please. Even under the *Uniting for Peace* resolutions,[20] by which the General Assembly arrogated to itself a wider power of making resolutions than is expressly contemplated in the Charter, and which would extend to measures necessary to maintain or restore international peace and security, the Assembly is only empowered to make recommendations to member states. The *Uniting for Peace* resolutions do not contain any equivalent of article 25, which requires member states to carry out the decisions of the Security Council. Nor do they exclude, as does article 2(7), the application of any domestic jurisdiction considerations, such as is provided for in the case of enforcement measures of the Security Council under Chapter VII of the Charter, or address the separate inhibitions on states intervening in the affairs of other states which are the subject matter of the General Assembly's own Declaration on the Inadmissibility of Intervention and Interference in the Internal Affairs of States; the Declaration on the Inadmissibility of Intervention in the Domestic Affairs of States and the Protection of their Independence and Sovereignty; and the Friendly Relations Declaration.[21] All three declarations only except action taken under the relevant provisions of the Charter relating to the maintenance of international peace and security, two of them instancing Chapters VI and VII which relate to the Security Council, not the General Assembly.

Resolutions of the Security Council under Chapter VI

The Security Council, as described in article 24 of the Charter, has the 'primary responsibility for the maintenance of international peace and security', and for that purpose it has 'specific powers' for the peaceful settlement of disputes (Chapter VI of the Charter) and to take action in respect of threats to the peace, breaches of the peace and acts of aggression (Chapter VII). The Council is encouraged to develop and utilise regional arrangements both for the settlement of disputes and for enforcement action under its authority, and it has done so noticeably in cooperation with the Organization of American States and the Organisation of African Unity; recently it gave its support to the 'collective efforts for peace and dialogue in Yugoslavia undertaken under the auspices of the member states of the European Community with the support of the States participating in the Conference on Security and Co-operation in Europe . . .'[22].

The specific powers of the Security Council for the peaceful settlement of disputes under Chapter VI of the Charter are exercisable not only as regards disputes which are likely to endanger the maintenance of international peace and security, but extend to situations which might lead to 'international friction'. It may investigate a dispute or situation which may give rise to a dispute; it may call upon the parties to settle their disputes by negotiation, mediation, conciliation, arbitration, judicial settlement, resort to regional agencies or arrangements or other peaceful means; it may recommend appropriate procedures or methods of adjustment or settlement. It has done all these things: appointing a committee of investigation into the situation on the borders of Greece with Albania, Bulgaria and Yugoslavia in 1946;[23] and a committee to mediate between India and Pakistan in 1948;[24] recommending the United Kingdom and Albania to refer their dispute over the Corfu Channel incident to the International Court of Justice;[25] urging the Group of Five Central American States to spare no effort to find solutions to the problems of Central America and appealing to all interested countries to cooperate fully with the Group 'through a frank dialogue so as to resolve their differences' in 1983;[26] and urging Chad and Libya to settle their differences 'without undue delay and by peaceful means on the basis of the relevant principles of the Charter of the United Nations and the Charter of the Organisation of African Unity' in 1983.[27]

While still acting under Chapter VI of the Charter, or in any event short of Chapter VII (the Council is sometimes reluctant to spell out what it conceives as its authority for acting, even, on occasions, when it acts under Chapter VII), the Council has been no less assertive than the Assembly in giving a wide interpretation to its power to make recommendations to states. It clearly assumes power to express itself and to judge in respect of, and to deprecate, deplore and condemn what it determines are violations of the Charter, its own resolutions and those of the General Assembly; doing so even though the particular issue is one of self-determination, civil or political rights and not of international peace and security or 'international friction'. In its resolutions 180 and 183 of 1963 and 218 of 1965 on territories under Portuguese administration, it deprecated, and later deplored, 'the attitude of the Portuguese Government, its repeated violations of the principles of the Charter and its continued refusal to implement the resolutions of the General Assembly and the Security Council' and urged, among other things, 'the immediate recognition of the right of the peoples of the Territories under its administration to self determination and independence . . . the immediate cessation of all acts of repression [and] the establishment of conditions that will allow the free functioning of political parties'. It has followed the lead of the General Assembly in deploring loss of life in South Africa and the policies and actions of its government, and in calling on South Africa to abandon its policies of apartheid[28] and, without making a Chapter VII determination, in calling on states to impose sanctions on South Africa – the non-mandatory arms embargoes of 1963 and 1970.[29] This was followed by calling upon states to impose diplomatic, commercial and financial sanctions – another non-mandatory resolution – in respect of Namibia.[30] It has consistently deplored and condemned Israeli actions in the occupied territories and called upon Israel to correct them and to observe the Fourth Geneva Convention on the Treatment of Civilians in Time of War.[31] By resolution 752 (1992) it demanded that all forms of interference in Bosnia and Hercegovina, including those of the Yugoslav National Army and the Croatian army, cease and that the units of those armies withdraw, put themselves under the authority of the government of Bosnia and Hercegovina, or be disbanded and disarmed.

But, like the recommendations of the Assembly, the powers of the Council under Chapter VI are essentially recommendatory not mandatory; even when the Council seeks to exercise a mediatory or conciliatory role or carry out an inquiry, or the Secretary-General, acting in conjunction with the Council or on his own initiative, exercises his good offices or engages in preventive diplomacy in the interests of peace, what is involved is dialogue, not compulsion or unilateral physical intervention on the territory of the country concerned.

Physical intervention with consent

However, the United Nations does take action which involves the physical presence within a state of its representatives or agencies, or the specialised agencies, non-government organisations, or military forces or civilian agencies of other member states. Both the General Assembly and the Security Council have sought to relieve human suffering and distress in many parts of the world resulting from natural causes – famine or flood, earthquake or drought – by encouraging relief operations and the provision of emergency food supplies and other aid. Such humanitarian operations are mounted at the request and with the consent of the state concerned and, as the Secretary-General notes in his 1991 report on the work of the organisation, 'generally create no legal or political problems'.[32] They are not, however, without danger to the participants; in early 1992 a staff member of UNICEF was killed in Somalia and a staff member of UNHCR in Ethiopia. The Security Council called on all parties in Mogadicio 'to respect fully the security and safety of the [United

Nations] technical team and personnel of the humanitarian organizations' (resolution 746). Nevertheless, the guidelines adopted in
General Assembly resolution 182 of 19 December 1991 provide that
'The sovereignty, territorial integrity and national unity of States
must be fully respected in accordance with the Charter of the United
Nations. In this context, humanitarian assistance should be provided
with the consent of the affected country and in principle on the basis
of an appeal by the affected country.' A much more complex matter
is the role that the United Nations has devised for itself for peacekeeping operations which involve the organisation authorising various forms of physical intervention within states in response to
situations other than those brought about by natural causes.
Peacekeeping, what has been termed 'Chapter VI and a half', provides for a gap in the Charter between the essentially conciliatory
text of Chapter VI and those enforcement provisions of Chapter VII
which follow a determination by the Security Council of the existence
of a threat to the peace, a breach of the peace or act of aggression.[33]
In the majority of cases, the responsible organ has been the Security
Council, but in three instances, the United Nations Emergency Force
1956–67 (UNEF I), the United Nations Security Force in West New
Guinea 1962 (West Irian), and the United Nations Observer Group
for the Verification of the Elections in Haiti 1990 (ONUVEH), the
operations were established by the General Assembly.

The United Nations divides peacekeeping operations into observer
missions (as in the case of the United Nations Truce Supervision
Organization – UNTSO – established to help in supervising the
observance of the truce in Palestine in 1948) and peacekeeping forces
(for example, the United Nations Emergency Force – UNEF II –
established in 1973 to supervise the cease-fire between Egypt and
Israel, to supervise the redeployment of forces and to control buffer
zones). Both forms of operation have usually required military personnel provided by member states on a voluntary basis but, whereas
observers are not armed, peacekeeping forces have light weapons
which may only be used in self defence. Both have the same ground
rules. They come under the direction of the Secretary-General, who,
in parallel with the mission or force concerned, will himself offer his
good offices with a view to resolving both the practical problems
consequent upon UN intervention and the underlying issues which
have occasioned it. They require the continuing support of the
Security Council. Perhaps most important of all, a peacekeeping
force must have the consent of the governments on whose territory it
operates, a factor that was emphasised and elaborated recently when
the Security Council gave consideration to the principles of peacekeeping. At the end of the Council's meeting, the President reported:

the members of the Council, while recognising the principle that peace-keeping should only be undertaken with the consent of the host countries and the parties concerned, urge the host countries and all parties involved to assist and facilitate in every way the successful and safe deployment and functioning of the United Nations peace-keeping operations in order to fulfil the mandate, including the early conclusion of status of forces agreements with the United Nations and the appropriate infra-structure support.[34]

(The first United Nations Emergency Force – UNEF I – was withdrawn, despite the efforts of the Secretary-General to retain it, following a unilateral Egyptian decision.)

Finally, consistent with the generally accepted principle that 'every state has an inalienable right to choose its political, economic, social and cultural systems',[35] peacekeeping forces must not be used to favour one party against another in internal conflicts in the territories in which they are stationed. Even when it is urged by the Security Council, as in 1960–61, 'to take all appropriate measures to prevent civil war in the Congo', a UN force is 'not to be a party to or in any way to intervene in or be used to influence the outcome of any internal conflict, constitutional or otherwise'.[36]

Following the United Nations Truce Supervision Organization in the Middle East, observer missions were established in India and Pakistan in 1949, Lebanon in 1958, Yemen in 1963, India and Pakistan again in 1964, the Dominican Republic in 1965, Iran and Iraq in 1988 and Angola in 1988.[37] Peacekeeping forces have been established on the Egypt Israel border from 1956 to 1967 and 1973 to 1979, in the Congo from 1960 to 1964, in West Irian from 1962 to 1963, in Cyprus since 1964, on the Golan Heights since 1974, in Lebanon since 1978 and for Afghanistan and Pakistan in 1988.[38] These missions and forces were, for the most part, established to monitor cease-fire agreements and stand-off arrangements between different states or forces from different states and thus the operations fell squarely within the responsibility of the Security Council for the maintenance of international peace and security. However, in West Irian and the Congo, their presence in what was a final or immediate post-colonial stage in the history of the territory involved the United Nations in a more extensive role; and the functions of the Secretary-General's representative in the midst of a civil war in the Dominican Republic in 1965 included reporting to the Security Council on violations of human rights.

The Security Council had been involved in the transfer of power and the establishment of political rights at an early stage in

Indonesia. In 1947 it had established a Committee of Good Offices which, renamed the United Nations Commission for Indonesia in 1949, was instructed to assist Indonesia and The Netherlands in making provision for the transfer of sovereignty and

> to observe on behalf of the United Nations the elections to be held throughout Indonesia and . . . in respect of the territories of Java, Madura and Sumatra, to make recommendations regarding the conditions necessary (a) to ensure that the elections are free and democratic and (b) to guarantee freedom of assembly, speech and publication at all times . . .[39]

In 1954, the role of the UN Security Force in West Irian was essentially to act as the police arm for a parallel United Nations Temporary Executive Authority which took over the administration of the territory from The Netherlands and subsequently handed it over to Indonesia.

The position of ONUC, the UN Operation in the Congo, was considerably more complicated. Initially responding to a request by the government of the Congo to provide military assistance in the face of armed Belgian intervention, and subsequently authorised by the Security Council to prevent the occurrence of civil war, using force if necessary to do so, and to remove mercenaries from the Congo, it was from the first engaged in assisting the Congolese government to maintain law and order and to protect life.[40] In the absence of effective Congolese security forces, ONUC had itself to provide for ordinary police and security functions and to ensure protection to persons threatened whether by the agencies of the Congolese government or by their opponents. At various times and places ONUC established neutral zones and protected areas as places of safety. In 1961 it provided its good offices to bring about agreement between the contending groups to a reconvening of the Congolese parliament and itself made arrangements for the reopening of the parliament and the protection of the parliamentary members. As part of the UN operation, there was an extensive civilian component of ONUC to restore and maintain public, financial and technical services, to provide temporarily, and to train, an administrative and legal infrastructure, and to provide for the relief of refugees. In all, the operation involved the United Nations not only in seeking to restore and maintain peace in the Congo, but in providing physical assistance to curb violations of human rights and humanitarian assistance to the victims of civil war and such violations.[41]

The intervention in the civil war in the Dominican Republic in 1965 was an unusual peacekeeping mission. The Security Council called for a cease-fire and invited the Secretary-General to send a representative to the Dominican Republic for the purpose of reporting to the Council on the situation. The mission consisted of the Secretary-General's representative and at most four military advisers. The presence of the representative enabled the Secretary-General to inform himself and the Security Council of the progress of the civil war, the deteriorating situation in the Republic, the ineffectiveness of civil authority and complaints of widespread violations of human rights, of executions and the disappearance of persons who had been arrested. But although the President of the Security Council noted the violations of human rights and that statements made by members of the Council had 'condemned gross violations of human rights'[42] no resolution to that effect was adopted and the United Nations was unable to take any steps to provide any protection to those who suffered or were threatened by such excesses.

The purpose of a number of the more recent peacekeeping operations established by the United Nations has been political, or as much political as holding the ring militarily, and in that respect it has been engaged in assisting in the establishment of political rights and, to a lesser extent, monitoring agreements for the observance of human rights. One of the roles of the United Nations Observer Group in Central America (UNUCA), which was established in 1989, was to monitor the cessation of armed hostilities, including the demobilisation and repatriation of the members of the Nicaraguan resistance; but the UN intervention also includes the agreement of the Secretary-General to provide UN observers to 'verify the electoral process in Nicaragua'.[43] Observer groups were established in Haiti in 1990 (ONUVEH) with the function of observing the electoral process and in the Western Sahara in April 1991 (MINURSO) to observe the referendum on the future of that territory. A UN observer mission was established in El Salvador in 1991 (ONUSAL) to monitor all agreements made between the government of El Salvador and the dissident *Frente Farabundo Martí para la Liberación Nacional*, which included agreements on human rights and the electoral system.[44] The missions in Cambodia – UNAMIC and UNTAC – are designed to provide a UN presence to assist in the destruction of weapons and to facilitate the implementation of a comprehensive political settlement in Cambodia.[45] The UN operation in Namibia in 1989 and 1990 (UNTAG) has been described as a UN operation with a military component. Designed to assist in bringing Namibia to independence, its first task was to ensure that the cease-fire between the South African forces and SWAPO was maintained. Thereafter it set about organising and holding elections to a Constitutent Assembly which was to decide the constitutional structure of the new state and laying down rules for the conduct of the parties contesting that election. The change of direction in these recent operations calls into question whether the United Nations should seek another description for them rather than continue to classify them under the term 'peacekeeping operations'.

Before undertaking these recent operations, as with the earlier ones, the United Nations has always sought the consent of the governments or de facto authorities of the territories in which UN personnel have operated. The delay in the deployment of the UN peacekeeping force in Yugoslavia in 1992 (UNPROFOR) was due to the fact that the Secretary-General's plan had 'not yet been fully and unconditionally accepted by all in Yugoslavia on whose cooperation its success depends' (resolution 740 (1992)). Such consent is not a necessary factor where the Security Council acts under Chapter VII.

Chapter VII

Chapter VII of the Charter makes provision for action with respect to threats to the peace, breaches of the peace and acts of aggression. The Security Council is empowered to determine the existence of any such act or threat, to call on the parties to comply with 'such provisional measures as it deems necessary or desirable' to prevent any aggravation of the situation, to decide what measures not involving the use of armed force shall be taken to maintain or restore international peace and security and to call on member states to apply those measures. Under article 25 of the Charter, member states have agreed to carry out the decisions of the Council. If peaceful measures 'would be inadequate or have proved to be inadequate, [the Security Council] may take such action by air, sea or land forces as may be necessary. . . '. The Council, however, has no armed forces of its own and must rely on the forces of those member states which are willing to answer its call for the assistance of armed forces in taking such action.[46]

Surprising as it may seem, in the 46 years since the United Nations came into existence, the Security Council has taken action under Chapter VII in only ten instances and, despite the frequent resort to force in the Levant, only once in respect of that area. In 1948, the Council determined that, in view of a renewal of hostilities, the 'situation in Palestine constitutes a threat to the peace within the meaning of Article 39. . . '.[47]

In 1950, the Council noted 'with grave concern the armed attack on the Republic of Korea by the forces of North Korea' and determined that 'this action constitutes a breach of the peace', though there was no express reference in that case to Chapter VII or any article of the Charter.[48]

In a preambular paragraph of its resolution on the Argentine invasion of the Falklands Islands in 1982, the Security Council determined that 'there exists a breach of the peace in the region of the Falkland Islands (Islas Malvinas)', but again there was no express reference to Chapter VII or any article of the Charter.[49] The resolutions on the Iran–Iraq war in 1987 and the Iraqi invasion of Kuwait in 1990 similarly made determinations of the existence of a breach of the peace in preambular paragraphs, but their operative paragraphs were prefaced by a statement that the Council was acting under articles 39 and 40 of the Charter.[50]

These five instances were all cases where there was war or invasion – a use of armed force by one country against another. In two of them, the determination of a breach of the peace was followed, immediately in Korea (a case where peaceful measures 'would be inadequate') and after an intervening period when economic sanctions had been imposed on Iraq (a case when they had 'proved to be inadequate'), by the Council recommending or authorising member states to repel the attack or to force the withdrawal of the aggressor 'and to restore international peace and security in the area'.[51] In the other three instances, the Council ordered 'the Governments and authorities concerned, pursuant to Article 40 of the Charter, to desist from further military action and to issue cease-fire orders to their military and paramilitary forces' (Palestine), demanded the immediate cessation of hostilities and the withdrawal of all Argentine armed forces from the Falkland Islands, and demanded an immediate ceasefire, a discontinuance of all military activities and a withdrawal of all forces to the internationally recognised boundaries (the Iraq–Iran war), but took no action of a coercive nature.

The resort to Chapter VII in the other five instances, Southern Rhodesia between 1966 and 1980, South Africa in 1977, Yugoslavia in September 1991 and May 1992, the arms embargo in respect of Somalia and the Libyan resolution of March 1992, was not of a pattern with the cases referred to above.

On 11 November 1965, the government of Southern Rhodesia, a self-governing colony of the United Kingdom, unilaterally declared its independence. On the following day, the Security Council decided to condemn 'the unilateral declaration by a racist minority in Southern Rhodesia' and called on all states not to recognise the 'illegal minority regime in Southern Rhodesia'.[52] Eight days later, on 20 November, in a resolution which was designed to get as close as possible to a Chapter VII resolution without actually coming within that Chapter, the Council determined that the 'continuance in time [of the situation resulting from the unilateral declaration of independence] constitutes a threat to international peace and security', and called on all states to refrain from any actions which would assist the regime in Rhodesia, to desist from providing it with arms and military material and 'to do their utmost to break all economic relations with Southern Rhodesia, including an embargo on oil and petroleum products'.[53] Five months later, on 9 April 1966, without citing any Charter provision, the Council determined that the 'resulting situation [presumably in that resolution the supply of oil to the Rhodesian regime] constitutes a threat to the peace'. It was not until 16 December 1966, however, that the Council expressed, itself as acting 'in accordance with Articles 39 and 41', determined that the situation in Southern Rhodesia constituted a threat to international peace and security, and decided that members of the United Nations should impose selective sanctions against Southern Rhodesia.[54] There followed over 20 Security Council resolutions, a number imposing further sanctions, before legality was resumed and Rhodesia/Zimbabwe attained majority rule and an independence acceptable to the United Nations.

Although the resolutions of 20 November 1965 and 16 December 1966 determined that the situation in Southern Rhodesia constituted a threat to international peace and security – a determination that was repeated or recalled in a number of later resolutions – what concerned and motivated the Council in adopting those resolutions and the principal sanctions resolutions was not any external or outwardly aggressive acts of the authorities in Southern Rhodesia or their armed forces. From the very begining, the objective of the Council was, expressly, to put an end to the power of a 'racist settler minority' (resolution 217), to reaffirm 'the inalienable rights of the people of Southern Rhodesia to freedom and independence in accordance with the Declaration on the Granting of Independence to Colonial Countries and Peoples contained in General Assembly resolution 1514 (XV)', and to recognise 'the legitimacy of their struggle to secure the enjoyment of their rights as set forth in the Charter of the United Nations' (resolution 232). In the course of these resolutions it addressed various internal acts of the regime in Southern Rhodesia, repeatedly condemning 'all measures of political repression, including arrests, detentions, trials and executions which violate fundamental freedoms and rights' and 'all attempts and manoeuvres by the illegal regime . . . aimed at retaining and extending a racist minority rule and at preventing the accession of Zimbabwe to independence and genuine majority rule'.[55] It was not until 1973 that the Council addressed an external act of the regime when it condemned 'all acts of provocation and harassment, including economic blockade, blackmail and military threats, against Zambia'; this was followed in 1976 by a condemnation of 'all provocative and aggressive acts, including military incursions, against the People's Republic of Mozambique' and in 1977 by a more specific condemnation of acts of provocation and harassment, military threats and attacks, against Botswana.[56]

But these were incidental to the main purpose of the Council. Sanctions were imposed 'in furtherance of the objective of ending the rebellion' (resolution 253) and were increased when 'the measures so far taken [had] failed to bring the rebellion in Southern Rhodesia to an end' (resolution 277). The Council was explicit in declaring that 'the speedy termination of the illegal regime . . . constitute[s] the first prerequisite for the restoration of legality in Southern Rhodesia so that arrangements may be made for a peaceful and democratic transition to genuine majority rule and independence' (resolution 423), and right up to the end of the Lancaster House Conference, it continued to emphasise its original objectives by reaffirming the rights of the people to 'self-determination, freedom and independence as enshrined in the Charter of the United Nations, and in conformity with the objectives of the General Assembly resolution 1514 (XV)'.[57] It is, therefore, difficult not to view the determination of the Security Council in this instance of a threat to international peace and security as a legal fiction which enabled it to resort to Chapter VII in order to further the policy of the United Nations of self-determination for colonial peoples and the objective of ensuring the purposes of article 24 of the Universal Declaration of Human Rights that everyone has the right to take part in the government of his country. But the fiction was connived in by the majority of the UN members and the action was taken with the consent of the United Kingdom, the metropolitan power, which, itself, had taken the initiative in introducing the first 'sanctions' resolution, SC resolution 221 of 9 April 1966.

The resort to Chapter VII in the case of South Africa paid a little more regard to external factors and the terms of that chapter. The Security Council had progressively adopted the position that the situation in South Africa 'is one that has led to international friction and if continued might endanger international peace and security'[58] and in its non-mandatory arms embargo[59] in 1963 expressed itself as convinced that 'the situation in South Africa is seriously disturbing to international peace and security'. The Chapter VII resolution itself (418 (1977)) recited that the 'military build-up by South Africa and its persistent acts of aggression against neighbouring states seriously disturbs the security of those states', and expressed the concern of the Council that South Africa was on the threshold of producing nuclear weapons, its condemnation of South African 'attacks on neighbouring independent states', and its view that 'the policies and acts of the South African Government are fraught with danger to international peace and security'. The Council, expressly acting under Chapter VII of the Charter, determined, 'having regard to the policies and acts of the South Africa Government, that the acquisition by South Africa of arms and related matériel constitutes a threat to the maintenance of international peace and security' and decided that 'all States shall cease forthwith any provision to South Africa of arms and related matériel of all types . . .'.

The genesis and purpose of resolution 418 were, however, the determination of many members of the United Nations to bring about the total eradication of the policy of apartheid and to affirm the right of self-government for all the people of South Africa. Following the Sharpeville shooting, the Council had called on the government of South Africa to abandon the policy of apartheid. In a series of resolutions thereafter it had deprecated or condemned the policy and repeated the call for its abolition. In 1973, the General Assembly had adopted and opened for signature and ratification a Convention on the Suppression and Punishment of the Crime of Apartheid which, among other things declared apartheid a crime against humanity.[60] Five days before the Security Council adopted resolution 418, it had adopted another resolution on South Africa in which it referred to and condemned the resort to massive violence, wanton killings and repression against 'black people' which it was convinced would lead to 'violent conflict and racial conflagration with serious international repercussions'; it reaffirmed the legitimacy of the struggle for the elimination of apartheid and racial discrimination and affirmed 'the right to the exercise of self-determination by all the people of South Africa as a whole, irrespective of race, creed or colour'; and it demanded that 'the racist regime of South Africa' end violence and repression, abolish the policy of bantuization, abandon apartheid and 'ensure majority rule based on justice and equality'.[61] Some of these points re-emerge in the preambular paragraphs of resolution 418; but the operative determination in the resolution is postulated on the policies of the South African government, and it is these policies (together with the acts) of the government which are declared as 'fraught with danger' and, when linked with the acquisition of arms, are the basis of the determination of the threat to the maintenance of peace. In the context of this resolution, it is difficult to read that reference to policies other than as a reference to apartheid and the other internal policies of the South African government. And the connection between apartheid and the considerations which justify a resort to Chapter VII continue to be drawn in later resolutions. Resolutions 473 of 1980, for instance, re-affirms that the policy of apartheid is a crime against the conscience and dignity of man, the Charter of the United Nations and the Universal Declaration of Human Rights and seriously disturbs international peace and security' and calls on the 'South African regime to take measures immediately to eliminate the policy of apartheid'.

As in the case of Southern Rhodesia, it is apparent that Chapter VII is being used to give effect to the political rights of self-determination and the right to take part in the government of one's country in the terms of the Universal Declaration of Human Rights and to bring about changes in the internal regime of a country. The assertion, and determination, of a threat to the peace seems no more than a legal fiction to assist in that process. The official reference book of the United Nations at least has no doubt about the matter:

The racial policies of the Government of South Africa have been a major concern of the United Nations for more than 35 years. During this time United Nations organs have agreed on a wide range of measures for action by the international community with the aim of ending apartheid.

Chief among these measures is an arms embargo designed to halt the build-up of arms in South Africa, some of which, the Security Council has noted, have been used to further the Government's racial policies. A voluntary arms embargo, in effect since 1963 was made mandatory by the Council in 1977.[61]

The mandatory arms resolutions in respect of Yugoslavia (September 1991) and Somalia raise further questions about the use made of Chapter VII. The Security Council acted under Chapter VII in resolution 713 (1991) when three of the constituent republics of the Yugoslav Federation had resorted to armed force: Slovenia and Croatia to seek their independence, Serbia to prevent them, or, at least in the case of Croatia, to limit the territory it could call its own. In one sense this was a civil war; in another it was a conflict between different nationalities seeking to exercise a right of self-determination and self-rule. The representative of Austria on the Security Council certainly had no difficulty about widening the concept of 'self-determination' from its traditional UN context as a process of decolonisation when he referred to the 'implementation of the right to self-determination in keeping with the aspirations expressed by the peoples of Yugoslavia' as one of the principles on which the future relations among the people of Yugoslavia should be based. In that respect, this resolution is in line with those relating to Southern Rhodesia and South Africa. But it is clear that some representatives on the Security Council were uneasy; this was not a decolonisation issue and Chapter VII action was being proposed in respect of what they saw as an internal dispute in an established state. The only 'external' fact noted in the debate was a flood of refugees and, although the Council expressed its concern that the continuation of the situation constituted a threat to international peace and security, for the first time when taking action under Chapter VII, it failed to recite or make a determination to that effect. Indeed, its actual decision of measures under Chapter VII was tucked away, unannounced, in a fifth operative paragraph instead of being highlighted in the resolution. What then was to be the justification for action under Chapter VII in this civil war? For China, India, the USSR and Zimbabwe, the essential factor which justified a resort to Chapter VII was the request for action by Yugoslavia itself.[63] Welcome as such a request may be in invoking the assistance of the international community, and relevant as it may be to peacekeeping operations, and whether or not this is a case of 'intervention' in a state's internal affairs, the fact of such a request has no basis in Chapter VII. One particular result of this approach is that the request of a particular state for coercive action under Chapter VII in respect of itself, in circumstances where the invocation of a threat to international peace and security is highly questionable, can mean the Security Council taking action, the principal effect of which is to impose binding obligations as to the conduct of all other members of the United Nations rather than to address directly the situation in the country concerned. By May 1992, however, in response to the fighting in Bosnia–Hercegovina, Yugoslavia (by then consisting only of Serbia and Montenegro) had assumed, in the eyes of the Security Council, the role of aggressor and a more classic resolution was adopted which determined that the situation in Bosnia and Hercegovina and other parts of Yugoslavia constituted a threat to international peace and security and, expressly acting under Chapter VII, decided on economic, financial and other sanctions (resolution 757 (1992)).

In the meantime the first Yugoslavian resolution on the supply of arms had been adopted as a precedent four months later in a resolution (733 (1992)) on the civil war in Somalia. The later resolution was principally directed at humanitarian concerns, which are the subject of the initial operative paragraphs; the only 'external' factor was the outflow of refugees. Again, although the Council expressed its concern that the continuation of the situation constituted a threat to international peace and security, there is no recitation or determination to that effect, and again the decision of Chapter VII measures is tucked away in a fifth operative paragraph. Although the Council had been invited by the Somali chargé d'affaires at the United Nations to intervene in the crisis to save lives, the Council apparently felt itself unable to envisage coercive physical action *within* the country and confined its mandatory paragraph to an arms embargo.

The resolution on Libya (748 (1992) of 31 March 1992) provides a further departure from precedent. In resolution 731 (not a Chapter VII resolution) Libya had been asked to provide a response to requests by the United Kingdom and others to cooperate in establishing responsibility for the terrorist acts which led to the destruction of Pan Am flight 103 and UTA flight 772. Libya's failure to cooperate resulted in the March resolution which determined 'in this context, that the failure of the Libyan Government to demonstrate by concrete actions its renunciation of terrorism and in particular its continued failure to respond fully and effectively to the requests in resolution 731 (1992) constituted a threat to international peace and security', and in decisions of the Council expressly under Chapter VII requiring Libya to commit itself to cease all forms of terrorist action and all assistance to terrorist groups. The Security Council had moved from invoking Chapter VII in cases of external aggression to invoking it in cases of self-determination, civil war and now state participation in, or assistance to, terrorism.

Sanctions

Following its invocation of Chapter VII in respect of Southern Rhodesia, South Africa, Iraq in 1990, Yugoslavia, Libya and Somalia, the Security Council decided that member states should take certain measures. In the cases of South Africa, resolution 713 on Yugoslavia, and resolution 733 on Somalia, mandatory measures were confined to an embargo on the supply of arms and related matériel. In the case of Libya, a ban on aircraft flights and the supply of aircraft and aircraft components, and a requirement to reduce diplomatic staff, were added to the arms embargo.

In the other two cases the measures decided by the Council were considerably more extensive. Under the Rhodesian resolutions, member states were required to prevent the import into their territories first of all of selected products, and subsequently of all commodities and products originating in Southern Rhodesia, to prevent the sale or supply by their nationals or from their territories of any commodities or products to Southern Rhodesia or to any person or body for the purposes of a business carried on in or operated from Southern Rhodesia, and to prevent the use of their ships or aircraft for any such purposes. No funds for investment or any other financial or economic resources were to be made available to Southern Rhodesia from their territories or by their nationals, and their airlines were to be prevented from operating to or from Southern

Rhodesia or from linking with Rhodesian airlines or aircraft. In due course, states were required to end all economic or other relations with Southern Rhodesia and to pass legislation forbidding the insurance of flights to, and excluding cover of goods transported to or from, that country. The resolutions imposing these measures were spread over a number of years; comprehensive sanctions on imports and exports had to wait a year after the first Chapter VII resolution and the latest sanctions resolution was adopted 11 years after the Security Council had first condemned the unilateral declaration of independence. In the case of Iraq, the Council's response was more immediate. Four days after the invasion of Kuwait the Council adopted a resolution requiring member states to take measures to prevent imports from, and exports to, Iraq or Kuwait, the use of their ships and aircraft for such purposes, and the provision of any funds or other financial or economic resources to Iraq or Kuwait.[64] The Bosnia Hercegovina resolution followed much of the Southern Rhodesia precedent. Although there was much in common in the sanctions resolutions as respects Southern Rhodesia and Iraq, there were particular provisions which took account of the unique circumstances of each case; an innovation as regards Iraq was a requirement that states should deny aircraft bound for Iraq permission to overfly their territory unless they first landed outside Iraq or Kuwait to allow verification that it was not in breach of the sanctions measures, and to detain any Iraqi ships which had been used in violation of the sanctions measures. In all these cases, the Security Council established a committee of the Council to monitor compliance with its resolutions.

None of these sanctions resolutions purported to authorise physical action by states generally within the territory which was the subject of the resolution, though a number of the Rhodesian resolutions also called on the United Kingdom, as the administering power, to bring the rebellion to an end and do other things which could only be effected by intervention with armed force. To the greater extent, sanctions measures decided on by the Security Council were confined to requirements for member states (and requests to non-member states) to act, and to impose restrictions, within their own territorial jurisdiction or in respect of their own nationals; and they fell within article 41 of the Charter which provides for measures 'not involving the use of armed force'.

However, in the cases of both Southern Rhodesia and Iraq the Council authorised measures for the policing and enforcement of its article 41 measures which went beyond that article. Resolution 221 (1966), which constituted the first determination of a threat to the peace in the case of Southern Rhodesia, not only called on 'all States to ensure the diversion of any of their vessels reasonably believed to be carrying oil destined for Southern Rhodesia which may be en route for Beira' but also called on the United Kingdom 'to prevent, by the use of force if necessary, the arrival at Beira of vessels reasonably believed to be carrying oil destined for Southern Rhodesia . . .' In reliance on this resolution, the United Kingdom instituted a naval patrol in the Mozambique channel stopping ships which might be suspected of carrying oil for Southern Rhodesia; in one case shots were fired across the bow of a vessel which failed to comply with a request to stop.

Resolution 665 (1990), which anticipated by three months the Council's authorisation of member states to use force to ensure the withdrawal of Iraq from Kuwait, recorded its alarm at the use of Iraqi-flagged vessels to export oil in contravention of earlier resolutions and called upon

> those Member States . . . which are deploying maritime forces to the area to use such measures commensurate to the specific circumstances as may be necessary under the authority of the Security Council to halt all inward and outward maritime shipping in order to inspect and verify their cargoes and destinations and to ensure strict implementation of the provisions relating to such shipping laid down [in the principal sanctions resolution].

In resorting to article 42 of the Charter to restore international peace and security in the Korean case,[65] the Council recommended that 'the members of the United Nations furnish such assistance to the Republic of Korea as may be necessary to repel the armed attack and to restore international peace and security'. In its resolution 678 of 29 November 1990, the Council authorised 'Member states co-operating with the Government of Kuwait . . . to use all necessary measures to uphold and implement [the relevant resolutions] and to restore international peace and security in the area.' The end of the fighting in the latter case brought more resolutions under Chapter VII to provide for the aftermath of the war, the return of prisoners, the identification of mines and weapons and the payment of compensation from Iraqi oil revenues.

In resolution 687 (1991), the most detailed of all resolutions adopted in this context, the Council made provision for a United Nations observer unit to be deployed in a demilitarised zone between Iraq and Kuwait, the functions of which were to deter violations of the boundary and to observe any hostile or potentially hostile movement. Unlike missions established under peacekeeping rules, this observer unit, established under a Chapter VII resolution, can only be terminated by a decision of the Council and the Council decided to review the question of termination or continuation every six months.[66] Resolution 687 also decided on the 'destruction, removal or rendering harmless' of chemical, biological and ballistic weapons remaining to Iraq and that 'Iraq shall unconditionally agree not to acquire or develop nuclear weapons', and established the necessary investigative machinery to implement those decisions.

In the cases of both Southern Rhodesia and Iraq, as in that of Bosnia–Hercegovina, some regard was had to limited humanitarian considerations. In the former case, resolutions contained exceptions for funds and foodstuffs for humanitarian purposes and, before the allied forces commenced military operations against Iraq, the Security Council adopted a number of resolutions concerned with the humanitarian aspects of Iraq's invasion of Kuwait and its subsequent treatment of Kuwaiti nationals and nationals of third states. The Council concerned itself with whether there was an urgent humanitarian need to supply foodstuffs to Iraq or Kuwait, the mistreatment and oppression of individuals in Kuwait, the attempts by Iraq to remove the population of Kuwait and the abduction of Kuwaiti and third-state nationals to Iraq. It also reaffirmed the responsibility of Iraq for its actions in Kuwait under the Fourth Geneva Convention on the treatment of civilians in time of war. All these resolutions were expressed to be made under Chapter VII.

However, when the fighting was over in Iraq/Kuwait and the Council expressed its grave concern over 'the repression of the Iraqi civilian population in many parts of Iraq' and noted the 'magnitude of the human suffering involved', the resolution it adopted not only omitted all reference to Chapter VII but it expressly recalled article 2(7) of the Charter and reaffirmed 'the commitment of all Member States to the sovereignty, territorial integrity and political independence of Iraq and all States in the area'. Security Council resolution 688 condemned the repression of the civilian population, demanded that Iraq, 'as a contribution to removing the threat to international peace and security in the region, immediately end this repression', and insisted that Iraq allowed 'immediate access by international humanitarian organizations to all those in need of assistance in all parts of Iraq and to make available all necessary facilities for their operations'.

Notwithstanding that it had up to then been acting explicitly under Chapter VII, it drew back at this stage. Resolution 688 was only one of two resolutions out of the 19 affecting Iraq adopted by the Council between 2 August 1990 and 17 June 1991 which did not expressly or implicitly rely on Chapter VII; the other exception, resolution 669, was concerned with extending the terms of reference of the committee of the Council charged with the supervision of the sanctions resolution. As a consequence, when the allied forces sought to turn over to the United Nations the administration and responsibility for the protection of the 'safety-zones' which they had established in Northern Iraq as they claimed 'consistent with United Nations Security Council resolution 688',[67] the Secretary-General insisted that he required an agreement with the Iraqi authorities before he could take on that kind of function. Whatever the humanitarian need, in the absence of an appropriate resolution under Chapter VII, the only precedents then to hand, the only procedures under which he could operate, were those applicable to peacekeeping or relief operations. A Memorandum of Understanding authorising UN humanitarian operations along Iraq's northern border was signed by the Secretary-General's representative and Iraq on 18 April 1991. The lack of accord between the Secretary-General and the Western powers over this issue clearly caused the former some concern. In his report for 1991, he writes:

> a reminder has been rendered necessary by the experience gained in addressing the humanitarian emergency that occasioned Security Council resolution 668 (1991). The Secretary-General cannot be expected to use powers that are not vested in him and deploy resources that are not available. For large-scale field operations, the Secretariat needs clear mandates, with assured financing, in accordance with the provisions of the Charter and under established procedures.

Conclusion

This review of what the United Nations has in practice done in the field of providing humanitarian relief or protecting human rights leads to four conclusions:

- the United Nations does take up, consider and pass judgement on, allegations of serious violations of human rights in states and will adopt condemnatory resolutions when it thinks appropriate; the issue insofar as taking matters into consideration and passing judgment is no longer a perception in the organisation of a lack of power, but is a question of the threshold of the violation and a matter of choice; the United Nations and its membership are not consistent and their inconsistency is not always creditable;

- the United Nations has not sought to intervene, and has not authorised states to intervene, physically in a state except with the consent of that state or following a Chapter VII determination;

- with two exceptions (Yugoslavia in 1991 and Somalia), the United Nations has not authorised coercive measures in respect of a state or territory which are binding on its members without first making a determination of a threat to the peace, breach of the peace or act of aggression. However, in addition to recommending voluntary sanctions, it has twice (three times if Yugoslavia is included) acted to impose mandatory sanctions under Chapter VII in order to further the rights of populations to self-determination and the right of people to participate in their own government. In two of those cases, the determination under Chapter VII was of questionable validity and in the third was ignored in favour of a request from those authorities in the country concerned which the United Nations decided to recognise as having appropriate authority. Its decision to require Libya to commit itself to cease all forms of terrorist action and all assistance to terrorist groups is without doubt the most significant departure in recent years;

- it would not appear that considerations of lack of formal authority to intervene physically is a significant factor in providing material aid and relief to the victims of natural disasters, refugees or dispossessed persons in a country of refuge. The country concerned is usually only too anxious to invoke the assistance of the international community in humanitarian operations. The inhibiting or restricting factors here are lack of money and other resources and difficulties and dangers of access, sometimes man-made. Where, however, the cause of distress or oppression is the action of a governing authority or civil war, the deep-seated objections, particularly in the Third World, to the United Nations involving itself, or interfering, in the internal affairs of a member state would appear to inhibit intervention except on a request from some domestic organ which it is prepared to recognise as having national authority. It would be highly optimistic to put any hope in the United Nations being able to take action in such cases by the adoption of such legal fictions by which action was justified under Chapter VII in the decolonising decades. The resort to what may be considered a marginally relevant external arms embargo in the Somali resolution 733 would seem to emphasise the powerlessness of the United Nations to take action to intervene in a civil war unless, as in El Salvador, the internal parties have become disposed to seek assistance.

Subject to these restraints, the United Nations has intervened physically in the territories of states in cases of civil wars to monitor the terms of disengagement between the parties, agreements for a cease-fire, truces and arrangements for demobilisation and resettlement (Yemen, Dominican Republic and Nicaragua). In addition to its action under Chapter VII to further the policy of self-determination and the establishment of political rights in Southern Rhodesia and South Africa, the United Nations has been engaged (on occasions in the aftermath of a civil war) in the establishment of political rights by providing for, or observing, the conduct of elections in Indonesia, Namibia, Nicaragua and Haiti and has undertaken a similar role in the Western Sahara and in El Salvador.

The United Nations has, not surprisingly, never been engaged within the territories of a state with the sole mandate of providing protection against violations of human rights. Its role in Iraq is essentially humanitarian in providing for the relief of those who have suffered as a result of war and oppression. In some cases, where it has been asked to monitor agreements for bringing an end to a civil war and the ensuing political arrangements (the Dominican Republic and El Salvador), the United Nations has also been charged with an observer role as regards violations of human rights. The experience of the Dominican Republic, where the UN observer was the recipient of well-attested complaints of serious violations but the organisation was unable to do anything to remedy the situation, is typical of the impotence of the United Nations, even when they have an authorised presence in the country, to act against the authorities of a state or insurgents however gross or extensive their oppression of their own populations.

The only case prior to 1991 in which the United Nations was able to act to provide physical protection against government or insurgent violations of human rights by establishing safe zones was in the Congo in an operation on which it embarked initially at the request of the Congolese authorities and in which, at its height, it disposed of a force of 20,000 officers and men. In 1991, notwithstanding that there were effective military forces available to the north and south of Iraq which had, on unilateral national initiatives, already taken steps to provide safe havens for refugees and victims of oppression, and notwithstanding the adoption of resolution 688 in the wake of so many Chapter VII resolutions, the United Nations still felt itself unable to mount an operation for relief in Iraq without the agreement of the authorities there.

Notes

1. UN doc. A/36/462, 8 October 1981.
2. Between 1945 and 1989, China cast 3 vetoes, France 18, the Soviet Union 114, the United Kingdom 30 and the United States 67.
3. Up to 30 April 1991, 95 UN members had ratified or acceded to the ICCPR.
4. There is a danger of confusion between the Human Rights Committee and the Commission on Human Rights. The former is established by the International Covenant on Civil and Political Rights solely for the purpose of ensuring compliance with that Covenant by those states which become parties to it; the latter is a subsidiary organ of the United Nations itself and, in addition to having drafted the Covenant and other human rights instruments, it exercises many of the United Nations' own functions as regards inquiries into alleged violations of human rights.
5. ECOSOC res. 1/5.
6. '1. Everyone has the right to take part in the government of his country, directly or through freely chosen representatives.
   2. Everyone has the right to equal access to public service in his country.
   3. The will of the people shall be the basis of the authority of government; this will shall be expressed in periodic and genuine elections which shall be by universal and equal suffrage and shall be held by secret vote or equivalent free voting procedures.'
7. GA res. 1514 (XV).
8. 'All peoples have the right of self-determination. By virtue of that right they freely determine their political status and freely pursue their economic, social and cultural development.'
9. GA res. 637A (VII).
10. Article 13 (1.b) and Chapters IX and X.
11. Article 14.
12. Which can have the effect of restricting or controlling the exercise of the functions of the Security Council; e.g. on 29 April 1991, by res. 690 the Security Council established the UN Mission for the Referendum in Western Sahara (MINURSO); the financing of the Mission required the approval of the General Assembly which was forthcoming on 17 May.
13. GA res. 1005 (ES-II).
14. GA res. 1353 (XIV).
15. GA res. 37/184.
16. GA res. 45/127.
17. For recent resolutions calling on states to provide aid to refugees see GA res. 43/8 (Sudan), 43/9 (Bangladesh), 44/239 (Romania), 45/12 (Afghanistan), 45/159 (Malawi) and 45/161 (Ethiopia).
18. UN Yearbook for 1974, p.117.
19. *Everyone's United Nations*, p.83. UN Department of Public Information, New York. (This is the official reference book of the United Nations.)
20. GA res. 377 (V).
21. Declaration on the Inadmissibility of Intervention in the Domestic Affairs of States and the Protection of their Independence and Sovereignty, GA res. 2131 (XX); Declaration on Principles of International Law concerning Friendly Relations and Co-operation among States in accordance with the Charter of the United Nations, GA res. 2625 (XXV); Declaration on the Inadmissibility of Intervention and Interference in the Internal Affairs of States, GA res. 36/103.
22. SC res. 713 (1991).

23. SC res. 15 (1946).
24. SC res. 39 (1948).
25. SC res. 22 (1947).
26. SC res. 530 (1983).
27. Statement by the President of the Council, 6 April 1983, *Resolutions and Decisions 1983*, p.8.
28. SC res. 134 (1960).
29. SC res. 181 (1963) and 282 (1970).
30. SC res. 283 (1970).
31. See for example SC res. 592 (1986), 605 (1987), 608 (1988) and 672 (1990).
32. Among the responsibilities of the UN Office for Research and the Collection of Information is the monitoring of information and developments relating to possible flows of refugees in order to strengthen the capacity of the organisation, and the Secretary-General in particular, to respond to emergencies: see UN Doc. A/45/6 (Prog.1).
33. *Everyone's United Nations* (note 19 above) states that: 'From a legal standpoint, United Nations peace-keeping operations can be considered to be based on Article 40 of the Charter.' Whatever argument may be adduced in support of that proposition so far as the Security Council is concerned, it ignores the fact that three operations were authorised by the General Assembly, and in no case was the establishment of a peacekeeping operation immediately preceded by, or based on, a prior determination under article 39. The Secretary-General's report (A/45/6 Prog.1) goes no further than to quote as the legislative authority for peacekeeping operations 'resolutions and decisions, particularly of the Security Council . . .'
34. Statement by the President of the Security Council, 30 May 1990.
35. GA res. 2131 (XX).
36. SC res. 146 (1990) and 161 (1961).
37. Known respectively as the UN Military Observer Group in India and Pakistan (UNMOGIP), the UN Observation Group in Lebanon (UNOGIL), the UN Yemen Observation Mission (UNYOM), the UN India–Pakistan Observation Mission (UNIPOM), the Representative of the Secretary-General in the Dominican Republic (DOMREP), the UN Iran Iraq Military Observer Group (UNIIMOG) and the UN Angola Verification Mission (UNAVEM I and II).
38. Known respectively as the UN Emergency Forces (UNEF I and II), the UN Operation in the Congo (ONUC), the UN Security Force (UNSF), the UN Peace-keeping Force in Cyprus (UNFICYP), the UN Disengagement Force (UNDOF), the UN Interim Force in Lebanon (UNIFIL) and the UN Good Offices Mission for Afghanistan and Pakistan (UNGOMAP).
39. SC res. 67 (1949).
40. See SC res. 161 and 169 (1961). The authority to prevent civil war was expressed in the somewhat strange form of '*Urges* that the United Nations take immediately all appropriate measures to prevent the occurence of civil war in the Congo . . .'
41. For a brief account of the Congo operation, see *The Blue Helmets*, pp.215–57. UN Department of Public Information, New York (1985).
42. Statement by the President of the Security Council, 26 July 1965.
43. See SC res. 637 and 644 (1989).
44. GA res. 45/2 and SC res. 690 and 693 (1991).
45. SC res. 717 and 718 (1991) and 745 (1992).
46. Articles 39,40,41 and 42.
47. SC res. 54.

48. SC res. 82.
49. SC res. 502.
50. SC res. 598 and 660.
51. SC res. 83 (1950) and 678 (1990).
52. SC res. 216.
53. SC res. 217 (1965).
54. SC res. 221 and 232 (1966).
55. SC res. 253 (1968), 277 (1970), 403 (1977) and 445 and 448 (1979).
56. SC res. 326 (1973), 386 (1976) and 403 (1977) 445, 448 and 460 (1979).
57. SC res. 134 (1960).
58. SC res. 181.
59. GA res. 3068 (XXVIII).
60. SC res. 417 (1977).
61. *Everyone's United Nations*, pp. 79–80.
62. Provisional Verbation Records of the SC, S/P 3009.
63. SC res. 661.
64. SC res. 83 (1950).
65. SC res. 689 (1991).
66. See Chapter 3 this volume.

CHAPTER 6

Military intervention and UN peacekeeping

RICHARD CONNAUGHTON

Given the recent profound change in international relations, it would be surprising had peacekeeping and the concepts of military intervention not been influenced by, or reflected in, this change. For example, only a short time ago it could have been argued quite reasonably that traditional peacekeeping opportunities (neutral soldiers armed only for self-defence and established on an inter-state border with the agreement of both states) had declined. It now appears that there will be an explosion of border disputes. For example, within the boundaries of the former Soviet Union alone, a January 1992 tally revealed 47 separate border disputes of which 22 involved external states.

What has also increased is the willingness of the United Nations to become involved in the peacekeeping activities in intra-state conflict. In the first 40 years of its life, the United Nations undertook 13 peacekeeping operations. Since 1988, including Cambodia, it has sponsored a further 13 such operations. Military intervention and UN peacekeeping has always been a prolific activity in international affairs but what has occurred of late is a change in its rationale and a move towards peace-enforcement.

Military intervention and UN peacekeeping is a political concept where the definition can change with the debate. Military intervention and UN peacekeeping often occurs when troops are sent into a divided society, generally against the wishes of the incumbent government. Where military intervention does occur at the invitation of the incumbent government, it will usually suppress the perceived right to self-determination of that part of the population threatening the interests of the government. Military intervention and UN peacekeeping is therefore closely linked to coercive interference but sometimes, as occurred with the Soviets in Czechoslovakia, it is difficult to separate the act of intervention

165

from the act of invasion. It is possible to say, therefore, that there is no neat and tidy definition of intervention which overcomes the complexities of international politics. The recommended course of action for those seeking a definition is to adopt common language usage applied to the specific situation. (That is, if the definition is not ambiguous, then use it.) This recommendation applies equally to the even broader term 'peace-making'.

The reader is warned by Alan James[1] that 'peacekeeping' as applied to the United Nations is a term which has been given a number of meanings. The International Peace Academy demonstrates the scope for confusion by describing peacekeeping as 'intervention' although, within the context given below, the use of the word is not inappropriate. Peacekeeping is:

> the prevention, containment, moderation and termination of hostilities between or within states, through the medium of a peaceful third party intervention organised and directed internationally, using multinational forces of soldiers, police and civilians to restore and maintain peace.[2]

It is Alan James who makes the distinction between peacekeeping and military intervention:

> Yet when compared with military intervention, there is a distinction between the two [which] was seen to lie in their attitudes towards the associated issues of force and consent, collective security relying, ultimately, on the mandatory use of force, while peacekeeping eschewed force, except in self-defence, and required the consent of the host state for the admission of UN personnel.[3]

The aim of this chapter is to describe the military considerations of collective peacekeeping and intervention. It will not attempt to indulge in political, legal or economic analysis unless such matters are directly related to the military art. The military implications of the demise of the Soviet Union and the ending of the Cold War have to be spelt out because, understandably, it is the military which has arguably suffered most the consequences of change, due to its fall from a position of undue privilege. The continuing application of old values and former understandings of military capabilities could have unfortunate consequences for the future. The ensuing discussion is set out as a continuum: the past; the present; and the requirement for the future. Within each of these three sections will be divisions examining Chapter VI of the UN Charter which deals with the pacific settlement of disputes and which has emerged to embrace the peacekeeping function; Chapter VII of the UN Charter, the enforcement chapter; and something lying between the two, known as Chapter VI and a half.

The Past

The Great War of 1914–18 was the first of two world wars fought this century by both sides as coalition operations. The distinction between a coalition and an alliance lies in the tendency of the former to be of shorter duration. Having suffered the most in the Great War and with the most residual fear for the future, it was France who took the lead in attempting to establish a collective security regime. It proposed the establishment of an International General Staff and the raising of standing forces to provide support to article 10 of the Covenant of the League of Nations. Article 10 was the forerunner of article 2(4) of the UN Charter and required of states the guarantee of the territorial integrity and independence of every other state. It was President Woodrow Wilson of the United States who interceded to block the French initiative. He had no wish to see the resurrection of the old military alliances which had been so instrumental in the origins of the First World War.

In view of the emergence of the United States as the only genuine, balanced (in political, military and economic terms) superpower, it is essential to understand its politico-military past in order to make any meaningful forecast for the future. Wilson broke away from the powerful US tradition of non-involvement and the avoidance of entangling commitments enunciated in the Washington and Jefferson declarations. Wilson was a visionary who played a leading role in promoting the setting up of the League of Nations. His famous Fourteen Points outlining to Congress the world aims of the United States (which were subsequently adopted verbatim by the Allied Powers) concluded with the statement that: 'A general association of nations must be formed under specific covenants both for the purpose of affording neutral guarantees of political independence and territorial integrity to great and small countries alike.'

The reason why the United States moved from isolationism to intervention, despite the reluctance of many Americans, was probably because it was becoming a world power and as such could not risk the whole of Europe falling under German hegemony in the event of an allied defeat. This fear and Wilson's belief in the need for a new world order were tailor-made factors which drew the United States into the vortex, thus ensuring an allied victory. A 'new world order' is not an invention of the 1990s but was very seriously considered in both Europe and the United States during the First World War. It was a tragedy for both Wilson himself and the future of the League of Nations that in 1920 isolationist elements in Congress blocked ratification of the League's Treaty and Covenant, thus preventing the United States from joining and, as a consequence, disastrously weakening the League from the outset.

The situation in 1919 was such that the necessary, restrictive rules circumscribing a state's previous sovereign right to go to war had, in theory, been put in place. The League delayed, rather than withdrew, a state's sovereign right to enter into armed conflict. Article 12 still permitted a state to go to war three months after the award by arbitrators or after the report by the Council. What the architects of the League of Nations had failed to do was to build in a compensating enforcement mechanism. This was not an oversight. The weakness was recognised. France repeatedly urged the need for an international force to be at the League's disposal in the event of a 'cooling off' period failing to work, but the progressively enfeebled League proved to be powerless as a result of its membership failing to carry out the League's recommendations.

The war had laid bare problems which still remain potential sources for destabilising the options for multilaterally based solutions. Multilateral military operations do not erase national aspirations or the need for separate states to demonstrate their own success. In the First World War, the Dominions of the British Empire sought their own military operational integrity. This was more particularly true of the United States. Wilson and General Pershing insisted that US troops should operate under separate command. It had been this problem of command authority which had so mortified the British. In 1914, while their military power was admittedly eroding, it was nonetheless substantial, and yet they had to subordinate their land forces on the western front to French command. The right to assume command is invariably quantity-related. Britain had begun the war with four divisions which soon expanded to six, but this compared with 62 French divisions. Out of this military Hobson's choice arose political discomfort. 'Are we', asked Lloyd George of Churchill in January 1915, 'really bound to hand over our troops to France as if we were her vassal?' The lesson is still pertinent today: despite the growing importance of economic considerations, a state's position in the world order is largely influenced by its effective power-projection capabilities.

Although not a fervent isolationist, President Franklin D. Roosevelt did not want war but, by 1938, he had concluded that the

United States could not cut itself off entirely from world events. In August, he admitted 'we are no longer a far-away continent'. General George C. Marshall summarised the difficulties facing the US military planners in 1938. They are equally true today:

> With us, geographical location and the international situation make it literally impossible to find definite answers for such questions as: who will be our enemy in the next war; in what theatre of operations will it be fought; and what will be our national objective at the time?

At Pearl Harbor on 7 December 1941, Japan answered General Marshall's riddle. 1941 was also the year in which the allied powers had begun to plan to rectify the shortcomings of the League of Nations in their blueprint for the future United Nations. But here again, there was a major flaw. The fault lay in the assumption that the sinking of ideological differences that had been so essential if Hitler were to be defeated, would be perpetuated in the peace. Sir Brian Urquhart wrote:

> The 'United' in United Nations came from the Atlantic Charter of 1941 and referred to nations united in war, not in peace . . . the Charter assumed, with a stunning lack of political realism, that they would stay united in supervising, and if necessary enforcing world peace.[4]

The enforcement measures drawn up by the drafters of the UN Charter are contained in Chapter VII but the onus is still placed on states to avoid the use of armed force. There are a number of incremental steps prior to ultimate military action (article 42) which include provisional measures, economic sanctions and demonstrations of the use of force. Some of the articles present conceptual difficulties which require an interpretation appropriate to the 1990s rather than to 1945. One such is article 43 whereby:

> 1. All Members of the United Nations, in order to contribute to the maintenance of international peace and security, undertake to make available to the Security Council, on its call and in accordance with a special agreement or agreements, armed forces, assistance and facilities, including rights of passage, necessary for the purpose of maintaining international peace and security.
> 2. Such agreement or agreements shall govern the numbers and types of forces, their degree of readiness and general location, and the nature of the facilities and assistance to be provided.

Another is Article 47 which establishes:

a Military Staff Committee to advise and assist the Security Council on all questions relating to the Security Council's military requirements for the maintenance of international peace and security, the employment and command of forces placed at its disposal, the regulation of armaments, and possible disarmament.

The Military Staff Committee (MSC) consists of the Chiefs of Staff of the permanent members of the Security Council. Any members of the United Nations can be invited 'to be associated' with the MSC and there is provision to establish regional sub-committees. The role of the MSC is to be 'responsible under the Security Council for the strategic direction of any armed forces placed at the disposal of the Security Council'. The question of who commands 'shall be worked out subsequently'.

The MSC did make an attempt after the Second World War to formulate a multilateral force structure comprised of the three principal services of the armed forces. The Committee was required, among other tasks, to indicate the strength and composition of the separate components and the proportion of the overall strength that should be provided on the basis of equality by the five permanent members. With the notable exception of the United States, the initial national proposals were broadly similar. In fact, in the interest of unanimity, Nationalist China supported the UK propositions. The United Kingdom, China and the Soviet Union each proposed that the air component of the international force should comprise 1,200 aircraft, France proposed 1,275, but the United States proposed 3,800 aircraft (excluding air transport). For the land component, the United Kingdom and China proposed 8 to 12 army divisions, the Soviet Union 12, France 16, and the United States 20. The recommended composition and strength of the naval forces was more convoluted but of similar disproportion.[5] The gap between the United States and the other four permanent members could not be bridged.

The Chairman of the MSC, British General R.L. McCreery, wrote to the Chairman of the Security Council informing him of the Committee's inability to agree. The year was 1948. The grand but impossible dream had failed, even before the obvious questions such as the funding in peacetime of such substantial armed forces had been addressed. The early chill of the Cold War had made its presence felt. The original objections and the original source of obstruction came from the Soviet Union which:

> saw no need for a large force if it was not to be used against a major power; insisted that the principle of equality should gov-

ern the contributions of the permanent members; and demanded clear definition of the conditions under which the force could be used.[6]

The problem areas cited were those concerned with command and parity. In essence, the Soviets did not wish to see a US-dominated United Nations wield such considerable military power. It was principally their deliberate obstruction which denied the United Nations the prospect of sponsoring an international collective security regime. The scene was now set for the United Nations to emerge as the sparring ring for the see-sawing fortunes of Western and Eastern ideologies.

Meanwhile, the MSC's inability to draw together the anticipated, international collective security regime had a number of consequences for the international community. First, there was a growth of regional, collective defence systems such as NATO, the Warsaw Pact, the Baghdad Pact (redesignated CENTO), SEATO (South East Asia Treaty Organisation), ANZUS (Australia, New Zealand and the US) and others. More important from this study's point of view, and deserving amplification, was the influence which the impasse had on peacekeeping and military intervention.

The collapse of the initiative to introduce a truly broad-based, international enforcement system led to a fortuitous compromise, with the emergence within the United Nations of the peacekeeping function, something not provided for in the Charter. The original peacekeepers who appeared from 1947[7] were military observers overseeing cease-fire agreements and truces. It was not until the 1956 Suez Crisis that forces were deployed on peacekeeping activities, and it was not until 1973 and UNEF II, a peacekeeping force deployed to Egypt and Sinai following the Yom Kippur War, that peacekeeping procedures were standardised into a format that is recognisable today.

The circumstances under which the 'blue berets' have been traditionally deployed have fallen within the ambit of three basic understandings. First, the troops are not normally drawn from among the permanent members of the Security Council; secondly, 'blue berets' only use force for the purpose of self-defence; and thirdly, the monitoring of inter-state borders and cease-fire lines is conducted with the consent of both states.

Statistics reveal how truly limited have been the past opportunities for the deployment of traditional peacekeepers. There have been over 150 limited wars since 1945 and the casualty toll has exceeded 20 million.[8] But 85 per cent of these armed conflicts have been intra- rather than inter-state wars, of which 95 per cent have been fought outside Europe.[9] It is in the field of inter-state conflict that peace-keeping will be more likely to succeed, but then only when there is peace to be kept and with the permission of both parties. The infin-itely more prolific intra-state conflict is less to do with territorial disputation than with ethnic, religious and ideological struggle. This is not an environment in which traditional peacekeeping sits easily because invariably there is factional, armed infighting and there is no peace to be kept. Even where these conflicts have territorial dimen-sions, the territorial patchwork across whose frontiers the peace is to be kept can pose formidable logistic problems.

Setting aside the special circumstances prevailing in Cyprus, the attempt to conduct peacekeeping activities within one state, notably the Congo and the Lebanon, has not been at all distinguished. Sometimes the peacekeepers' *raison d'être* has been called into ques-tion. Within the Congo, the central government collapsed following the precipitate withdrawal of the colonial power, leaving behind a chaotic situation. Provinces seceded and for a period the UN force lacked an effective mandate because neither the Security Council nor the General Assembly could reach agreement on a new mandate. Within the Lebanon, the UN Secretariat was strongly opposed to the deployment of a peacekeeping force. They had good reason because Israel was opposed to UN intervention from the outset and the Secretariat foresaw that casualties would be heavy for a peacekeeping operation. The peacekeepers did succeed in Namibia but the opera-tion was imperilled at the beginning because of inadequate funding.

During the Cold War, peacekeepers were drawn from small and very often neutral states. India was a notable exception in terms of size. The function these states have been called on to perform has been that of lightly armed gendarmes, with the emphasis placed on patience and control rather than on high levels of military com-petence and adeptness in the handling of lethal weapons. Traditional UN peacekeeping worked well and casualties were minimised because peacekeepers were accepted as neutrals, their aim being to help and to mediate between two sides. The absence of arms encour-aged the perception of a non-threatening body acting under the authority of the United Nations. The demands placed on the peace-keepers fell comfortably within what could be expected of small, often conscript armies. Yet it was as long ago as the Katanga epi-sode, 1961–63, that the peacekeeping function and the use of force first proved to be incompatible in potential conflict.

The Congo experience was exceptional. It remains the only occa-sion that the peacekeeping concept of using weapons only in self-defence was well and truly prejudiced. Not only did the United Nations virtually take over and run the country, but there also arose a schism between the UN troops due, in the main, to 'a definite degree of partisanship among African contingents in the Congo, which was not surprising in view of the vested interests involved'.[10] More recent peacekeeping operations, notably the UN Interim Force in Lebanon (UNIFIL), indicate that an obligatory abstention from the use of weapons, except in self-defence within an environment where the settlement of disputes with firearms is the norm, is becoming increasingly difficult to sustain. Nevertheless, what has been regarded as traditional peacekeeping will still continue in those environments where it can still function. The traditional peacekeepers have a proud and remarkable record of achievement in supporting UN peacekeeping and security initiatives.

Those not familiar with the peacekeeping process often ask whether the United Nations encounters problems of morale, discipline and training efficiency when sending young conscripts or volunteers to unusual and difficult environments such as South Lebanon, Namibia or Kashmir. Morale tends not to be a problem, for the personnel involved are usually volunteers. It depends on the mission. If the mission is seen to be impossible, as is arguably the case in South Lebanon, then morale will naturally suffer.

There is a very important point to be established here: whereas conscripts have proved to be of enormous value in traditional peacekeeping operations, they have consistently proved to be unsuitable for intervention actions. Out on the ground, each contingent operates according to its own level of discipline and competence. The planners within the deployed Force Headquarters tend to account for the variations by employing national forces according to their known strengths and idiosyncrasies. Thus there has been a somewhat negative tendency to employ on peacekeeping duties 'the devil you know'. Consequently, peacekeeping operations have become the preserve of selected, often non-aligned and small states. These traditional peacekeepers are rarely drawn from common collective security organisations such as NATO but rather, due to the presence of a high proportion of neutrals, the peacekeepers will represent as polyglot a bunch as is possible.

The central problem lies in training efficiency and the contradiction implicit in deploying lightly armed and slightly trained peacekeepers in hostile, sometimes warlike environments where host state and neighbouring state forces are of a higher level of military proficiency. It is, therefore, not so much a problem of how the peacekeepers feel but rather how reassured the host countries feel with the varying quality of UN-deployed peacekeepers.

Another recurring question is whether there are special problems of command and control arising from the multinational nature of the forces. These perceived difficulties have been largely ironed out through the experience of four decades of operations. Multinational peacekeeping forces are seldom well integrated and therefore the quality of the commander has a very direct impact on the operation and ultimate success of a particular force. Contingents tend to operate federally within the structure of the force and there is sufficient slack within the staff system for creative interpretation. The lessons of the Congo have been learned and military men are now consistently appointed to direct military operations. The degree to which donor states work around or through the appointed UN commander depends largely on that commander's ability and personality. He has to contend with the tension generated between national requirements communicated directly to forces under his command and, on occasions, poor direction from UN headquarters.

There have been studies into the upgrading of the peacekeeping function by giving the 'blue berets', where necessary, increased firepower. This higher profile peacekeeping was described by Secretary-General Dag Hammarskjöld as 'Chapter VI and a half' – i.e. lying midway between Chapter VI peacekeeping and Chapter VII enforcement. For example, if Palestine were to be divided into two states, the peacekeepers deployed in support of a United Nations settlement, assuming such a settlement were possible, would require a significantly more robust status-of-forces agreement and rules of engagement than those drawn up in 1973. This is now a practical proposition. So long as the permanent members continue to cooperate, there is likely to be more frequent resort to UN intervention in all its gradations, including peace-enforcement, if peacekeeping is deemed to be inappropriate. The Finnish General Hägglund, force commander in UNIFIL 1986–88, summarised the changing relationship between peacekeeping and peace-enforcement:

> Peace enforcement should not necessarily be opposed; it simply requires different forces and a completely different concept. An intention to deter and enforce requires forces which are as frightening as possible. For this kind of mission great-power battalions, professional soldiers and all the means at their disposal are preferable.[11]

The word 'intervention' embraces a whole variety of different meanings. Prefixing it with the word 'military' still leaves the subject open to comprehensive sub-division. Arms transfers and the imposition of a blockade are forms of military intervention. Clinical strikes (point attacks employing missiles or bombs), as occurred at Osiraq in 1981, intended against Libya in 1986, and achieved against Iraq in 1991 with Cruise missiles and laser-guided bombs, are also forms of military intervention. The more common impression of military intervention involves one or more states intervening within the territory or possessions of other states. The threat or intention of the use of significant force on both sides is implicit. Today, there is a probability that military intervention will be aimed at the securing of peace. This is a very recent development for in the post-1945 period it had invariably been conducted with a view to securing parochial, ideological goals.

Having divided into two ideological camps, the post-Second World War international order faced up to the inevitability of the looming struggle being accompanied by force or the threat of force. The late Hedley Bull recorded that 'intervention in the sense of coercive interference by outside parties in the sphere of jurisdiction of a state is an endemic or built-in feature of our present international arrangements'.[12] The statistics relating to the United States alone support these statements. When the occasions of threat of force are added to the occasions where force has been used, the total since 1945 exceeds 500, most of which have been in the Third World.[13] In the 1950s and 1960s:

> the United States used its military power or paramilitary power on an average of once every eighteen months either to prevent a government deemed undesirable from coming to power or to overthrow a revolutionary government considered inimical to America's interests.[14]

These power-projection operations were invariably unilateral, promulgated in the main by the United States and the Soviet Union. The hint of a move away from unilateralism was evident as long ago as the 1962 Cuban Missile Crisis, when the prominent American international lawyer, Louis Henkin wrote, albeit prematurely, 'but by 1962, in Latin America surely, the day of unilateral intervention by the United States seemed over, replaced by collective judgement if not by truly collective action'.[15] In those days, the United States and the Soviet Union informally recognised each other's spheres of influence in Central America and the Eastern bloc respectively. Within these areas, they were able to intervene in other states' affairs more or less to order. For example, President Johnson did not seriously seek a legal justification for the 1965 intervention in the Dominican Republic, nor President Brezhnev for the 1968 intervention in Czechoslovakia.[16] When *both* states perceived a territory to be within their own sphere of influence, however, as happened when the Soviet leadership deceived the United States and placed missiles in Cuba, the world was taken to the brink of war. Neither Vietnam nor Afghanistan, however, fell unequivocally within either superpower's recognised sphere of influence and the conflicts became high-intensity, ideological struggles. One of the reasons for the defeat of both states' armed forces in these intra-state armed conflicts was attributable in part to the active opposition of the other superpower.

Why, therefore, have so many interventions such as Vietnam and Afghanistan failed? There have been muddled aims, breakdowns in consensus and poor morale among the ranks of the intervenors but the failure has been due principally to an inability fully to comprehend the situation, the risks and the effort required. Too much emphasis was placed on the justification for intervention and too little analysis was devoted to the consideration of whether intervention could succeed. Almost without exception, intervenors cannot tolerate casualty levels that are acceptable to their opponent; interventions tend to polarise support within the target territory, carrying with them the seeds of their own destruction. Military intervention and UN peacekeeping is a most difficult warlike operation. It requires strategic mobility for the crossing of anything other than contiguous borders, which is one reason why coercive intervention has been almost exclusively the province of the super- or medium-powers.

There are the costs to consider, both financial and in human life. Vietnam cost the American taxpayer $190 billion, while the Soviets spent $3–4 billion for each of the years their forces were fulfilling no useful purpose in Afghanistan.[17] In the Vietnam theatre the Americans dropped a greater number of bombs than in the European theatre during the Second World War. The proportion of civilian casualties within the Second World War total was 48 per cent. In the Korean War it had risen to 84 per cent, but in Vietnam civilian casualties reached 90 per cent.[18] The 200,000 military casualties the United States suffered in that war was greater than their losses in the Pacific war. The Afghanistan total was small by comparison. Among the 100,000 declared deaths, the Soviets admitted to the loss of 13,310 troops.[19]

The impact of the Afghanistan war on Soviet domestic opinion was, however, dramatic. So much so that neither the new Commonwealth of Independent States nor the Russian Federation is likely to embark again on external intervention missions without the most overwhelming justification. The Vietnam War also had a dramatic influence upon American domestic opinion and military confidence. The national ego would receive further bruising resulting from the 1980 Iran hostage affair, the Multinational Force intervention in Lebanon in 1982–84 and the amateurish 1983 Grenada intervention. The 1989 Panama intervention heralded a change of fortune in national prestige and confidence, to be consolidated during the 1990–91 Gulf crisis.

In October 1987, as a reflection of the changing Soviet attitude to the United Nations, President Gorbachev dropped the old Soviet reservation about UN peacekeeping activities and won a significant propaganda coup by beginning the repayment of Soviet debts to the United Nations. This latter act contributed to the return of the United States to a more active UN role and to begin repaying its own debts which had grown to $500 million. Moscow now wanted the United Nations to become the guarantor of international peace and security through standing forces and the revitalisation of the Military Staff Committee. Further evidence of the Soviet desire to strengthen the power of the United Nations was reflected in its recommendation that the foreign ministers of the permanent members of the Security Council should attend Council meetings as envisaged in article 28(2) of the Charter. As to the operational function, the Soviets proposed what was then the new strategy of 'preventive diplomacy' whereby UN troops would be stationed along the border of a threatened state to act as an international trip-wire.

The Present

Our recent experience of peacekeeping and peace-enforcement has been influenced by three inter-related factors; first, the ending of the Cold War and the associated decline of the Soviet Union; secondly, the confirmation of the United States as the only all-round super-power; and thirdly, the role played by the United Nations, particularly in relation to the Gulf crisis of 1990–91. This central section takes as its foundation, therefore, the conclusion of the East West dispute and the transition from the Cold War to a new New World Order.

The end of the Cold War and the emancipation of the people of Central and Eastern Europe has established a number of dangerous domino effects within the region, the ramifications of which will also be felt elsewhere. Porous borders pose distinct problems, not least that of militant migration. It is true that conflicts cannot be wished away but have to be resolved and that the incidence and dangers of border disputation will worsen before they improve. Minorities will have to be disabused of the notion that third parties will automatically come to their assistance in a conflict. Intervention and non-intervention are different sides of the same coin. Just as there have to be rules or principles of multilateral military intervention, there have to be rules for non-intervention. The adoption of other means, or accepting the often unpalatable fact that nothing can be achieved by military intervention, may have to be faced up to.

In the case of Yugoslavia, arguments were presented that military action was essential, first to contain the crisis and secondly to make the point that force and aggression do not pay. Military intervention and UN peacekeeping is always a last resort but it is the assignment of ground forces which represents the ultimate commitment. In 1950 it was hoped that the Korean crisis could be resolved by the application of naval and air power. This still remains a sensible policy today, that is in those circumstances where it can succeed. Similar arguments were adduced in respect of protecting Croatia. It was reasoned that only light naval interventionist forces were required to raise the naval siege of Dubrovnik and that it was a relatively simple matter to intercept the federal air force during its attacks on Croatia's infrastructure. In view of the region's history, that would have been a recipe for disaster. Certainly, the reticence displayed by many states over becoming involved in Croatia was through fear of establishing a precedent.

The politically desirable goal of extracting peace dividends as a result of the ending of the Cold War has set in motion among the former adversaries, force reductions in the range of 25–50 per cent. The victors of the Gulf War are now set on a course whereby they risk suffering the penalty of their success. Historically, success often brings with it the seeds of future failure. While the victor demobilises, the defeated go back to the drawing board to be better prepared for the future. The ending of the Cold War and its associated, reassuring stability is giving way to the greatest prospect for turbulence since 1945. There will be fewer trained forces able to respond to future predictable calls for assistance. The inevitable implications of these changed circumstances are the certainties of coalition operations. In its report on the Gulf Crisis, the Washington Center for Strategic and International Studies gave the opinion that for the United States '[t]he option of going it alone simply does not exist, and all foreign and defence policy decisions must be made with this realisation'. Because the interests of Western states are closely interwoven, it does appear that they are unlikely to engage in further unilateral intervention operations. The inevitability of working within a coalition is already a fact for less powerful states who, as the peace dividend is taken, are obliged to examine functional force structuring or 'segmentism'.

NATO, meanwhile, adjusts to the new circumstances whereby threats of war have been replaced by the threat of turbulence. NATO has a crucial role to play in any future intervention scenario. It will not be under the NATO banner, however, that self-selecting constituent members will operate in support of regional actors. To adopt that course of action would be a presentational disaster: the North imposing its own political diktat or Brezhnev Doctrine on the South.

NATO's contribution to the Gulf crisis has been hugely underestimated. The principal achievement was not in keeping open the lines of communication or even defending Turkey, but rather in providing the mechanics of inter-operability and some aspects of commonality of approach and equipment.

NATO has confirmed that the organisation will not operate outside alliance boundaries. Nowadays, it is unrealistic to expect automatic unanimity among the myriad competing security organisations. It is more likely that each individual crisis will create its own coalition. For example, although NATO has never operated outside its area *per se*, it was nonetheless predominantly NATO forces that were located at Silopi and Incirlik for possible operations into northern Iraq. The subtle difference was that they were not under NATO command. It should also be noted that effective intervention would not have been possible from either Turkey or indeed Saudi Arabia without the support of the host nation. Saudi Arabia, for example, made available airfields, the modern port of al Jubayl, and also provided free petrol and water.

The NATO connection could be a mixed blessing. The pre-eminent states will be those whose procedures are inter-operable and whose forces not only 'dock' into one another but often also share a common language. This means, therefore, that echelons of excellence will be created. Some states will be content to draw the dividend of political esteem, aware that their forces do not face significant military risks. Other states will find such circumstances insulting. This is a feature of future coalition operations which will require early analysis and the adoption of palliative solutions.

Within Europe, the constituent NATO members are adapting to the difficult circumstances of the post-Cold War era. It remains an unsettled environment. The United Kingdom has accepted the Supreme Allied Commander Europe's (SACEUR's) request that they lead and allocate two divisions to a multinational rapid reaction corps for operations within NATO boundaries. The prospect of British command aroused no great enthusiasm in Bonn. In addition, France, not a member of NATO's military wing, has proposed the formation of a binational corps with Germany. The United Kingdom has addressed the question of the defence of European interests outside the NATO area. The proposition is the formation of a European Reaction Force (ERF) under the Western European Union (WEU) and autonomous from NATO. Both organisations, however, would draw from the same pool of available forces. The ERF's *raison d'être* would be to be deployed whenever European interests were threatened outside the NATO area and where a military response was considered appropriate.

The development of a WEU intervention capability is important. It will establish new possibilities. There are possible benefits for Britain and Europe in having a capability for multilateral European action outside the NATO framework either where it would be inappropriate for NATO to be involved or where it would not wish to be involved. Yugoslavia created difficulties for historical reasons and is considerably 'closer to home' than some of the other possible areas where WEU action might be contemplated. There are likely to be circumstances where it is easier to establish a minimum degree of consensus. In response to Germany's unilateral stance in recognising Croatia and Slovenia, rather than put the alliance at risk the other EC states chose to acquiesce in taking action about which some of them had serious misgivings.

A majority of strategists would agree that America's security interests are best served by a continuing presence in Europe and along the Pacific Rim. Both these regions are America's major industrial competitors. To the United States, but more important, to its Congress, it is essential that the burden-shedding/sharing exercise is equitable. Furthermore, if Europe does want the US forces to remain in Europe, it needs to take positive action now to persuade Congress accordingly. There is a compelling rationale for European powers to encourage America to remain within NATO for collective security contingencies both within and outside the NATO area.

In both the Gulf and northern Iraq interventions, the American concept of deploying unified commands, consisting of two or more services, worked well. The unified commands are each allocated global areas of operation in support of regional actors. The boundary between European Command (EUCOM) located at Stuttgart, and Central Command (CENTCOM) located at Tampa, Florida, runs through Turkey's south-eastern border. Thus it was that CENTCOM was assigned the Gulf War while EUCOM was responsible for operations from Turkey in support of Iraq's Kurds. It is difficult to offer a sensible recommendation that the Unified Headquarters should be internationalised in the interest of coalition operations and diplomacy. In the first place, there are few allied staff officers who could have integrated into the staff of these working headquarters and secondly, since the national headquarters worked well, it is difficult to refute the logic of 'if it works, why fix it?'

What the Gulf crisis confirmed was America's military ascendancy, but her relative economic decline was also exposed, as was her unwillingness and inability to fund even her own national, high-intensity military operations. There is a college of opinion which proposes the formation of a coalition of paymasters and fighters. Evidence shows these separate functions may be required to remain rigorously distinct. Blood is more emotive than treasure. Had the Gulf campaign not been conducted so expeditiously and with relatively few casualties, the relations between America and Japan and Germany would have become profoundly hostile. The American public sensed that the GIs had become Tokyo's and Bonn's mercenaries.

The question of Japan's and Germany's role in peacekeeping and intervention is raised regularly. Under their respective interpretations of Article 9 of the Japanese Constitution and the *Grundgesetz*, or basic law, neither state is permitted to play a role. Japan did deploy minesweepers into the Gulf at the conclusion of hostilities and an animated parliamentary debate discussed sending peacekeepers into Cambodia where the senior UN representative is Japanese. Germany sent ships into the Mediterranean to free allied warships for operations in the Gulf and, similarly, fighter aircraft into Turkey.

Although both states are economic superpowers they are politically frustrated, having as yet no obvious transregional role in international affairs. Japan is taking positive remedial action to press for a seat as a permanent member of the Security Council. Germany has been less assertive but is thought to be no less keen. Japan was present at the Heads of State summit meeting held at the United Nations on 31 January 1992, occupying one of the rotational non-permanent Security Council seats. She shares the responsibilities laid down by the relevant extract of article 43 of the UN Charter quoted on page 168 above. In view of Japan's presence at the January summit, the declaration issued by the Security Council is of more than passing interest:

> The members of the Council pledge their commitment to international law and to the United Nations Charter. All disputes between states should be peacefully resolved in accordance with the provisions of the Charter. The members of the Council reaffirm their commitment to the collective security system of the Charter to deal with threats to peace and . . . acts of aggression.[20]

Article 43 does ask for things other than armed forces, there being options to offer 'facilities and assistance'. There are, however, a significant number of states which would not welcome the encouragement of the development of German and Japanese power-projection capabilities. But with the possibility of worldwide demand for some sort of international forces exceeding the availability of suitable manpower, can German and Japanese military resources be overlooked in the future? Whereas there are those in Germany and Japan who sense a need for national global strategies, both the German and Japanese peoples have shown considerable opposition to changing respectively their basic law and constitution to enable them to fight overseas.

The United Nations has authorised Chapter VII military enforcement operations on two occasions,[21] both of which produced different models. The most recent was the Gulf model. Prior to that was the Korea model and there is a third, untried Dumbarton Oaks model which would involve article 43 action under the provisions of article 47, whereby the MSC undertakes strategic command of an operation. The circumstances of each intervention situation are rarely similar, nor are the reactions or composition of the intervention force ever the same. For this and other reasons, it is unlikely that the Gulf or Korea models will be duplicated or that the Dumbarton Oaks model will be followed. There can never be a standard format, but it is still preferable to have some loosely drawn plan in place, with parallel options arising from abstract contingency plans. If this is not achieved, planners will be obliged to meet every crisis hot-planning and at the gallop.

In the Gulf model, a basic flaw lay in the American leadership's insistence on emphasising national rather than international commitment, overlooking the fact that the mandate to lead arose from within the United Nations in New York rather than within Washington's political offices. Future coalition leaders will need to learn from this example the importance of the presentational dimension so as to avoid claims from the enemy that their foe is the lead intervention state rather than the international community as a whole. Once the Security Council had authorised the use of armed force under resolution 678, it had no control over the military operation which it had set in train. Moreover, once a resolution is adopted, its amendment can be frustrated by the veto of any one of the five permanent members of the Security Council. Again, presentationally it could appear to those who would wish to view it as such, that the United States had hijacked the United Nations. There was more than a hint of exasperation when Javier Pérez de Cuéllar said:

> The war is not a classic United Nations war in the sense that there is no United Nations control of the operations, no United Nations flag, [blue] helmet, or any engagement of the Military Staff Committee. What we know about the war, which I prefer to call hostilities, is what we hear from the three members of the Security Council which are involved – Britain, France and the United States – which every two or three days report to the Council after the actions have taken place. The Council, which

has authorised all this, [is informed] only after the military activities have taken place.

It is unlikely that the Gulf experience will be repeated, first because the United States is unlikely to wish to undertake again such a substantial commitment and secondly, because the international community is unlikely again to provide it with a blank cheque. It is the Korean experience which provides the most plausible model for the conduct of future military operations. UN Security Council resolution 84 of July, 1950 authorised the establishment of a unified command, gave the enterprise UN status and approved the flying of the UN flag. The command of UN forces was mandated to the United States. Since the United States funded the majority of the operation, provided half the ground forces and 85–95 per cent of the naval and air forces, her pre-eminent position as what may be described as the 'framework state' was incontestible. Fifteen other states provided forces while 48 of the then 60 members pledged assistance. For the future, the Security Council has to evolve a system of accountability to the United Nations but not such an all-pervading accountability as to inhibit sensible military operations.

When the Military Staff Committee was founded it was intended that it would plan and command collective security operations. What is important today is not the fact that these objectives were stymied by Cold War tensions but rather that the MSC still exists within the Charter. There has been reluctance and resistance to revitalise this moribund committee, but that does not take account of the need to take hold of a committee whose origins lay in the Dumbarton Oaks Conference of 1944, and to massage it to the circumstances appropriate to 1992. There are doubts today as to the feasibility of article 43 action upon which the MSC's *raison d'être* has been based. What has become clear is that the United Nations can legislate but it cannot direct military operations. It seems most unlikely that coalition states would agree to their forces being directed by states who were not associated with the coalition through the contribution of troops. But this is considering the operational end of the spectrum, for which a Korea model variant may prove to be suitable. It will be remembered that the MSC is authorised to co-opt other members on to its committee, or to activate regional subcommittee. As an indication of its democratisation, it could, if there was the will, change its title. An official of the former Soviet Ministry of Foreign Affairs, Boris P. Krasulin, argued that the MSC should be:

vested with broad powers and important functions under the Charter . . . and . . . in a position to provide on a permanent basis a comprehensive operational analysis of the politico-military situation in world trouble spots other than the Gulf and to prepare corresponding recommendations for the Security Council. We take the view that . . . MSC sessions should be put on a regular footing to deal with a whole set of issues involved in countering acts of aggression, including forecasts of possible scenarios, and specific ways to prevent the risk of unauthorized use of force or a massive conflict triggered by a provocation or an accidental development.

The strength of the MSC lies in the capabilities of its membership. States will increasingly look to the Secretary-General to take a lead in preventive diplomacy, deriving his authority from article 99: 'The Secretary-General may bring to the attention of the Security Council any matter which in his opinion may threaten the maintenance of international peace and security'. But UN headquarters is not established to fulfil this function. The Secretary-General's military adviser is a Major General from Ghana who does not enjoy the benefit of so much as a planning cell. Historically, the assets of the five permanent members of the Security Council have only been used in support of peacekeeping operations *in extremis*. It is quite evident that not to take advantage of their planning capabilities, intelligence resources, communications and transportation is nothing short of self-inflicted obstruction. The whole subject of military support operations within the United Nations needs to be fundamentally reassessed and pervasive self-interest set aside. Past attitudes and interpretations have to change to reflect the new realities in international relations.

There have been two distinct, profoundly important milestones in intervention and peacekeeping procedures following on from the Gulf crisis. The first confirmed the further erosion of article 2(7), the domestic jurisdiction article, when Security Council resolution 688 was able to serve as a basis for the despatch of 20,000 NATO troops into northern Iraq to support the Kurds without Iraq's consent. The second milestone lay in the establishment by the Security Council under resolution 689 of the United Nations Iraq–Kuwait Observer Mission (UNIKOM).

That the traditional concept of peacekeeping is capable of change is evident from the examination of the structure and *raison d'être* of UNIKOM. The military commander is an experienced UN officer, the Austrian Major General Günther Greindl, who was UNFICYP commander from 1981–89. The control zone runs the length of the Iraq–Kuwait border, extending 10 kilometres into the former state and 5 kilometres into the latter. The Mission, comprising 300 unarmed military observers from 35 states, has been established with the agreement of Kuwait and (reluctantly) of Iraq. Iraq's principal objection arose from the inclusion of members of the forces of the allied coalition countries within the UN force.[22] It is from this point that the traditional concept of peacekeeping and observer forces has its starkest variation.

General Greindl's staff consists of a Pakistani second-in-command, a British military assistant, a French operations officer and an American logistician. The commander's liaison officers in Baghdad and Kuwait are respectively Russian and Chinese. There are British troops among the observer group, which is provided in the main by the traditional donor states. The involvement of representatives of the forces of the five permanent members of the Security Council guarantees a more compliant response from Iraq and ensures that the peacekeepers do not become part of the problem. UNIKOM is not a traditional peacekeeping operation because it is backed by the guarantee of uncompromising force. Such 'battleship diplomacy' emphasises that UNIKOM was not intended to be impartial, owing its legitimacy not to Chapter VI but to Chapter VII of the Charter. The assigned forces may only be removed by the affirmative vote of the Security Council.

The question is whether the United Nations will build on this precedent. It is not just a matter of involving the forces of the superpowers in order to attract the attention and concentrate the minds of squabbling parties, but rather of returning to first principles. Collaborated standing operating procedures will ease the problems of command and control. A rules of engagement (ROE) register can be agreed, and the meaning of the use of force can be determined. A strengthened military staff within the United Nations could draw up and update contingency plans, engage in dialogue and thus, by building confidence, provide future commanders of peacekeeping operations with genuine international support. UNIKOM has finally laid to rest the notion that the involvement of the forces of the major powers represents a colonial imposition. Today, there is no need to avoid major power competition in the disputed arena.

The Future

On 31 January 1992, the UN Secretary-General was invited, through the medium of the Security Council Summit Declaration, to prepare, for circulation to the members of the United Nations by 1 July 1992, his analysis and recommendations on ways of strengthening and making more efficient within the framework and provisions of the Charter the capacity of the United Nations for preventive diplomacy, for peace-making and peacekeeping. In general terms, these functions can be roughly grouped under Chapter VI, Chapter VI and a half and Chapter VII.

Two years ago, it would have been possible to write with the benefit of statistical analysis to the effect that the prospects of traditional Chapter VI peacekeeping had all but vanished. The evidence would have included the demise of inter-state conflict and increasing intra-state violence where the peace has to be created in order to be kept. But now, the certain increase of inter-state border disputes in Europe, Africa and South America will offer, if it is the will of those states involved, further opportunities for traditional peacekeeping. The two central problems are likely to be the fact that there is not an infinite number of suitable troops and that the funds are not readily available.

'Preventive diplomacy' has emerged as the buzz phrase of the decade. With the benefit of hindsight it seems obvious that the deployment of UN troops on the Iraq–Kuwait border, prepared to use escalating degrees of force, would have drawn its own 'line in the sand'. By establishing such a trip-wire, the message conveyed to a would-be aggressor is not obfuscated in diplomatic language that can be misinterpreted, but conveys a clear warning that the crossing of the line risks bringing down upon the head of the potential aggressor unacceptable levels of force.

The British army, which is among the more doctrinally retarded of armies, finds itself in a unique position, having on its dusty shelves a doctrine to suit the occasion. *Keeping the Peace*, a British army manual, is a relic of a colonial era which had as its essential rationale the avoidance of the use of force but, where that proved to be impossible, made provision for the use of 'minimum force'. This is very much the philosophy of preventive diplomacy although today the prospect of escalation is more plausible than it was previously. There are two associated issues worthy of mention. First, the forces assigned in *Keeping the Peace* operations were not in any way earmarked or specially trained to carry out that function. It was but one arrow in the army's quiver of military skills. The second point is that the British army often conducted such operations with a significant conscript component, and it is here that one of the chief practical differences between Chapter VI and Chapter VI and a half operations lies. In the latter, some well-trained, intelligent and motivated conscripts and reservists might be found a role but others will prove to be unsuitable and certainly should not be placed in a situation of potential escalating violence from which they have to be withdrawn.

There are no really precise distinctions between Chapters VI, VI and a half and VII operations although what we are now going on to examine is more appropriate to Chapter VII. In assessing the relevant factors, two groups emerge: those which establish themselves as obvious prerequisites, and others which are less obvious. It is important that the relevance and subtle differences of the latter group should be understood by those charged with the production of a formula for the future. In the section on 'The Present' above, the reader was asked to accept that the future would be distinguished by the inevitability of coalition diplomacy and coalition operations. The Gulf crisis provides a fertile area for the enunciation of prerequisites. There can be little argument that the support of, and resolutions emanating from, the UN Security Council gave the coalition its authority and legitimacy. The request for assistance and the assistance provided by the host state, proved to be essential. The US Secretary of State James Baker was particularly adept at the necessary political coordination. It has also emerged that not only do potential enemies need to be assessed and analysed in detail but so too must the military capabilities of potential allies be examined, as well as their willingness to participate in future peace-enforcement operations. The peacetime coordination of intelligence with allies will require to be the same as during armed conflict. The importance of the right commander in the right place at the right time was established yet again. The often emotive subject of command has deeper implications which will emerge in the analysis of the second group of factors. It is becoming clear that liaison officers in national headquarters have a key function to perform. It is also clear that they have to be in position as a matter of routine prior to the emergence of the crisis. They also need good and reliable means of communication.

The perceived problem areas of coalition operations include the choice of the supreme commander; language; logistics; interoperability; recognition of religious and cultural differences; regard for the time required for coordination; workable channels and links with the media and all aspects of intelligence and security. This is by no means an exhaustive list and, indeed, it is the identification of these 'prerequisite' areas which is the first step towards a solution. In addition, an examination of the second group of less distinct features is necessary for a broader understanding of the issues at stake.

When a state is approached by the UN Secretary-General or other interested states to join a peace-enforcement coalition, the government will go through a process of analysis to reach its decision. Often the decision-making process will be abbreviated as states intuitively decline to become involved in another state's internecine warfare. More often than not, the decision will be based upon a finely balanced assessment of factors. There will be domestic and international factors to consider and they will rarely march in step.

The decision-making process will begin with an assessment as to whether national interests are at stake and, if they are, whether they are vital interests over which the government has a duty to act. If vital national interests are not at stake, the government concerned has to decide then upon its international responsibilities and consider the disadvantages of not intervening. For example, if State A declined to be associated with an intervention in which State B had a vital national interest, it could present problems in the future if State A wished to solicit the support of State B for an intervention which was in State A's national interest. It is this consideration of the pros and cons of intervention which is most likely to gain weight in the 1990s as other states, thus far seen to be sitting on the sidelines, come under pressure to take on 'world order' responsibilities more explicitly. Legality is becoming an increasingly important notion in the interaction between states, especially as regards UN activities. The would-be interventionist government will need convincing that there are clear moral and legal grounds for gaining legitimacy for any putative operation. The national aim has to be decided and, from this, there will invariably be a compromise as the coalition's political aim and military mission are agreed. A coalition can only be effectively constructed for a clearly stated purpose based on an unequivocal aim. Whereas the maintenance of the aim must be the first principle of coalition operations, it does not mean that the aim is to be slavishly pursued when, for example, the factors on which it was formulated are no longer applicable.

Inevitably, the coalition has to decide collectively how success should be measured and defined. The constituent coalition governments will examine the political and military consequences of success and failure. They will be aware of the failure of earlier interventions and the danger of descending the 'slippery slope' of expanding commitment. Expanding commitment raises the political risks in terms of increased casualties and costs. Above all, there has to be an assessment of both national and international consensus. The question policy-makers will ask is whether public opinion can be sustained and what effect national involvement will have on the standing of the government.

The requirement for consensus provides an appropriate example of the tension which can exist between domestic and international considerations. The United States learnt at Versailles in 1919, and again more recently in the Gulf from November 1990, that domestic and international consensus do not necessarily run in tandem. This scope for a disconnection to occur impinges most upon the framework, or lead, state. A coalition will inevitably only be as strong as the framework state. If, therefore, the framework state is deprived of its own domestic consensus to proceed, then it is more than likely that the multilateral peace-enforcement operation will also fail.

By examining the structures which evolved in Korea and the Gulf, it is possible to forecast a military structure for the future. On both occasions the framework state was the United States. The framework state is the one with the greatest military and political commitment and hence attracts the right to command. All the other coalition states will invariably subordinate their forces to the framework state. From among these subordinate states there will emerge what can be described as a secondary state. In both Korea and the Gulf, the secondary state was the United Kingdom. There is no formality in establishing the relationship and it is not dependent upon the quantity of troops made available to the coalition. The relationship arises from an empathy between the framework and secondary states. These are qualitative assessments based on the secondary state's political and military commitment, the reliability of its advice, the quality of its troops, and the strength of its supporting analysis teams. Language is also an important consideration.

The secondary state's position is no sinecure. Since the framework state will often find it convenient or desirable to establish links of substance with no more than one state, the secondary state becomes the spokesman for the other coalition members. It will assess the political and military intentions of the framework state and will offer comment. The framework state is not obliged to heed this advice. It is important, however, in such politically highly charged circumstances as a peace-enforcement operation, that the framework state has the option of assessing the advice of a trusted state that is examining problems from a different position. One of the secondary state's principal roles is to be the check and balance to the framework state. It should ensure that the other coalition states are treated as allies, not auxiliaries.

The perception that coalition doctrine and training have to be integrated is overstated. Within NATO, an integrated doctrine at the strategic level based on the American concept of air–land operations, a kind of updated *Blitzkrieg*, has come to fruition. The United States has had the resources to formulate this strategy and has proved that it works within the realms of high-intensity conflict. If the strategy has a weakness, that weakness lies in its silence on inter-operability.

It is at the operational and tactical level that an all-embracing doctrine becomes difficult to impose upon national forces whose own special characteristics and training methods afford them their own distinct military fingerprint. In Vietnam, Australia's approach to jungle warfare was so significantly different to that of the United States that it asked for, and was allocated, its own tactical area of responsibility. The problem Australia was unable to reconcile while operating with the Americans, was the latter's concept of control and application of firepower. This is a societal and historic phenomenon but it can cause nervousness among collocated allies. In both the Grenada and Panama interventions, where overall casualties were low, 60 per cent of those suffered by the Americans were attributed to friendly fire. Accidents will always happen in warfare. At Verdun, the French artillery killed three of their own for every ten Germans. However, in the Falklands campaign, the British Commando Brigade, which conducted most of its fighting at night and at close quarters, suffered less than 4 per cent to friendly fire. 35 of the 145 Americans killed in action in the Gulf and 72 of the 467 wounded were friendly fire victims. Moreover, seven M1A1 tanks and 20 of the 25 Bradley fighting vehicles lost, were lost to friendly fire. Separation makes sense.

In Germany's Central region, national corps planned to fight within their own boundaries in a NATO layer-cake. The cross-fusion of national forces from one corps to another, which may be desirable if not essential, rarely occurred as an unplanned contingency. Differences do exist in allied organisations: doctrine, language, logistics, terminology, and their management of armed conflict. So fundamental are these differences that it is sensible to maintain area separation between coalition forces for the ground war. Problems will arise when foreign formations are attached to another coalition force or where aircraft operate across constituent coalition members' boundaries. Potential problems can be minimised through coordination and liaison. Politicians and soldiers support the concept of separateness. The politician is encouraged by the simplicity of control and the ability to demonstrate to the public through the media the extent of the national effort and commitment. The soldier is encouraged by an understandable preference for distinct operational command arrangements.

Large numbers of participating states within military coalitions are never likely to be an efficient means of conducting operations. They may be a political expedient but there will always be practical problems in making them work. Time is a feature which has not been given the prominence that it deserves. The Gulf coalition had the luxury of five months to put itself in some semblance of order. Because it was a short campaign where the casualties did not approach the levels forecast, the coalition did not suffer undue stress. Under different circumstances, for example a long drawn-out campaign with high casualty rates such as Vietnam, the coalition would have been subjected to tension. Reference to military history is not helpful because, in the majority of cases, a state of war existed and the operations were not speculative. For example, towards the end of the Second World War, the coalition partners knew what they were trying to achieve, they had a known enemy, specific objectives and agreed missions. We have come no further forward from 1938 when General Marshall discussed his quandary, quoted on p. 168 above. So much is dependent upon the will of states.

The suggested solution is negotiations, bilaterally, multilaterally and within the Military Staff Committee. Planning inside the United Nations will have to be in the abstract because the confidentiality necessary for the planning and execution of military operations cannot be guaranteed within an open UN structure. The requirement of national representatives is to identify and analyse the threat or risks of conflict, define the common interest of parties and initiate military planning. Peace-enforcement planning has three functions: to assess the potential need to address the crisis; to draw up or revise existing contingency plans; and to earmark forces and resources. The overriding danger implicit in this course of action is reaction. If states from what has been described as the Third World sense that here is a clique of states mapping out its own vision of world order, then the enterprise may well falter. Regional actors have to be part of the planning process and, as an expedient, it would be reasonable to consider internationalisation of the American concept of unified commands. So much is dependent upon the will of states.

In the Gulf crisis, there was evident tension between the United States as framework state and the principal host state, Saudi Arabia. Eventually, a suitable solution to the vexed question of command did emerge, but who should judge as to which state had the greatest commitment and was exposed to the greatest risks? President Bush's implacable statement that no US forces would be placed under any other state's command, should not be interpreted as the United States having only two intervention options: total commitment or no commitment. It will not necessarily be the framework state in future peace enforcement operations. It would be unlikely to be the lead state in any operation undertaken in francophone Africa, for example, or indeed in most parts of Africa, nor where it has already had its fingers burned, as in Cambodia. And in the sensitive area of the Caribbean, it might well heed the wishes of the OAS to avoid an imposed solution by a superpower. For example, the restoration by intervention of the legitimate president of Haiti might, from a presentational point of view, be better if conducted by a coalition of OAS members.

So much of the decision-making process reflects the personality of the leadership, and leaderships change. However, the exercise of full command within alliances and coalitions is not a feature of modern times. SACEUR does not have full rights of command over NATO troops because, when assigning troops to NATO, nations assign only operational command or operational control. At the tactical level there is tactical control, which refers only to the local direction and control of movement and manoeuvre in order to accomplish the mission. Command should not be an emotive issue although theory and practice are not always the same. Charles de Gaulle would have been mortified by the prospect of French troops subordinating themselves to the Americans in the Gulf but, if the principle is accepted that the framework state commands, then that is militarily realistic and is all-embracing.

In 1986, the Goldwater–Nichols Department of Defense Reorganization Act streamlined the military chain of command. It was apparent that some believed it was this Act which enabled General Schwarzkopf in the Gulf and Lieutenant General Shalikashvili in northern Iraq to enjoy apparent military autonomy. A minor problem did arise in relation to the Kurds when the British Prime Minister, John Major, who had been foremost in the political direction of the initiative to protect the Kurds, gave an undertaking that troops would remain for as long as was required. General Shalikashvili, his mission completed, had initiated a partial rather than a general withdrawal. Coalitions are not like alliances such as NATO, with the generals and diplomats all sitting in one room. In coalitions, the orders come from different capitals. These directions will not be concurrent and there is therefore a risk that components within coalitions, although keen to present a united military front, will not always have received their directions from their government. The system needs a greater degree of finesse to achieve a more effective political system for coalitions coming together, otherwise the risk of getting out of step will continue. It is certainly essential that donor states should fully understand and agree the supreme commander's mission statement.

It was not, however, the Goldwater–Nichols Act – following on from the micro-managed, abysmal Lebanon intervention of 1982–84 – which gave the US commanders their power in the Gulf. Power was delegated to the in-place commanders because they enjoyed the confidence of the President, the Secretary of Defense and the Chairman of the Joint Chiefs of Staff. Such delegation of power is the sum of political experience and comprehension of the military task and, to a varying degree, a political determination not to be over-awed by media considerations. Other coalition members in the Gulf and northern Iraq did not allow their commanders so much latitude; it therefore became inevitable that states would be out of step. Coalition governments will always be concerned that adequate political control should exist over the supreme commander. General Schwarzkopf enjoyed a relatively free hand to fight the battle in the Gulf, but when he sought to extend the conflict northward into Iraq, it became immediately evident that political controls were in place and that this would not be permitted to become a repeat of Korea.

The future and success of peace enforcement as a constituent part of a global collective security regime is largely dependent on the attitude and role adopted by the United States. The moral indignation shown by Britain and France over the plight of the Iraqi Kurds could not be translated into military action without the active assistance and participation of the United States. America's undisguised reluctance to be drawn into the Kurdish relief operation only months after the President had wrapped up the successful Gulf conflict and spoken in terms of America as the undisputed world leader, did appear to be a contradiction in terms. It should not have been. What the world was seeing was the interplay and tension of, on the one hand, the American interventionist mission and manifest destiny and, on the other, the isolationist rejection of entangling commitment with a strongly emergent domestic 'America First' lobby demanding, 'why us, why there, why now?'.

> What, for example, shall the rest of the world do when America refuses to act or pursue a parochial interest? It was one thing to look to America for leadership when the nation was self-confident and public spirited; it may be quite another if America feels beleaguered, under siege economically, and too poor to act.[23]

If states see it as part of their national interest to invest in a global collective security system they need to pursue a policy of positive encouragement of the United States to be available to take the lead. However, there is justifiable cause for pessimism that the prospect for long-term world order is not good. The US administration seems unable and unwilling to grasp the problem of its overwhelming economic troubles. The American public is becoming less impressed by foreign intervention and a predominant foreign policy, as shown in a January 1992 *USA Today*/CNN/Gallup poll which revealed that 82 per cent of those questioned believed the resolution of international problems should take a back seat to the tackling of domestic ills. The American public is worried by extrapolations which suggest that by the year 2010, 35 per cent of the nation's gross national product will be absorbed by care-related budgets. It is also a public whose values and ethnicity are changing. In 1970, America's population comprised 83 per cent non-Hispanic whites. By the year 2010, the extrapolation suggests the white proportion will have declined to

68 per cent and this change may well influence whether and indeed where the nation will wish to intervene.

For reasons discussed earlier, the availability of troops for future peace operations will be influenced by the reduction of forces – the 'peace dividend' – following the end of the Cold War. For example, the number of British infantry battalions, the workhorse of any army, is to be reduced from 55 to 38. The impact of such reductions can be offset by states reviewing procedures for the deployment abroad of reservists and conscripts, which in the European context was related to the threat of general war within the NATO area. France's support of the Gulf War was affected by the presence of 40 per cent conscripts in its 47,000-strong Force d'Action Rapide (FAR). Legislation would have been necessary in order to deploy them to the Gulf and the lack of any such legislation necessarily meant breaking up divisions which influenced adversely such key combat elements as artillery support. France is now taking steps to reduce the conscript element in FAR to a minimum. Germany has no plans to abandon conscription. One reason has nothing to do with military operations: the German welfare organisation is dependent on the support of conscientious objectors and would therefore collapse if conscription ended.

There will be over 26,000 military personnel involved in the UN peacekeeping operations in Cambodia and Yugoslavia. If forces are available, are they suitable and who in the United Nations is able to make such professional judgements? There will be less of a problem in the future finding troops for peacekeeping operations (if there is no great proliferation of commitment and funds are available) than for the more dangerous preventive diplomacy or peace-enforcement. Soldiers do not exist in a vacuum and are influenced by change within the society to which they belong. A recent poll in a Spanish magazine indicated that only 8 per cent of those interviewed were prepared to die for Spain. How many would be prepared to die for peace in Cambodia or Yugoslavia? In Sri Lanka, a bemused Indian officer said: 'Things would be different if we were fighting for our country but here it's difficult to explain to the troops why we are in it at all.' Undoubtedly, troops will put their lives on the line where there is a clear national interest, or even where there is an identifiable humanitarian cause. The concept of the just war is important. If, in future, troops are asked to risk their lives by separating parties in a civil war with whom they have no sympathy, the outcome is difficult to predict.

Both the United States and the Soviet Union learnt through their intervention experiences in Vietnam and Afghanistan that conscripts were unsuitable for military operations, making political and military demands similar to those made by multilateral peace-enforcement operations. It is likely that the states of the former Soviet Union will increase the professional proportions in their forces but this will take time and, in view of the difficulties currently being experienced in most of those states, the availability of Russian, CIS or other troops for assignment to peace-enforcement operations this decade should be discounted.

There is a need within the United Nations to exercise shrewd judgement in accepting from a state its offer of armed forces. It is not a numbers game, but rather one of matching forces to courses. If selection is not based on sound military judgement, there is always the possibility that the UN troops become part of the problem. This was the case with the League of Nations in relation to the Japanese troops in Siberia in 1918–22 and with Ghanaian and Guinean troops in the UN operation in the Congo. The characteristics of forces must be matched to the environment and circumstances of the area to which they are assigned.

American force characteristics are arguably unsuitable for peace-keeping operations, which tend to be drawn-out, and require inordinate patience and the ability to turn the other cheek. Until now, there have been few political possibilities of deploying Americans on peacekeeping operations. Moreover, the US administration has opposed such commitment. American forces are more suited to the exercise of preventive diplomacy and peace-enforcement. Troops on preventive diplomacy missions are deployed to deter, but if that fails they will escalate their military response to an aggressor by calling on 'over the horizon' war-fighting assets until the situation is remedied. It is in this field of peace by deterrence that important states will find acceptable conditions for participation in UN peace initiatives.

There have been recent suggestions that states should earmark standing forces for employment in support of the United Nations. Such an idea is more idealistic than realistic. If a national brigade were to be earmarked, there is no guarantee that it would be manned, trained or equipped to counter the problem it was called on to confront. The 1979 Soviet invasion of Afghanistan illustrates this point. The Soviets invaded, buoyed by confidence derived from the 'great patriotic war'. They assumed, based on the experience of Poland and Czechoslovakia, that they would be unopposed. The response of the insurgency took them completely by surprise. Moscow was more aware of what was happening in Washington and London than among its own Central Asian people. The Motor Rifle divisions despatched from the Turkestan Military District were category C divisions, only 10–25 per cent permanently manned, and topped up by conscripts recruited for service in Afghanistan. Not until much later in the campaign did they backload Frog missiles, air defence systems, chemical defence equipment and other kit irrelevant to their task.

The slimmed-down forces of the future will be multi-roled to suit national requirements. It is wasteful and expensive to have standing forces on call to the United Nations; nor is it necessary. Despite British forces being assigned to NATO, they were never employed in earnest on duties for which they trained in support of the Alliance in Europe. Nevertheless, on 70 occasions since 1945 they were engaged in intervention operations outside Europe. Professional forces have the ability to adapt. They need to be backed by sound intelligence of the area to which they are to deploy, strategic lift transportation, logistics, communications and host nation support.

When the UN Secretary-General reports back to the Security Council, there should be evidence in his plan of the shake-up of the UN's recalcitrant bureaucracy. There is now a wave of enthusiasm for the United Nations but the organisation will have to work very hard to rise to the challenge before the moment passes. There is a suspicion that in the peacekeeping and peace-making fields it is attempting too much with too little talent. The contributors to UN peacekeeping operations find its sketchy military organisation inadequate. Each state has a different degree of suspicion of UN competence for a variety of reasons, but it is now time for the Secretary-General to ask for the professional advice available through the MSC. The UN Charter establishes the principle that peace-enforcement measures may be legally sanctioned and initiated through UN headquarters. If force is to be applied at the behest of the United Nations, it surely needs a dedicated, professional military staff to consider contingency and ongoing planning. It is incongruous to maintain fully staffed headquarters in a central region where it has been agreed that minimal prospects of general conflict exist, while the one organisation legally empowered to deploy forces is embarrassed by a poverty of military support staff.

Notes

* At the time of writing Richard Connaughton was head of the British Army's Defence Studies, but this chapter reflects an entirely personal point of view.

1. Alan James, *The Politics of Peacekeeping*, p.1. Chatto & Windus, London (1969).
2. *Peacekeepers' Handbook*, p.22. Pergamon Press, New York (1984).
3. Alan James, *The Politics of Peacekeeping* (note 1 above), p.3.
4. Brian Urquhart, *A Life in Peace and War*, p.93. Weidenfeld & Nicolson, London (1987).
5. *Yearbook of the United Nations, 1947–1948*, p.495.

6. Leland M. Goodrich, *The United Nations*, pp.164–5. Thomas Y. Cromwell, New York (1959).

7. In 1947 the United Nations had used observers in Greece and also employed military attachés in Indonesia to observe the cease-fire between the Dutch and Indonesian freedom fighters.

8. Lawrence Freedman, *Atlas of Global Strategy*, p.5. Macmillan, London (1985).

9. Harvey Starr and Benjamin A. Most, 'Patterns of conflict: quantitative analysis and the comparative lessons of third world wars.', in Robert E. Harkavy and Stephanie G. Neumann (eds), *The Lessons of Recent Wars in the Third World, Vol. 1: Approaches and case studies*, Lexington (1985).

10. Michael Harbottle, *The Blue Berets*, p.44. Leo Cooper, London (1975).

11. Gustav Hägglund, 'Peacekeeping in a modern war zone', *Survival*, XXXII (3), p. 240 (May/June 1990).

12. Hedley Bull, *Intervention in World Politics*, p.181. Clarendon Press, Oxford (1984).

13. William J. Olson, *Military Review*, February 1989, 7.

14. Richard J. Barnet, 'The costs and perils of intervention', in Michael T. Klare and Peter Kornbluh (eds.), *Low Intensity Warfare*, p.210. Methuen, London (1989).

15. Louis Henkin, *How Nations Behave*, p.219. Columbia University Press, New York and London (1968).

16. Thomas M. Franck and Edward Weisband, *World Politics*. Oxford University Press, New York (1971).

17. R.L. Sivard, *World Military and Social Expenditures 1987–88*, p.30. World Priorities, Washington DC (1987).

18. Ingrid Detter de Lupis, *The Law of War* (Cambridge: Cambridge University Press, 1987), p.241.

19. General Alexei Lizichev, head of the Soviet army and navy's Chief Political Directorate, reported in *The Times*, 26 May 1988.

20. *New York Times*, 1 February 1992.

21. Military enforcement under Chapter VII was also authorised in resolution 221 (1966) on Southern Rhodesia which led to the setting up of the Beira patrol. The UN also invoked Chapter VII in applying arms embargoes on Yugoslavia and Somalia.

22. Edward Fursdon, 'UN Successes in 1990', *Army Quarterly*, 121 (4) (Summer 1991).

23. David Gergen, *American Perspectives after the Gulf War*, (Report of the Meeting of the Trilateral Commission, Tokyo, 20–22 April 1991), p.43.

CHAPTER 7

Spoiling the ship for a ha'porth of tar: the financial crisis at the United Nations

ANTHONY PARSONS

The gush of anti-United Nations propaganda which streamed out of governmental and right-wing quasi-academic sources in Washington and associated capitals in the early 1980s created a widespread impression that the organisation was a prodigal, incompetent form of outdoor relief for otherwise unemployable bureaucrats of many, mainly Third World, nationalities. It was also alleged to be burdened with unnecessary and expensive programmes voted into existence by the non-aligned majority who contributed only a tiny fraction of the budget. Governments in the major donor countries, especially the United States, were thus being put on notice that, unless this bloated monster could be halted and reduced to a manageable size, Western economies would suffer grievous decline.

There may be grains of truth in the above caricature, but its dissemination tended to destroy all sense of proportion. The regular budget of the United Nations for 1991 was assessed at a mere $1 billion, approximately 25 per cent of the annual aid contribution of the United States to Israel alone, about $3^{1}/_{2}$ per cent of the British defence budget, and slightly less than the annual budget of the British Foreign and Commonwealth Office including overseas representation. The total expenditure in 1984–85 (a bad year in the view of the anti-UN lobby) of the United Nations and its 'family' – all the specialised agencies such as FAO, ILO, UNESCO, WHO, etc – drawing on both assessed and voluntary contributions, was about $10.5 billion, still well short of the British defence budget and a drop in the ocean compared with the budgets of spending departments in the United States. Hence the first point to bear in mind is that the discussion relates to very small sums when compared with national budgets.

Contributions to UN budgets are levied on the basis of a formula which takes into account overall national income, per capita national income, population and ability to pay. Under this calculation the United States pays by far the lion's share: in the early 1970s, this was limited to a ceiling of 25 per cent of the total budget although a precise assessment would put the US contribution at probably closer to 30 per cent. The following figures give a rough cross section of percentage payments by representative states in 1991:

Representative percentage contributions to the UN budget 1991

United States	25.00	China	0.79
Japan	11.00	India	0.37
Germany	9.30	Kuwait	0.29
Russia	10.00	Saudi Arabia	1.02
Ukraine	1.25	Argentina	0.66
Belorus	0.33	Brazil	1.45
France	6.25	Nigeria	0.20
United Kingdom	4.80		

Half the membership (80 out of 159 states when the August 1991 figures were available) paid the minimum of 0.01 per cent, i.e. $92,000 for 1991 as opposed to the $250 million of the United States, $86 million of Germany and $44 million of the United Kingdom. By the spring of 1992 the membership had risen to 175, with further applications in sight – all likely to have low to minimal assessments.

It is of course these disparities which have provided the fuel for the flames of those in the West who argue that it is intolerable that each member state should have equal voting power, and who propose that voting should be weighted proportionately to contributions. This overlooks the fact that the doctrine of sovereign equality of states as manifested in article 18 of the Charter – 'Each member of the General Assembly shall have one vote' – was formulated by the Western democracies with the United States at the forefront. It presented no problem for the first 10 years or so of the existence of the United Nations when the West could command a parliamentary majority in all major organs. It was only with decolonisation (vigorously supported by Washington), the emergence of the Non-Aligned Movement and the shift unfavourable to the West in the parliamentary arithmetic, that voices were raised calling for a move of the goalposts and for a more archaic relationship between the piper and the tune.

Peacekeeping operations have historically been financed in four different ways:

1. *From the regular UN budget*. This applies to small observer and other operations such as UNTSO in the Middle East ($310,521,300 from 1948–89), UNMOGIP in India/Pakistan ($67,709,300 from 1948–89) and UNOGIL in Lebanon in 1958 ($3,697,742).

2. *Contributions from individual states*. Examples are UNYOM, the Observation Mission in the Yemen from 1963–64, which was paid for in equal parts by Egypt and Saudi Arabia and UNSF in West Irian (1962–63), paid for by the governments of Indonesia and The Netherlands.

3. *Voluntary contributions*. UNFICYP in Cyprus is, I believe, the only peacekeeping force supported entirely by voluntary contributions with the troop and other contributors absorbing most of the costs of their contributions. It was established in 1964 and had cost $635.7 million by December 1990.

4. *Assessments in special accounts*. Under this method, all member states pay a certain amount, with the major proportion paid by four of the five permanent members (China is assessed far lower than the others) for their 'special responsibilities' under the Charter.[1] This covers the majority of the larger operations such as UNEF-I, UNEF-II, UNDOF (Golan), UNIFIL (Lebanon), ONUC (Congo), UNIIMOG (Iran/Iraq) and UNTAG (Namibia), plus one or two smaller ones such as UNAVEM (Angola) and ONUCA (Central America).

By the end of October 1991 the aggregate deficit of all these accounts was of the order of $463 million. For example, $287 million was owed to UNIFIL, only $88 million of the $140 million assessed for MINURSO (supervision of the Western Sahara referendum) had been paid, and only $40 million of the $60 million needed for UNIKOM (Iraq–Kuwait demilitarised zone) had been raised.

In mid-September 1991 the Secretary-General wrote to all member states thanking those 51 (including the United Kingdom) that had paid their 1991 assessments to the regular budget but pointing out that the UN was 'in the midst of its worst financial crisis since it had been founded'. He had been obliged to borrow from peacekeeping funds to meet the basic operating costs of the organisation. He stated that 'either we manage effectively to address the financial problem, or the United Nations will be rendered incapable, for lack of resources, to perform its far-reaching functions, with the required effectiveness, especially for the maintenance of international peace and security'. He added that, as of 1 September 1991 (i.e. with the year two-thirds gone), unpaid assessments to the regular budget totalled $809.5 million of which $471.4 million related to the current year and $338.1 million to previous years. (The US proportion of this debt was $531 million.)

As regards defaults on previous annual contributions and late payments of current assessments on peacekeeping accounts, the load was more widely spread. By September 1991, 57 states had paid their regular assessments in full, and only 18 had cleared their peace-keeping debts. The United States and the Soviet Union owed $267 million of the $463 million shortfall on the peacekeeping account.

The peacekeeping figures disclose that financing UN military operations, when not paid for by individual states, has been a constant struggle. The following total is misleading because it does not take into account general inflation, the rising costs of equipment or the decline in the value of money over the past four decades. The uncorrected statistics show that all 17 UN peacekeeping operations mounted since 1948 had, up to the end of 1990, cost $4 billion. Even taking the necessary adjustments into account, this would amount to only a tiny fraction of the cost of each of the two military enforcement actions launched under the authority of the UN since 1945, namely the Korean and Gulf Wars. In the first case, the costs were borne by the troop contributors, principally the United States. In the Gulf War, as is well known, a substantial proportion of the cost was borne by the super-rich Gulf states and Saudi Arabia with additional contributions from Japan and Germany.

It is true that when the devil drives, the money is found, as with UNEF I (post-Suez) and UNEF II (after the superpowers had nearly clashed on a Middle Eastern battlefield). Generally speaking, however, the devil is the perceived 'vital interests' of great powers. If Saddam Hussein had not threatened Israel's security and the status quo in Saudi Arabia, and if payment for Desert Shield/Desert Storm had been on the basis of an assessed special account, it is doubtful whether General Schwarzkopf and his legions would have left Florida.

It is only realistic to assume that military enforcement action on anything but a minimal scale will have to be paid for, in future as in the past, by special *ad hoc* arrangements outside the UN financial system. The costs of modern warfare are so astronomical that it would be fanciful to expect the United Nations to meet them out of a 'special account' assessed on any basis which might be acceptable to the membership. Nor would it be practicable to raise contingency funds which would do more than scratch the surface of expenditure on the scale required.

However, it would be complacent to assume that the need for military enforcement on any scale in the future will be centred on the richer areas of the world or that Germany and Japan, both dependent on Middle East oil, will be ready to foot bills over and above a normal level of assessment as they did in the Gulf crisis. It is more likely that future crises, be they civil or inter-state, will erupt in poorer areas of the world: indeed the financing of the substantial UN military and civilian presence to buttress the Cambodian peace settlement provides an early test of the willingness of the membership to put its money where its mouth has been in praising the new-found ability of the United Nations to function effectively in the post-Cold War world. (Press estimates in early 1992 suggest that the cost of UN intervention in Cambodia will be in the order of $1.9 billion.) The same is true of the incipient UN peacekeeping and peace-making operations in Yugoslavia and El Salvador.

It goes without saying that early payment of assessed contributions, both to the regular budget and to peacekeeping accounts, would make a world of difference. Given the relatively small sums involved, there seems no reason why this should not happen, particularly as, in the case of the major contributors in default, their stand was primarily a political gesture. However, if more is to be expected of the United Nations by way of peacekeeping, peace-making and enforcement in all contexts including those hitherto excluded by pedantic adherence to article 2(7), extra funds must be made available on a contingency basis. Such funds, which could be raised on an assessed basis similar to that used for peacekeeping accounts, could be used for sudden emergencies – for example, the need to deploy personnel immediately to cope with a man-made crisis. The tardiness of the creation of the 500-person lightly armed security unit to help protect the Kurds in northern Iraq in 1991 comes to mind. Several weeks after it had been decided to deploy them, only 10 per cent were on the ground because only $3 million of the $35 million required for the whole operation had been forthcoming. The Secretary-General had no reserve on which to draw. Equally a contingency fund could be used to put in place, for example, a small military force on a potential victim's side of a frontier in the case of a threat of inter-state aggression. Such a force on Kuwaiti territory from July 1990 might well have given Saddam Hussein pause.

Secretary-General Pérez de Cuéllar, by the end of his term of office, had reached similar conclusions. In a report to the General Assembly dated 19 November 1991 he reverted to the financial crisis in detail, and in strong language. The budgetary situation had changed only marginally since his earlier appeal in mid-September. Specifically he recommended that: (1) he be given permission to charge interest to all members on unpaid assessments; (2) that governments, the private sector and individuals should contribute to a $1 billion peace endowment fund, the income from which would finance fresh peacekeeping operations at their outset; (3) a Humanitarian Fund of $50 million should be raised for humanitarian and disaster relief operations until regular contributions had been levied; and (4) that he be authorised to borrow on the commercial market in a last resort.

Some of these proposals which are very much in line with the thoughts of the group (including a $50 million emergency fund to be financed by voluntary contributions) were shortly afterwards incorporated in GA resolution A/46/L55 and Corr.1 on humanitarian assistance which was adopted by consensus. Following its adoption the UK representative announced that his government had decided to contribute $5 million to the new fund. He added that if other potential donors would announce their contributions soon, the fund would be able to come into existence quickly.

In addition to the above developments the flotation of interest-bearing UN bonds would also be a possibility. Another suggestion worth serious consideration is the adoption of an international disaster relief insurance scheme as proposed by Ambassador Ernst Michanek in the Swedish journal *Development Dialogue*. The intention would be to secure funding for relief operations and assured benefits in certain contingencies. The insurance would be financed primarily by governments through fees and contributions agreed for long periods of time, the premiums to be assessed on the normal basis. The scheme would be organised as a non-governmental agency and existing relief organisations and institutions would be asked to undertake most of the operations under the insurance. The full text of the article is reproduced here as an appendix to this chapter.

APPENDIX

An International
Disaster Relief Insurance*

ERNST MICHANEK

Insurance and international cooperation

A most important method of financing and organization is that of insurance
– private or social – which is by definition a system of ensuring/securing
predictable cash payments (or services in kind, or both) in contingencies
that may be unexpected or continuous. The idea is to share certain risks
that all or many of the insured are exposed to, and to level out the costs for
at least certain basic services, e.g. medical treatment and food supplies,
between the insured persons or between periods of time over the long-term
in each insured person's lifetime. The system is meant to stabilize, and often
equalize, fees and to guarantee benefits within the insured population by
automatic payments and, usually, by the build-up of funds and buffer
stocks. In many cases what began on a voluntary basis as a small-scale,
local undertaking for mutual benefit in particularly disastrous situations,
has developed into a national system with 'universal coverage' and with
more or less pronounced characteristics of income redistribution within the
population covered.

International emergency aid programmes of a general nature have been
proposed from several quarters, e.g. by UNCTAD and the United Nations
for the 'poorest' countries, and by the Brandt Commission. In these contexts the financial and organizational questions have been treated fairly
conventionally, while more radical ideas of global taxes and automatic
mobilization of resources have been put forward in rather vague terms.
Admittedly, these questions are to be seen in a more long-term perspective
than the need for reforms in international disaster relief, which is urgent.
However, a discussion of international disaster relief that is based on the
automaticity characteristics of an insurance, should serve as a point of
departure for a discussion of automaticity in a wider context. The ultimate
aim should be to arrive at proposals for a system of international conventions on the organization and financing of the developments towards the
attainment of specific international targets such as a truly universal system
of primary health services, drinking water provision, basic food supply and
elementary education.

Global targets for social achievements should be both long-term and
short-term; short-term targets being based on realistic undertakings by
governments and parties to conventions on measures to reach the long-term
targets. This means that a 'universalisation' of a basic human right, such as

primary education, is coupled to a global sharing of the costs involved. This cost-sharing would imply varying degrees of automaticity in the transfer of resources from richer to poorer parts of the global community, similar to present arrangements at the national level for the equalization of opportunity between the different parts of one country.

International disaster relief

International cooperation in national and regional disaster situations is an accepted moral obligation and an established practice. The need for such cooperation is increasing but the organization of international disaster relief operations is deficient and so is the financing of such relief, being still almost totally dependent upon voluntary contributions collected for each specific disaster after it has occurred. And as new kinds of disaster occur (caused by previously unforeseen environmental or industrial factors, e.g. in the field of nuclear power production) a more elaborate system of disaster relief and new kinds of assistance operations are required.

Disaster relief requires a high degree of preparedness and speed of operation. Non-governmental organizations, which rely on and respond to the willingness of people to assist the victims of disasters, have built up a considerable capacity for relief. This should continue to form the basis of disaster relief. But governments should jointly create the financial framework that could guarantee basic services in poorer countries in disaster situations. This should take the form of an insurance, which would mean that finance for disaster relief could be provided 'on a continuous, predictable and assured basis' Among insurable contingencies, harvest losses as well as oil pollution damages seem to lend themselves to insurance schemes irrespective of a general disaster insurance scheme, and they could provide ideas or models for a wide system of indemnities.

The membership of the disaster insurance should be universal, all countries being invited to register under a convention outlining the duties and rights of the insured. The paying of fees and contributions should apply to all members, with due regard to their individual capacity to pay. The countries which today carry the main burden of disaster relief should be expected to pay the bulk of the costs for a build-up phase; in return they should expect the development of a more efficient relief service and, in the longer run, a planned and more equitable system of cost-sharing by all members. Damage resulting from a disaster should be evaluated by a central body and the level of indemnities paid (in cash and/or in kind) on the basis of the availability of funds and other resources. The present relief pattern can provide a basis for working out a system of priorities and definitions of and criteria for compensation. A clear priority is that the least developed and most disaster-ridden countries are net beneficiaries from the beginning and are likely to remain in that category, while richer and less disaster-prone countries are net contributors.

Countries should be insured against the effects of natural and man-made disasters, and against the cost of inflows of refugees fleeing disaster and conflict in other countries. A higher degree of disaster prevention and of preparedness for disasters is being developed, and the insurance rules should promote preventive control and planning activities aimed at reducing the effects of natural disasters.

The organization of disaster relief

A great many organizations deliver disaster relief, and many have their own field activities. The most efficient international disaster relief of a short-term nature is at present delivered by the non-governmental League of Red Cross Societies in Geneva (founded in 1919), consisting of 126 national Red Cross and Red Crescent societies around the world. The League in certain cases cooperates with the International Committee of the Red Cross (ICRC) in Geneva, and in many cases it coordinates its efforts with other major non-governmental bodies active in humanitarian aid. The League to a great extent makes use of donations given by governments and of public services offered in response to its appeals for funds when disasters occur, but its real base is the voluntary contributions from its membership and from the general public.

The organization of Red Cross disaster relief activities in the field also reflects the non-governmental character of the movement, relief missions being organized for each disaster case on its own merits and with administrative resources being drawn from a roster of field workers available at short notice. The League cooperates closely with governmental institutions and other public bodies in those countries where the disasters occur.

Within the UN system a number of organizations give assistance in disaster situations. UNHCR handles the refugee problems of man-made disasters, UNICEF the disaster needs of children and young mothers, FAO/WFP agricultural relief and emergency food assistance, and WHO the public health aspects of disasters. A number of other specialized agencies cover particular aspects. The Office of the United Nations Disaster Relief Coordinator (UNDRO), established in 1971, has a coordinating role and certain resources for the purpose, and cooperates closely with the UNDP and its field offices. The IBRD and the IMF – as well as the regional development banks – may also play important roles in economic disaster situations.

Among the intergovernmental organizations outside the UN system, the European Community (EEC) and the Organization of American States (OAS) have increasingly important roles in disaster situations. The EEC has developed an elaborate (and complicated) system for emergency aid and food aid. On the whole, however, emergency aid at the international level is in strong need of better coordination and probably reorganization. The organization and financing of such aid should be seen as interdependent.

Governments which finance disaster relief through the UN bodies, and often directly to countries of need, have in some cases their own disaster relief organs (sometimes cooperating closely with their military set-up, particularly in the field of transport). The governments of the disaster-stricken countries, which require international aid in many or most cases, have to carry the bulk of the burden of the disaster themselves, in so much as it is not left to the victims to overcome it on their own. In a number of cases governments of poor countries also take part in disaster relief to their neighbours.

The volume of disaster relief

In a recent evaluation of UNDRO, the Joint Inspection Unit (JIU) of the United Nations referred to an estimate that, between 1965 and 1975, disasters occurred at a worldwide rate of about one a week, killing more than 3.5 million people, affecting more than 400 million, and causing national damage running into tens of billions of dollars.[A1] These disasters necessitated almost US$5.3 billion for disaster relief within the affected countries and US$1.6 billion of assistance from the international community.

International disaster relief activities have grown rapidly and are likely to continue to do so. Rapid population growth has increased the severity of disasters: sudden natural catastrophes such as floods, hurricanes, earthquakes and fires affect more people, as do more long-term ones such as droughts and epidemics, and man-made ones such as wars between or within countries, while environmental or technological factors as well as weakened national development programmes add to the risk of disasters.

In these circumstances, aid to meet the mounting need for international disaster relief is likely to be financed from available funds presently allocated to development efforts; moral imperatives and public opinion contribute to this. Disaster relief as such may be given, firstly, as far as possible for the immediate 'impact phase' (when the disaster strikes), secondly, for the following 'emergency phase' during which life-securing measures are taken, and thirdly, for the 'rehabilitation phase', in which the basic elements of medical care, food, clothing, shelter and community services are provided. Such aid will probably have to continue to an increasing degree during the fourth and final 'reconstruction phase', i.e. the return to normality with opportunities for improvement and adjustment. In this way, resource transfers for development may in the future even more than is now the case, be influenced by disasters rather than by development planning.

The 'non-system' of disaster relief

Hundreds of donor governments and inter-governmental and voluntary organizations have in fact evolved a chaotic 'non-system' of independent responses to disaster needs, resulting in waste, omission, duplication and inefficiency in the delivery of relief supplies, equipment and personnel. There is concern that relief efforts even restore or deepen the poverty of the vulnerable groups in Third World countries, rather than contribute to positive longer-term reconstruction. The coordinating mechanism of

UNDRO has not had the capacity to coordinate effectively the disaster relief efforts of the various UN organizations, let alone those of other bodies. Most UN organs have not wanted UNDRO to play a leading role. UNDRO's own relief assistance, financed from the UN regular budget and from small donations, amounts to an insignificant part of the total relief assistance (in 1978–79 about 1 per cent).

New attempts at coordination

The conclusions and recommendations of the JIU do not build on the feelings voiced by some observers that UNDRO should simply be abolished (like its predecessor, the International Relief Union, created in 1927 under the aegis of the League of Nations). Rather they aim at a more clearly defined role for UNDRO, limited primarily to immediate relief assistance in sudden natural disasters, and at its inclusion in the UNDP set-up. As for the UN system as a whole, it is proposed that the urgent need for improved international relief coordination to deal with the many fund-raising, managerial, logistical, and policy problems generated by recent long-term emergency situations (Kampuchea, East Africa, the Sahel) be met by a new coordinating machinery: an inter-agency Emergency Assistance Committee within the UN system, which would invite appropriate voluntary organisations to attend its meetings and carry out disaster relief operations.

While this report is being considered within the United Nations, the League of Red Cross Societies is about to undertake a study on disaster relief, covering relief principles and rules, the present relief system, and the question of the progressive development of relief law and organization. The outline of the study deals with the practical and the human rights aspects of disaster relief as seen against the background of the experience of the Red Cross, the United Nations and other organizations.

At the same time, the efforts continue of the various bodies active in disaster relief in order to meet the increasingly pressing needs. One example was the April 1981 conference to solicit financial pledges from governments and aid agencies towards meeting the immediate problem of refugees in Africa, now totalling five million. The UNHCR and the Red Cross were the principal actors and potential distributors of funds; in all, US$560 million were reported as pledged.

The case for an international insurance

Disasters are both predictable and unpredictable. We never know exactly when, where and how a disaster will strike, but they do occur to a great extent in areas and in forms that we know fairly well from experience. We *can* prepare for them, minimize their impact, organize aid to the victims, and assure the financing of such aid. Rich nations do this for themselves; poor nations need international cooperation to do it. This would be to the mutual benefit of all.

As disasters increase in severity, so disaster relief and its costs rise. The organization of disaster relief today is too dispersed and uncoordinated. As more disasters occur and new numbers are added to the 12–13 million people already seeking refuge from areas of natural catastrophes, war and political unrest, the inadequate level of efficiency of the relief efforts may deteriorate further. Those who contribute now to international disaster relief will pay more in the future for relatively less efficient services. If the contributions were secured with a degree of automaticity by an international convention, and equally the risks covered, all parties would benefit.

An international disaster insurance should thus be created, financed primarily by governments but organized as a non-governmental agency. The beneficiaries should be primarily the poorer and disaster-prone countries or rather the actual disaster victim.

An important advantage of even a modest beginning to an insurance system would be that the individual donor country would not have to make its own instant evaluation of the likely damages caused by a disaster that has just struck, or of the political eligibility of a particular country at the actual time of disaster. After all, it is not a particular government that should be rewarded or punished at the moment of a disaster caused by outside forces; it is the disaster-struck people that should be helped irrespective of their leadership at the time.

Another advantage is that certain indemnities would be paid as of right and not on the basis of charity. Because of the pooling of funds and their ensuing anonymity, there could be no bargaining for political favours at the moment of disaster. At the same time, the insurance is not likely to cover more than a part of the losses that have occurred; the room for politically motivated gestures of friendship would still be considerable.

There would also be ample room for continued voluntary service to alleviate the plight of the disaster's victims and for the collection of funds for voluntary activities. In fact, disasters at present cause damage of such size and scope that in many cases both public and voluntary aid to the victims is close to totally inadequate for real relief and rehabilitation; this can cause feelings of helplessness and passivity on the part of potential donors to voluntary programmes. Insomuch as the insurance covers a basic indemnity, voluntary additions may be just as worthwhile as they are now or even more so.

The utilization of existing bodies

The disaster insurance agency should commission the services under the insurance to be rendered from the most efficient organizations and firms, as with health services under a national insurance or tax-financed scheme or salvage operations under a marine insurance. As things stand at present, the Red Cross and other non-governmental organizations and institutions would be very likely to be in great demand as executive relief agencies.

Control of benefits

Indemnities or benefits of the disaster insurance should be clearly directed towards the actual victims of the disaster. Payments should not be made directly to governments, except for the kind of services that are normally provided by them. The indemnities or benefits should be delivered in such a way that they genuinely restore the situation to what it was before the disaster, or rehabilitate the victims. The indemnities would thus take very much the same form as now, and they would be directed so as to prevent, as far as possible, the same calamity occurring again or striking as severely.

Disaster victims in a country that has its own social insurance system (one that covers risks connected with natural disasters) are at an advantage compared to those who are not so covered.

As shown by reports from the International Social Security Association on the evolution of social security,[A2] the social security trends in Third World countries, although not without encouraging features, are in no way comparable to the trends observed in the industrialized countries; they reflect the existing stage of socio-economic development of Third World countries. In these countries, the rural population in particular and the non-wage-earning population as a whole are generally not covered, or only poorly, by national social security schemes and are thus particularly hard hit by disasters. Thus one of the aims of the disaster insurance agency should be to promote the growth of domestic social security systems in disaster-prone countries, corresponding to their level of development, so as to contribute to their disaster preparedness.

A non-governmental body

The disaster insurance agency can be built up as a cooperative enterprise by organizations (non-governmental, mixed and governmental) that currently exist in the field of disaster relief and refugee aid. It should not be an inter-governmental agency, but an independent institution working under an international convention on disaster relief, responsible to a board of trustees of its own, as a foundation or similar entity. This body should have the power to carry out, on behalf of a number of currently existing organisations, both central and field functions that could be more efficiently performed if they were not spread among so many. All existing functions would remain with inter-governmental or non-governmental organizations of the type which now exist, but they would not all have to carry out field work on their own. For poor countries in disaster situations, this would mean an easing of the burden they currently sometimes encounter: a flood of helpers that is not much easier to cope with than a sudden flood of their main river.

Securing contributions

A degree of automaticity is introduced into disaster relief finance by providing the insurance scheme with a basis of additional assessed and negotiated contributions from all governments. Disaster relief finance would thus be secured at three levels:

1. There should be assessed fees from governments, agreed for long periods and to be revised at given intervals. Corresponding to the present small

allocations for such a purpose within the United Nations, these contributions would cover the most essential services including basic administration, coordination and cost of permanent institutional infrastructure.

2. There should be a level of additional standing contributions by all governments, negotiated over a number of years (e.g. for three years like the periodic replenishments of the IDA, the IBRD affiliate) on the basis of past trends of contributions by governments to international disaster relief operations. These contributions would be used to finance the first, most immediate relief measures in a particular disaster area including procurement of most urgently required goods and services as well as organization of transport, other logistical measures and liaison with local authorities, enabling all non-governmental and governmental relief organizations to launch their operations in the area in an orderly, complementary and effective manner, as and when they decide to do so. Contributions at the first and second levels should provide for annual payments in the order of US$500 million at the outset.

3. There should continue to be a voluntary level of contribution from both governmental and non-governmental sources.

The body responsible for the insurance should be in a position to appeal for additional contributions from governmental and non-governmental sources in cases of extraordinary requirements. In most cases, however, the non-governmental organizations would be expected to use their own funds for relief actions which they wish to undertake, as a supplement to the basic services provided for by the insurance or in cases where the insurance is not active. Extraordinary governmental donations would be expected to be added to and, through donor action, coordinated with the services from the insurance.

The first practical steps

Action towards the creation of an international disaster relief insurance should begin outside the UN system. The first step to take is to organize a group to study a specific case of a 'typical' disaster (e.g. Somalia).

The group should analyse the present deficiencies, as demonstrated, and the potential remedies under a system of more automatic reaction to that same disaster by a body with an insurance-like system of finance and organization at hand.

The study should be undertaken in close cooperation with the League of Red Cross Societies, without asking them to take responsibility for its conduct and conclusion. As a part of the study, a draft convention on an international disaster relief insurance should be worked out.

Notes

1. This amounts to 56.155 per cent of peacekeeping bills according to Michael Littlejohns, UN correspondent, in the *Financial Times*, 28 February 1992.

Notes to Appendix

* Reprinted from *Development Dialogue* (journal of the Dag Hammarskjöld Foundation, Uppsala, Sweden) 1981 (1). The Study Group is grateful to both Ambassador Michanek and the Dag Hammarskjöld Foundation for granting it permission to reproduce this interesting proposal.

A1. *Evaluation of the Office of the United Nations Disaster Relief Coordinator*, prepared by the Joint Inspection Unit, JIU/REP/80/11.

A2. *International Social Security Association, Report 1, Evolution of social security and ISSA activities 1974–1977* (Geneva: UN, 1978).

CHAPTER 8

Conclusions and recommendations

ANTHONY PARSONS

As Peter Calvocoressi points out in the first chapter, the UN Charter is a multilateral treaty voluntarily subscribed to by its original signatories and subsequent adherents. In this context it resembles regional organisations such as the Organization of American States, rather than institutions such as the European Community which have aspirations for closer political unity amongst the membership. The United Nations is not and was never intended to be an embryonic world government. The rhetorical phrase 'We the Peoples of the United Nations' with which the Preamble to the Charter opens could more realistically have read 'We the Governments of Member States of the United Nations'. The organisation is grounded in the notion of state sovereignty, a notion jealously guarded as the membership has increased from the original total of 51 to the present figure of 178, largely through the collapse of the European empires, a process now nearing completion with the disintegration of the former Soviet Union.

The inviolability of this sovereignty is, as Nigel Rodley makes clear in Chapter 2, safeguarded in principle by article 2(4) of the Charter, which forbids the threat or use of force against the territorial integrity or political independence of any state and, more particularly, by article 2(7) which states that

> Nothing contained in the present Charter shall authorise the United Nations to intervene in matters which are essentially within the domestic jurisdiction of any state or shall require the Members to submit such matters to settlement under the present Charter; but this principle shall not prejudice the application of enforcement measures under Chapter VII.

This final phrase representing a qualification of which many are unaware. Little emphasis was laid in the early years on the contradiction

213

apparent to the non-legal mind between article 2(7) and articles 55 and 56. Under these two articles, members and the organisation itself are pledged to promote *inter alia* observance of human rights and fundamental freedoms. Yet it was taken for granted that the United Nations was debarred by article 2(7) from action against a member state which broke the pledge in article 56 by violating the human rights of its citizens. Human rights were regarded as falling within 'domestic jurisdiction'. Promotion rather than correction was the purpose.

As the earlier chapters indicate, there has been a considerable erosion of this bulwark against international action over the past 30 years. General Assembly resolution 1514 of 1960 effectively torpedoed the position maintained by colonial powers in the 1940s and 1950s that the process of decolonisation, however turbulent as in the cases, for example, of Algeria, Cyprus, southern Africa, Indochina and many others, lay within domestic jurisdiction and was therefore no business of the United Nations. From the 1960s apartheid in South Africa, regardless of its essentially domestic nature, was taken up by the General Assembly and the Security Council as a result of international outrage. In 1965 Britain took the initiative in bringing the internal rebellion in Southern Rhodesia before the Security Council. In 1968 Britain announced that it would not invoke article 2(7) where questions of human rights were concerned. The adoption in 1948 of the Universal Declaration of Human Rights had already called this restriction into question. The coming into force in 1976 of the International Covenants on Civil and Political and Economic, Social and Cultural Rights accelerated the process of erosion of 2(7) while the Commission on Human Rights and its subordinate bodies have for years regularly scrutinised and condemned human rights violations both thematically and in regard to individual states (see Chapter 5 for detailed analysis).

There has not been a comparable change in the attitude towards civil conflict, in spite of UN involvement in such situations in relation to decolonisation since 1960. There have in fact been far more civil wars than inter-state wars in the past 30 years. But the international community has resolutely turned its back on most of them, on article 2(7) grounds. Burma, Nigeria, Sudan, Mozambique, Angola (until outside powers such as South Africa, Cuba and the United States intervened on different sides), Rwanda, Burundi Somalia, Chad, Sri Lanka come to mind; and there are others. Yugoslavia may come to represent an important turning point.

Nor, until very recently, has the world reacted with anything beyond emergency relief to cases of man-made disasters arising out of massive human rights violations and/or civil war. Famine, and the displacement of peoples by the million, have resulted from these evils but, except in a handful of cases, no international attempt has been made to redress the causes when they have fallen technically within the domestic jurisdiction of states. The international community has found itself, as in Sudan and Ethiopia, in the bizarre position of mobilising large sums of money and sending personnel into exacting and sometimes dangerous situations while denying itself the opportunity of bringing together cause and effect in an attempt to ameliorate both.

Indeed, up to the end of the 1970s, the United Nations and the regional organisations recognised as such under Chapter VIII of the Charter (the Organization of American States (OAS), the Arab League and the Organisation of African Unity (OAU)) had little to congratulate themselves on in the above regards. Coercive action against South Africa to bring an end to apartheid was limited to an arms embargo by the threat of Western vetoes. Non-aligned solidarity, citing article 2(7), had helped to immunise abominable dictatorships such as those of Idi Amin in Uganda, 'Emperor' Bokassa in the Central African Republic, Macias Nguema in Equatorial Guinea and, above all, Pol Pot in Cambodia against international criticism, let alone action, as they tortured and massacred their populations. The great powers, paralysed by East–West competition, did little or nothing to break this silence except where a point could be scored against an adversary without fear of reciprocity. The well-tried saying that 'he may be a sonofabitch but he's our sonofabitch', led to a general self-denying ordinance over arraignment for human rights violations of regimes such as the Ba'athists in Syria and Iraq, the Pahlavi monarchy in Iran and the military regimes in Central and South America which were prosecuting 'dirty wars'. (I was Ambassador in Teheran from 1974–79 and thereafter UK Permanent Representative to the United Nations in New York. I have not forgotten the statements made in the General Assembly in 1979 by the representatives of the new governments of Uganda, Equatorial Guinea and Iran. 'Where were you, the United Nations, when we were crying for help?' they were in effect saying. An uneasy silence fell on the Assembly Hall.)

It is also significant in terms of the general desire to protect the continuing validity of articles 2(4) and 2(7) that states which were ultimately compelled to intervene unilaterally to depose monstrous regimes felt obliged to do so under the fiction of self-defence under article 51 of the Charter – the Tanzanian invasion of Uganda in 1979 to topple Amin and the Vietnamese invasion of Cambodia in 1978 which drove out the Khmer Rouge. By the same token, as Paul Fifoot has pointed out in Chapter 5, British recourse to the mandatory provisions of Chapter VII of the Charter against the rebel regime in Southern Rhodesia in 1966, and the arms embargo against South Africa in 1977 both necessitated recourse to a more or less tenuous threat to international peace and security. Otherwise external interventions in civil wars usually took place only at the invitation of a recognised government – Britain, Iran and Jordan in Oman from 1970–75, the United States in Lebanon in 1958, Egypt in the Yemen in 1964 (countered by Saudi Arabia on the opposite side), as well as 'regional' involvements – the Arab League in Kuwait in 1961, the Arab Defence Force in the Lebanon from 1976 and the unsuccessful OAU intervention in Chad in 1979 and again in 1981–82. The American engagement in Vietnam from 1963 to 1973 is in a class by itself.

The above were instances of military action or of mandatory non-military measures, i.e. of enforcement. The elaborate human rights structure of the United Nations, based on the Charter itself, the Universal Declaration, the Human Rights Commission and its subordinate bodies and the two Covenants, is wholly recommendatory. Within this framework there is no shortage of fora for debate, for the adoption of resolutions, for condemnatory statements, for investigations (with the consent of the party or parties concerned). But there is no provision for compulsion or coercion. It is entirely up to those at the receiving end of the admonitions of the UN human rights machine to accept or ignore its exhortations and recommendations.

It is impossible precisely to evaluate the impact on human rights violators of this non-mandatory international machinery. It has to be considered in conjunction with the effect of criticism in Western public media, the activities of campaigning non-governmental organizations such as Amnesty International and bilateral diplomatic representations. It is almost certainly true that the Pol Pots and Idi Amins, even if not shielded from UN scrutiny by superpower patrons or the voting strength of regional blocs, would have been, indeed were, deaf to any manifestations of disapproval. It is equally unlikely that, in the pre-*glasnost* years, regimes like those of Iraq and Syria would have been exposed even to private criticism from their Soviet patrons.

It is more difficult to judge retrospectively whether more could have been done by external persuasion and pressure to improve the human rights record of states friendly to the West in which there were major abuses falling short of the horrors perpetrated by some of the monsters mentioned above. I served as a diplomat in many such states, monarchical Iran being the most vivid case in point. I inclined to the view that the Shah's performance should be compared not with that of a Western democracy but with that of regional neighbours such as Iraq (much worse) or Afghanistan (equally bad if not worse); that Iran, autocratically governed for millenia, could not be expected to turn overnight into Scandinavia and that the Shah was at least doing his best for the economic and social rights of his people, even at the expense of the civil and political. I was therefore disposed to recommend that high-level private lectures by visiting VIPs were not only a waste of time but would infuriate the audience and thus benefit our competitors and adversaries at the expense of our commercial, strategic and political interests. I was also cautious of recommending private representations on behalf of individual political prisoners: success could not be guaranteed. On one occasion the person on whose behalf I appealed was, shortly afterwards, 'shot while trying to escape'.

This policy may not have been edifying but it is impossible with the passage of years to conclude that a more vigorous attitude would have been more effective. Since it was common to most Western governments, there is no empirical evidence either way. By the same token, criticism in the UN human rights machinery was too scantily publicised to have much impact, although it was clearly not totally ineffective. Otherwise states would not have made such intense efforts to avoid condemnation.

However, it is true that media exposure and public criticism by non governmental organisations such as Amnesty International, however vociferously resented, did on occasions lead to improvements in thematic terms, for example as regards torture and detention without trial, especially when the offending government believed that such criticism would generate public condemnation in the West which would reach a scale likely to damage its relationship with countries whose friendship and support were important.

The foregoing chapters note and reflect the profound changes which have taken place in the international configuration over the past five or six years and especially since 1989. Chapters 5 and 6, by Paul Fifoot and Richard Connaughton, set out in detail the range of persuasive and coercive instruments at the disposal of the United Nations from Chapter VI mediation to the imposition of mandatory sanctions or, as a last resort, the use of force under Chapter VII. Chapter 2 examines the legal context in which these steps and measures could or could not be put into effect against the background of article 2(7) as modified by the passage of time. Chapter 1 poses the question 'are illegal and criminal acts to be condemned and prohibited but not redressed or punished?'

There is no doubt that the international climate is more propitious than ever before for international action to redress massive human rights violations, to intervene to bring about peaceful settlement of civil conflicts and to address the causes of man-made disasters arising out of either or both these manifestations. This is not to say that the sovereignty provisions in the UN Charter will be formally amended. They will not. But an opportunity is at hand for the further dilution of their rigour, or rather to find ways of reinterpreting them short of structural breach. This would be in accordance with the way in which the application of the Charter has evolved pragmatically and without formal amendment over the decades even in the bleakest years of the Cold War. As it became clear that military enforcement action as envisaged in Chapter VII was impossible, peacekeeping – blue helmets and blue berets – developed under Chapter VI, presupposing the consent of parties to a dispute or conflict: in certain cases peacekeeping has taken place in a grey area between Chapter VI persuasion and Chapter VII enforcement, an area known as 'Chapter VI and a half'. The Congo operation was the first example of this. The Uniting for Peace procedure was adopted to give the General Assembly greater authority when the Security Council was blocked by vetoes; the 'enemy states' articles remain in the Charter (articles 77 and 107) but the states in question are now leading members of the organisation; and I have already touched on the developments in the interpretation of article 2(7).

Now the Cold War is over, the worldwide East–West confrontation is at an end: except in China and one or two insignificant states, communism has collapsed across the globe. American paranoia about the Red peril already seems as unreal as the accusations of witchcraft against the ladies of Salem. The 'our sonofabitch' doctrine, unsavoury at the worst of times, has lost validity even to the doughtiest exponents of *realpolitik*. With no clearly defined East to set against a clearly defined West, the solidarity consequent on group loyalty may crumble and bloc voting on a North vs. South or East vs. West pattern in UN organs may begin to wither. The staggering developments in mass communications over the past decade have brought a searchlight to bear on the darkest corners of the earth. Politically, the fresh tidal wave of ethnic nationalism released by the collapse of the Communist empire has been mirrored by complementary pressure towards pluralistic democracy. Even in areas most resistant to such change, such as Latin America and sub-Saharan Africa, the tide is flowing; tyrannies are falling and single party dictatorships such as Castro's Cuba are becoming the exception rather than the rule. Only parts of Asia continue to resist the tide. For the first time probably since 1945 there are at the moment no active inter-state wars in progress, while the withdrawal of superpower or regional outside support from one side or both has helped

to bring about peace in some of the bloodiest civil wars of the 1980s –
Angola (linked to the independence of Namibia), Lebanon, El
Salvador and Ethiopia are examples. Even in Afghanistan and
Cambodia the direction of events is towards peaceful settlement.

Against this background of growing global convergence, both political and economic, there is a nascent mood of public intolerance of
the notion that concern for human rights should stop at national
borders and that only inter-state wars and natural, not man-made,
disasters should be of concern to the international community.
Pedantic invocation of article 2(7) as buttress for the doctrine of non-
interference in domestic affairs is unacceptable to Western public
opinion as we saw in the aftermath of the Gulf War, admittedly a
very special case. The public media, with its unprecedented power
both to lead and to reflect public concern, refused to allow governments to stand back and ignore the plight and suffering of the Kurds
of northern Iraq under pressure of the persecution of Saddam
Hussein's military and security apparatus, the incident described in
detail by Lawrence Freedman and David Boren in Chapter 3. The
occupation of areas of Iraqi Kurdistan by coalition forces and the
establishment of 'safe havens' was the result. By the same token it is
difficult to imagine, for example, the OAU throwing a protective
screen around another Idi Amin or Bokassa, or even the Chinese, for
all their unreconstructed behaviour in Tiananmen Square and
general policy of domestic repression, shielding another Pol Pot from
international censure.

However, an age of sweetness and light is not just over the horizon.
There are between 15 and 20 civil wars going on as I write. One – in
Sudan — has caused casualties and displacement of people by the
million. Others have been scarcely less bloody relative to size of
population. One UN member state, Somalia, has almost unnoticed
collapsed into anarchy. Amnesty International's report for 1991 cata-
logues a lamentable list of worldwide human rights abuses, although
its general tone is less apocalyptic than in previous years. There are
plenty of regimes in the world which, while preaching freedom and
democracy, practise repression, while events in Yugoslavia (see
Chapter 4 by James Gow and Lawrence Freedman) demonstrate
that, as previous civil conflicts are settled, ethnic nationalism is
bound to give rise to fresh ones. A new world order based on peace
and democratic freedom is still a very long way away.

It is more than likely that the powerful governments which could
do something about situations within the domestic jurisdiction of
states as traditionally understood will be reluctant to involve themselves gratuitously in fresh endeavours. The states of the former
Soviet Union will be too preoccupied with trying to construct a new

dispensation out of the ruins of involuntary decolonisation. The diplomatic and military resources of the European democracies are already at full stretch in dealing with the controversial issue of the future of the European Community, with relations with Eastern Europe, the future of defence structures and transatlantic links forged in Cold War times, turbulence in the Balkans and a multitude of other pressing concerns. They will be disposed to take the view that there is more than enough on their plates to risk unnecessary involvement in situations in which they are more likely to attract kicks than ha'pence. The United States, the sole superpower, is already shouldering massive burdens and there are signs of domestic resentment at the notion that America should be a 'world policeman'. Voices are being heard arguing for closer concentration on solving the economic and social problems of the United States rather than neglecting them in favour of more glamorous foreign involvements. Non-aligned states (whatever that phrase may now mean) are already showing signs of resistance to the opening of further cracks in the wall of article 2(7).

The general attitude of the Non-Aligned Movement (NAM) towards the new dispensation has yet to crystallise. Resentment at American domination of the Security Council and the General Assembly (viz. the corridor clamour that the United States 'hijacked' the Council in the Kuwait crisis and uneasiness over the American stage management of the repeal of the 'Zionism is Racism' resolution in December 1991) is bound to develop and is likely to be fanned if the Western democracies show too strong an inclination to brush aside the sanctity of domestic jurisdiction in the Third World. At the same time the 1991 Accra summit meeting of the NAM revealed an awareness of a relationship between domestic performance, for example in the espousal of human rights and political pluralism, and foreign policy credibility in relation to the developed world. Equally, with no Eastern bloc for the recipients to turn to, Western donors are becoming less inhibited about linking development aid to 'good government', and it is likely that economic development will be the principal preoccupation of the NAM majority in the years to come. In a nutshell, the 1990s are likely to witness within the NAM, if not its collapse or merger with the economic Group of 77, a continuing struggle between a growing group of 'moderates' and a dwindling band of 'old fashioned radicals', as well as unpredictable swings of the pendulum between expressions of resentment at the unchallengeable power of the American-led West, and acceptance of the reality of the need for Western economic support.

Whatever happens, all governments in all geographical and functional groupings, should bear in mind that, if neglected, situations in 'far-away' countries can deteriorate to a point where crisis action of major proportions is demanded. For example, the great powers were not inclined to take action against Iraq's invasion of Iran in 1980 and were indifferent to the continuation of the war so long as neither side was likely to win an outright victory. But we are now conscious that if, for example, the Security Council had demanded Iraqi withdrawal from Iranian territory in September 1980 with a credible threat of mandatory economic sanctions in the event of non-compliance and if, as was likely at that time, Saddam Hussein had complied, the chain of events which led 10 years later to the Iraqi invasion of Kuwait in August 1990 would not have occurred. It is also clear from Chapter 4 that there was plenty of warning of the current situation in Yugoslavia but that no attempt was made to forestall the outbreak of civil war.

What happens in the future will thus depend more on the attitude of mind of governments and publics in the international community, whether in the context of the United Nations itself or of regional and sub-regional organisations, than on the letter of the law as understood heretofore. It is easy to hide behind article 2(7). It is equally easy to conclude that almost any civil conflict or man-made disaster arising out of human rights violations has a transnational dimension and should be tackled internationally. The civil war in Sudan, for example, has spilt over the borders of Chad, Uganda and Ethiopia, posing in practice a more realistic threat to 'international peace and security' than the Southern Rhodesian rebellion did in 1966. But the United Nations, for a whole series of reasons, has chosen to regard it as a strictly internal matter, of concern only to Sudan and, by a stretch of imagination, to the Organisation of African Unity.

The most vivid contemporary example of the other side of the coin has been, as already mentioned, the adoption of Security Council resolution 688 (1991) and the consequent intervention by the UN Secretariat and armed forces of the allied coalition in the domestic affairs of Iraq. Resolution 688 may not, strictly speaking, have been a Chapter VII resolution but it was adopted against the background of a Chapter VII situation arising out of Iraq's aggression against Kuwait. But the oppression which it condemned and the cessation of which it demanded had arisen out of the internal rebellions of the Kurdish and Shia Muslim communities, the violation of Iraq's sovereignty being excused by the impingement on international peace and security of the cross-border flight of hundreds of thousands of refugees. But it is also significant that, of all the dozen or so resolutions adopted by the Security Council following the Iraqi invasion of Kuwait, resolution 688 received the lowest positive vote (10), the highest negative vote (3) and an abstention by a permanent member

(China). The 2(7) skeleton was rattling in the cupboard.

This operation took place without benefit of the invitation or acquiescence of the party concerned, the government of Iraq, although the humanitarian activities of Secretariat personnel required prior negotiation with Baghdad. In what may be described as a Chapter VI context, the most dramatic recent example of the setting aside of article 2(7) in the interest of peace and democratisation has been the combined OAS/UN exercise in Central America dating from the Esquipulas Agreements of 1987 between the presidents of the five Central American states. The Agreements dealt with issues of national reconciliation, an end to hostilities, democratisation, free elections, termination of aid to insurrectionist movements, etc. and provided for international verification. In this overall framework, with the endorsement of the General Assembly and the Security Council as appropriate, the United Nations has, at the invitation of the Central American presidents, engaged in a series of activities which would normally be regarded as strictly within the domestic domain: monitoring elections in Nicaragua in 1989, the disarming and demobilising of the Nicaraguan contras, mediation between government and rebels in El Salvador, and verification of human rights in El Salvador. A combined civilian and military organisation, ONUCA, was established in 1989 for these and other analogous purposes, and an offshoot, ONURSAL, is currently active in El Salvador.

In the same part of the world the United Nations was invited to supervise elections in Haiti in 1990. Although the Security Council responded cautiously when asked to react firmly to the overthrow of the elected government by a military coup in October 1991, it went as far as to issue a presidential statement condemning the coup. Furthermore the General Assembly, on 11 October 1991, adopted by consensus a resolution condemning the coup, affirming the unacceptability of the military junta, and appealing to all member states to support the action being taken by the OAS to redress the situation.

Again in 1991, the international community, first the European Community and the Western European Union, then the UN Security Council, has been relatively uninhibited in involving itself in the internal conflict in Yugoslavia, to the extent of the Council adopting resolution 713 'deciding under Chapter VII' on an embargo on military supplies to Yugoslavia. This resolution also, for the first time in the history of the Security Council, invokes Chapter VIII of the Charter – Regional Arrangements. In this case the liberal interpretation of article 2(7) has been based on the positive attitude towards Security Council involvement of the effectively non-existent Yugoslav federal authorities. Subsequently the Council decided in principle to deploy a substantial peacekeeping force to separate Serbs from Croats and to monitor demilitarised zones in Croatia.

The above are valuable precedents but, in general, the international response to the question of intervention in the domestic affairs of states will continue to be patchy and to depend on a number of factors. The letter of article 2(7) will be most strictly adhered to in countries remote from great power interests – Burma, Sudan and Somalia – and most readily bypassed in more sensitive locations – the Middle East, South East Europe and the Caribbean. Much will depend on the attitudes of individual states or groups of states. The Central American presidents rated peace higher than strict adherence to the doctrine of non-intervention. President Assad of Syria, if faced with another rebellion analogous to what happened in Hama in 1982, could be expected to take a different attitude. Regional groups of states will decide on physical intervention in the light of practicalities. It was relatively easy for the ECOWAS states of West Africa to send troops into Liberia in 1990 when all authority collapsed; to mount an operation physically to separate Serbs from Croats even with the apparent agreement of both has presented greater problems. In this context the Security Council, in resolution 721 of 21 November 1991, agreed to the despatch of a peacekeeping force to Yugoslavia only if a cease-fire was in place and respected.

It is arguable that intervention to deal with another Idi Amin or Pol Pot would be easier than to disentangle combatants in the labyrinth of a civil war: on the face of it, in such cases, the cure lies in the simple expedient of toppling the offending regime. But subsequent events in Uganda and Cambodia demonstrate that this argument is flawed. Equally, some situations lend themselves more readily to external involvement than others. It is hard to see what outsiders could do to help over the Shining Path insurrection in Peru except to offer technical assistance to improve the shocking human rights performance of the security forces which at present more than matches the brutalities of the guerrillas. It is equally difficult to see, after the bloody fiasco of the Indian 'peacekeeping' intervention, what the international community could usefully do to bring reconciliation and peace to Sri Lanka. The present level of anarchy and violence in Somalia is probably beyond redemption, whereas there is a valid solution to the civil war in Sudan – federal autonomy between the two distinct halves of the country – if the right levers could be brought to bear on the parties. I could give other examples supporting or opposing the desirability and practicality of external intervention. In UN terms much will depend on developments in China. The other permanent members have less reason than before to be inhibited by article 2(7) either in terms of their own records (the former Soviet Union) or of protecting client states. But China is still domestically repressive and determined to allow no freedom to the peripheral provinces of the Empire, particularly the Tibetans; and it would be an uneasy partner in any discussion *à cinq* of these matters.

Against this tangled background, it would be artificial and unrealistic to recommend hard and fast rules for governments confronting the multitudinous challenges of the post-Cold War world. But certain guidelines suggest themselves.

Policy trends

Governments which deploy global or region-wide foreign policies should not swim against the present tide which is flowing in the direction of greater international involvement in matters hitherto regarded as falling within the domestic jurisdiction of states. The argument that such a policy invites reciprocal interference, for example over Northern Ireland in the case of Britain, has lost much of its force with the end of the Cold War and the erosion of bloc voting in multilateral organisations. Fear of losing profitable commercial contracts to less scrupulous competitors by offending touchy dictators has, or should have, become less of an inhibition as views about grave human rights violations and other comparable outrages have converged, not only in the First World. The cut-throat nature of commercial competition in, for example, the Middle East in the great oil boom of the 1970s is probably fading into the past. Less credence is given in the changing world of mass communication to 'Orientalist' argumentation that human rights standards and systems of government are so deeply rooted in historical cultures that what would be regarded as intolerable in one part of the world must be accepted as normal practice in another.

The criterion for the future should therefore be an objective analysis of whether external involvement would be effective or counterproductive and, if the former, by which means and by which state or group of states, and under the authority of which international organisation or organisations it should be set in train. As already suggested, where there is a will to intervene, a way can always be found around the legalistic obstacles.

This proposal does not amount to advocacy of unrestrained international busybodying by purportedly high-minded Western democracies. As discussed above, there are many instances in which outside involvement would be useless, if not harmful. It is rather a reflection of recognition that the global mood is changing, as recent events have suggested, and that governments, like it or not, are going to come under increasing public pressure to regard article 2(7) and all its works as a formulation capable of redefinition rather than a respectable defensive redoubt. The multilateral reaction to Saddam Hussein's persecution of Kurds and Shi'ites, to the civil war in Yugoslavia and to the military coup against the democratically elected President Aristide of Haiti amount to more than simple straws in the wind. Indeed, the former UN Secretary-General, Javier Pérez de Cuéllar, shortly before leaving office, spoke of the need for the establishment of a 'kind of court' comprising unbiased persons free from governmental control to decide episodically on circumstances in which the right of the international community to intervene in the domestic affairs of a state was justified.

Furthermore, on 18 December 1991, the General Assembly adopted a resolution appointing a high-level humanitarian aid coordinator with authority to organise the efforts of many different UN agencies involved in efforts following natural or man-made disasters and to pressurise recalcitrant governments denying aid to suffering people or using relief assistance for political ends.

Pre-emptive diplomacy

The avoidable failure by the United Nations to pre-empt catastrophic conflict over the past decade has underlined the need to develop this neglected instrument. For some years voices have been crying in the wilderness advocating pre-emptive action before crises explode into conflict. It is encouraging that, at long last, this innovation was endorsed in a public statement by the five permanent members in New York, in October 1991 and further confirmed in the Heads of Government meeting of the Security Council at the end of January 1992.

Firm, coordinated action by the permanent members could, for example, almost certainly have aborted the Iraqi invasion of Iran in 1980, the Israeli invasion of Lebanon in 1982 and the Iraqi invasion of Kuwait in 1990. In all these cases there was a period of months in which tension rose and hostilities became more likely. For different reasons no diplomatic attempts to prevent the drift to war were made: in the case of Kuwait, the divisions in the regional organisation, the Arab League, were a contributory factor. In all cases, either no signals or the wrong signals were sent. No warnings were issued, publicly or privately, of the international consequences of precipitating war. International silence was received as acquiescence.

It is to be hoped that the lesson has been learnt and that a regular practice will be put in place in New York under which the UN Secretary-General and members of the Security Council can monitor potential trouble spots on a regular basis and, if necessary, take action with potential aggressors or to protect potential victims before it is too late. Regional organisations should by the same token establish analogous mechanisms, the Conflict Prevention Centre set up by the CSCE in Vienna being a good example (although it was too recently created to do anything about the incipient conflict in Yugoslavia).

Such mechanisms should also focus on nascent developing civil conflicts analogous to that in Yugoslavia and on incipient large scale human rights violations in order to bring pre-emptive pressure to bear wherever practicable. This pressure could take the form of collective *démarches* to governments to make clear that the international community would not turn its back if the situation degenerated into open warfare or massive human rights violation. If sufficient goodwill existed, international mediation or conciliation could be offered (as in Central America since 1989) or a 'deterrent' force to separate communities heading towards conflict with each other (something of this kind might have been attempted in Yugoslavia before the outcome of fighting made it impossible). It could be made plain that if international efforts consistent with the terms of Chapter VI of the Charter (pacific settlement of disputes) were unavailing, recourse would be had to enforcement measures under Chapter VII in which the protection of article 2(7) does not apply (the mandatory arms embargoes against Yugoslavia and Somalia are useful precedents) and that, if the worst came to the worst, these would not be confined to non-military measures (sanctions) if the international community agreed that military enforcement was both practicable and desirable (the precedent here being the protection of the Kurds in northern Iraq).

In the light of the quick, decisive and effective action by the Security Council in response to the Iraqi invasion of Kuwait on 2 August 1990, it is not difficult to envisage pre-emptive action of this kind being taken by the Council in regard to future potential international causes, the corollary being that if the warnings were rebuffed or went unheeded, the Council would translate threat into action if ultimately necessary.

It is of course much harder to envisage prior agreement on the structural replication on a contingency (or actual) basis of the incremental steps in Chapter VI and the measures in Chapter VII in cases of civil conflict, etc. This would make explicit the pragmatic assumption already tacitly made that the more relaxed interpretation of article 2(7) evident in the examples of northern Iraq, Yugoslavia and Somalia will in the 1990s become the rule rather than the exception where it is judged that external involvement will be beneficial. This would amount to a great leap forward which China for one, and certain non-aligned and non-permanent members of the Security Council, let alone a majority in the General Assembly, may well prove to be reluctant to take.

This problem would be considerably eased if the regional organisations were to give higher priority to pre-emptive diplomacy within their own terms of reference and if there were close and more continuous liaison on such matters between the regional organisations and the main organs of the United Nations. In cases of incipient civil conflict or human rights violations it is right that the regional organisation concerned should be the first to intervene and, if practicable, to shoulder the main burden. This has been the case with the OAS and Haiti, the EC, WEU and CSCE and Yugoslavia, and, with hindsight, the Arab League should have been more vigorous in its efforts to prevent Saddam Hussein from invading Kuwait. It is true that not every member state of the international community is embraced in an effective regional organisation, but if sub-regional bodies such as ASEAN and the South Pacific Forum are included, there are only a few left out in the cold. Indeed, in 1990 we saw a sub-regional organization which had been created entirely for economic purposes, ECOWAS, take military enforcement action to restore order in a purely domestic crisis in a member state, Liberia.

In a nutshell it would make it easier for the more reserved members of the Security Council if notionally domestic questions were brought to the Council's attention either by a regional organisation or after all efforts by that regional organisation had failed.

Arms transfers

The Gulf crisis revealed in vivid fashion the consequences of the pursuit of commercial, financial and industrial advantage, combined with East–West competition and the need for medium-sized powers to secure major export markets if they are to retain indigenous military industries, all at work in a conflict-ridden area possessing great wealth in which militarism and territorial ambition are commonplace. While the international community concentrated on nuclear disarmament and the Non-Aligned Movement condemned as neo-colonialism any political restraint on the transfer of conventional weaponry from the industrialised to the non-industrialised world, Iraq succeeded in building up by purchase and technology-transfer a military inventory exceeding that of any NATO member except the United States, including more main battle tanks than those possessed by Britain and France combined, plus comparable numbers of combat aircraft, artillery pieces, armoured personnel carriers and ballistic missiles as well as a chemical capability. This is not to mention

Iraq's more clandestine acquisitions such as a near-nuclear capability and the 'supergun'.

Iraq may have outstripped all other Middle Eastern states in terms of quantity and in some respects quality of armaments but many others were not far behind – Israel, Egypt, Iran, Syria and Saudi Arabia come to mind.

The consequent fact that it took half the world in arms to face down the aggressive dictator of a small, relatively unindustrialised country compelled the industrialised world, in particular the principal arms-exporting states (the five permanent members of the Security Council) to accept that arms exports carry risks as well as benefits. At the urging of the United States, the five have begun a series of meetings to work out ways to prevent the further transfer of weapons of mass destruction and to exercise restraint over the transfer of conventional weapons to conflict-ridden areas of the world. Moreover, on 9 December 1991, at UK and thereafter European Community initiative, the General Assembly unanimously resolved to establish a public register of international arms sales, an important step in the direction of 'transparency' in this hitherto secret area of international commerce.

At the same time a major restocking operation is underway in the Middle East and the rubric has been heard that 'friendly countries are entitled to fulfil their legitimate self-defence needs'. Coupled with Soviet and Eastern European dependence on the military industrial complex for hard currency and employment, there is a risk that, regardless of the lesson of 1990–91, another arms sales spree may get underway, and that the public protestations of the immediate post-crisis period will be severely modified in practice. Chinese export of nuclear technology to Iran is a dangerous example.

However, even if the flow of conventional arms resumes internationally, there is a strong case for total embargoes to parties in civil conflicts and to major human rights violators. South Africa was rightly singled out for a mandatory arms embargo on human rights grounds from 1977 at a time when China was supplying the Pol Pot regime in Cambodia. Not surprisingly the Soviet Union continued to saturate Syria and Iraq with military equipment through the 1970s and 1980s regardless of their human rights records, as did the United States and Britain with the Shah of Iran. In these cases East–West competition was an ingredient, albeit by no means the only one.

In today's world, it should be possible to secure the agreement of the dozen or so significant arms exporters to stop supplying major human rights violators and combatants in civil wars. The mandatory arms embargoes on Yugoslavia and Somalia mentioned earlier are steps in the right direction as is the OAS and other nations' boycott of Haiti.

If such a policy is put into effect it will be accompanied by the inevitable sanctions-busting on the part of the international private sector arms trade. The world has already been alerted to the need for greater vigilance in this area by the revelations of Iraq's nuclear and other acquisitions. For a whole series of reasons the private sector international arms trade must be brought under control. Governments should include in the UN arms register not only government-to-government contracts but also private sector deals. Moreover there must be a genuine tightening up of control over 'dual purpose' exports.

The above proposals are more readily applicable to civil wars and man-made disasters such as flights from persecution across national boundaries than they are to massive human rights violations within the borders of a state. One has only to read Amnesty International's annual reports to see that no country has a spotless human rights record. But at what point along the spectrum of offenders between, say, Iraq ('Torture of prisoners was routine and widespread . . . hundreds of people . . . "disappeared" in custody . . . There were hundreds of extra-judicial executions'[1]), and Sweden ('Amnesty International reiterated concern that the government's decision to place indefinite restrictions on the [six Kurdish] refugees' freedom of movement was not open to judicial scrutiny. In October the organisation welcomed the lifting of restrictions on the six refugees.'[2]) should international concern express itself in action rather than criticism and recommendation for improvement? What are the criteria for defining 'massive' violations and who should set them? What action can be taken short of toppling an offending regime? A ruthless dictator is not going to welcome 'negotiation, mediation, concilia- tion', etc (article 33 of the Charter) between himself and his people, which would serve only to weaken his grip on power. If diplomatic representations, public criticism, condemnation by regional and UN human rights machinery prove either totally ineffective or only mar- ginally effective, where does the international community go next? Does it, as happened with South Africa, proceed to diplomatic isolation and economic sanctions or does it, as in so many past instances, confine itself to the wringing of hands?

There are no easy answers to these and other related questions. As with civil conflict, regional organisations are best qualified to influ- ence and if necessary to coerce human rights violators. Belated though this may be, we are now seeing a gratifying invigoration of the relevant machinery and political will within the OAS as the rule of law and a commitment to civil liberty spreads through Latin

America. The reaction to the coup in Haiti is an indication that the traditional Latin American way of changing governments, the military coup d'état, is no longer acceptable. Over the past few years there has been a marked improvement in human rights standards throughout Central and South America.

In Europe, human rights machinery is well established and will no doubt become more deeply entrenched and widespread as the pan-European CSCE develops. In sub-Saharan Africa the trend is positive and it is not impossible to imagine major violators in the future being exposed to pressure and even coercion at the hands of the OAU. The basic structure has existed since 1981 in the African Charter on Human and People's Rights. But there is no sign of movement within the Arab League against major, or indeed any, offenders, although some of the worst in the world are to be found within that organisation. The old saying about the pot and the kettle is regarded with respect in Arab circles, and in the wider Islamic world there is no regional organisation to take up the cudgels on behalf of sufferers from human rights violations in, for example, Iran (a major offender), Pakistan or Indonesia. The Organisation of the Islamic Conference (ICO) has drafted a declaration on human rights 'in accordance with the Sharia'. It has not yet been approved. It is ironic that in 1992 Iran, Iraq, Indonesia and Syria were all members of the UN Human Rights Commission.

Where there is room for improvement below the UN machinery is in the Commonwealth. In 1979, at the initiative of Gambia, a Commonwealth summit meeting debated a proposal to establish a Commonwealth Commission on Human Rights with judicial powers not dissimilar to the European Court of Human Rights. The proposal was watered down to the creation of a two-person Human Rights Unit in the Commonwealth Secretariat, whose task was the promotion of human rights rather than the protection of victims against violations. At the Harare summit in October 1991 the final communiqué failed to match advance publicity about concentration on human rights. Fine rhetoric and exhortation appeared in the communiqué on 22 October 1991 but no fresh machinery was created to strengthen the hand of the Secretariat.

Even in today's world, the melancholy conclusion is inescapable that, at the level of the UN Security Council and General Assembly, adherence to the essence of article 2(7) is still so strong that enforcement action, non-military or military, is unlikely to be authorised unless there is an identifiably international dimension to a massive human rights violation, such as the transborder flight of refugees or assaults by the violating government against opposition elements in neighbouring countries. The main UN organs will be ready to support action by regional organisations as in the case of Haiti. But the veto-bearing power of China on the Council and the apprehensions of influential states in all the continents about dangerous precedents for involvement in their own domestic affairs will continue to inhibit anything beyond pressure and persuasion exercised through the existing human rights machinery which, to be fair, is far more extensive and intrusive than anyone could have imagined possible 20 or 30 years ago. Hence influential states should not be inhibited about continuously battering against the wall, notwithstanding rebuffs. As suggested earlier, ways round can frequently be found. It should be borne in mind that if the Security Council is blocked by veto, the Uniting for Peace procedure is available for transfer of the debate to the General Assembly. This is particularly relevant in that the original Uniting for Peace resolution, adopted on 3 November 1950, in Section E (adopted unanimously with one abstention), makes the point that enduring peace will not be secured solely by collective security arrangements but 'especially upon respect for and observance of human rights and fundamental freedoms for all'.

War-Crimes and Crimes against Humanity

In the first chapter Peter Calvocoressi deplores the lack of an international tribunal to try crimes against humanity, in effect a permanent successor to the Nuremberg Tribunal. Debate on this question has been reopened by the crimes committed by Saddam Hussein and his myrmidons. During the Gulf crisis there were strident calls from certain political quarters for Saddam to be brought to trial.

In spite of the well-known difficulties – including the taint of 'victor's justice' surrounding the Nuremberg proceedings and the difficulty of bringing offenders to trial – the present international configuration provides an unprecedented opportunity for serious and positive consideration of such a proposal. Even among former adversaries there would be widespread agreement across the UN membership that a head of state guilty of a flagrant breach of article 2(4) of the Charter, of ordering torture, mass executions, the firing of oil wells and missile attacks on neutral states, should not escape responsibility; nor should those more immediately responsible for the commission of such acts. Should such a court be established, the question of retroactivity would have to be dealt with. Should Pol Pot, Idi Amin and Bokassa be arraigned as well as Saddam Hussein? What action should be taken against a government which, as would certainly be the case with Iraq, refused to surrender its nationals to face trial by the tribunal? Would such recalcitrance warrant action under articles 41 and, if necessary, 42 of the Charter? Would a tribunal immediately become a political football with Arab states voting to arraign Israeli leaders for actions carried out in the Occupied Territories and Israel responding by bringing a charge against, for example, President Assad of Syria for the 1982 Hama massacre?

In spite of all these problems, the Security Council and/or the General Assembly should consider adopting a resolution confirming the view that such a tribunal should be created and instructing the International Law Commission to accelerate its work on the Draft Code of Offences on the Peace and Security of Mankind, perhaps setting an early target date for completion. This process will be arduous and has already been long drawn-out, but the gap should be filled and the disappearance of East–West confrontation plus the hoped-for amelioration of its North–South counterpart at last makes this feasible. There can be no doubt that the existence of such a tribunal with powers of condign punishment, however difficult to formulate still more so to apply, would have a deterrent effect.

Finance

The thrust of this book, and of statements made over the past four or five years by world leaders, most recently by the outgoing Secretary-General in his annual report to the General Assembly, is that, in the post-Cold War world, more rather than less will be expected of the United Nations. In his seminal article published in *Pravda* and *Izvestia* on 17 September 1987, Mr Gorbachev advocated a system of global security based on the Security Council, the establishment of a 'hot line' between UN headquarters and the capitals of the permanent members and the chairman of the Non-Aligned Movement, mechanisms under UN auspices for verification of arms control agreements, wider use of UN military observers and peacekeeping forces, encouragement of the use of the Secretary-General's good office and much more. Four years later, in his statement to the General Assembly on 23 September 1991, President Bush spoke with pride and hope of the opportunities to make the Charter work for the purposes for which it was designed. He noted that, in the previous 36 months, the United Nations had mounted more peacekeeping missions than in its first 43 years. Similar sentiments have been expressed by many heads of state and government and foreign ministers.

And yet, in mid-September 1991 (and again in mid-November) the Secretary-General was obliged to write to all members informing them that the United Nations was in the midst of its worst financial crisis ever and that he had been forced to borrow from peacekeeping funds to meet the basic operating costs of the organisation. Only 51 states had paid their 1991 assessment in full. 'Either we manage effectively to address the financial problem, or the United Nations will be rendered incapable, for lack of resources, to perform its far-reaching functions, with the required effectiveness, especially for the maintenance of international peace and security.'

The plain fact was that, at the end of August 1991, nearly half the assessed regular budget of $1 billion was outstanding, as well as nearly $5 billion from previous years. Nearly half the assessed contributions ($430 million) for six current peacekeeping operations had not been paid. A further $215 million was owing for assessed contributions from previous years, in some cases for operations already wound up.

For the regular budget the principal debtors, including outstanding payments for previous years, were the United States ($531 million), the Soviet Union ($46 million), Japan ($61 million), Brazil ($17 million) and Argentina ($15 million). Most of these debts amounted to late payments of 1991 assessments. The United Kingdom was fully paid up, although the British record of prompt payment is not so shining where peacekeeping accounts are concerned (on 31 August $17 million owing out of $24 million assessed).

The recommendation is simple. If the international community wants more from the United Nations, the members must be prepared to pay. Considering that the sums involved are trifling in relation to national budgets, late payment is inexcusable. In democracies as well as autocracies and dictatorships, 'We the peoples' are accustomed to the existence of a wide gap between the rhetorical promises of politicians and their performance in reality. In this particular area it would be neither financially painful nor administratively difficult to bring the two into common focus.

Notes

1. *Amnesty International Report*, 1991.
2. *Ibid.*

Appendix

Boutros Boutros-Ghali

AN AGENDA FOR PEACE[1]

Preventive Diplomacy,
Peacemaking and
Peace-keeping

Report
of the Secretary-General
pursuant to the statement adopted
by the Summit Meeting of the
Security Council on
31 January 1992

1. SC Doc. S/24111, 17 June 1992
(New York: United Nations)

Introduction

In its statement of 31 January 1992, adopted at the conclusion of the first meeting held by the Security Council at the level of Heads of State and Government, I was invited to prepare, for circulation to the Members of the United Nations by 1 July 1992, an 'analysis and recommendations on ways of strengthening and making more efficient within the framework and provisions of the Charter the capacity of the United Nations for preventive diplomacy, for peace-making and for peace-keeping.'

The United Nations is a gathering of sovereign States and what it can do depends on the common ground that they create between them. The adversarial decades of the cold war made the original promise of the Organization impossible to fulfil. The January 1992 Summit therefore represented an unprecedented recommitment, at the highest political level, to the Purposes and Principles of the Charter.

In these past months a conviction has grown, among nations large and small, that an opportunity has been regained to achieve the great objectives of the Charter – a United Nations capable of maintaining international peace and security, of securing justice and human rights and of promoting, in the words of the Charter, 'social progress and better standards of life in larger freedom'. This opportunity must not be squandered. The Organization must never again be crippled as it was in the era that has now passed.

I welcome the invitation of the Security Council, early in my tenure as Secretary-General, to prepare this report. It draws upon ideas and proposals transmitted to me by Governments, regional agencies, non-governmental organizations, and institutions and individuals from many countries. I am grateful for these, even as I emphasize that the responsibility for this report is my own.

The sources of conflict and war are pervasive and deep. To reach them will require our utmost effort to enhance respect for human rights and fundamental freedoms, to promote sustainable economic and social development for wider prosperity, to alleviate distress and to curtail the existence and use of massively destructive weapons. The United Nations Conference on Environment and Development, the largest summit ever held, has just met at Rio de Janeiro. Next year will see the second World Conference on Human Rights. In 1994 Population and Development will be addressed. In 1995 the World Conference on Women will take place, and a World Summit for Social Development has been proposed. Throughout my term as Secretary-General I shall be addressing all these great issues. I bear them all in mind as, in the present report, I turn to the problems that the Council has specifically requested I consider: preventive diplomacy, peacemaking and peace-keeping – to which I have added a closely related concept, post-conflict peace-building.

The manifest desire of the membership to work together is a new source of strength in our common endeavour. Success is far from certain, however. While my report deals with ways to improve the Organization's capacity to pursue and preserve peace, it is crucial for all Member States to bear in mind that the search for improved mechanisms and techniques will be of little significance unless this new spirit of commonality is propelled by the will to take the hard decisions demanded by this time of opportunity.

It is therefore with a sense of moment, and with gratitude, that I present this report to the Members of the United Nations.

Boutros Boutros-Ghali

I. The Changing Context

In the course of the past few years the immense ideological barrier that for decades gave rise to distrust and hostility – and the terrible tools of destruction that were their inseparable companions – has collapsed. Even as the issues between States north and south grow more acute, and call for attention at the highest levels of government, the improvement in relations between States east and west affords new possibilities, some already realized, to meet successfully threats to common security.

Authori.rian regimes have given way to mor democratic forces and responsive Governments. The form, scope and intensity of these processes differ from Latin America to Africa to Europe to Asia, but they are sufficiently similar to indicate a global phenomenon. Parallel to these political changes, many States are seeking more open forms of economic policy, creating a worldwide sense of dynamism and movement.

To the hundreds of millions who gained their independence in the surge of decolonization following the creation of the United Nations, have been added millions more who have recently gained freedom. Once again new States are taking their seats in the General Assembly. Their arrival reconfirms the importance and indispensability of the sovereign State as the fundamental entity of the international community.

We have entered a time of global transition marked by uniquely contradictory trends. Regional and continental associations of States are evolving ways to deepen cooperation and ease some of the contentious characteristics of sovereign and nationalistic rivalries. National boundaries are blurred by advanced communications and global commerce, and by the decisions of States to yield some sovereign prerogatives to larger, common political associations. At the same time, however, fierce new assertions of nationalism and sovereignty spring up, and the cohesion of States is threatened by brutal ethnic, religious, social, cultural or linguistic strife. Social peace is challenged on the one hand by new assertions of discrimination and exclusion and, on the other, by acts of terrorism seeking to undermine evolution and change through democratic means.

The concept of peace is easy to grasp; that of international security is more complex, for a pattern of contradictions has arisen here as well. As major nuclear powers have begun to negotiate arms reduction agreements, the proliferation of weapons of mass destruction threatens to increase and conventional arms continue to be amassed in many parts of the world. As racism becomes recognized for the destructive force it is and as apartheid is being dismantled, new racial tensions are rising and finding expression in violence. Technological advances are altering the nature and the expectation of life all over the globe. The revolution in communications has united the world in awareness, in aspiration and in greater solidarity against injustice. But progress also brings new risks for stability: ecological damage, disruption of family and community life, greater intrusion into the lives and rights of individuals.

This new dimension of insecurity must not be allowed to obscure the continuing and devastating problems of unchecked population growth, crushing debt burdens, barriers to trade, drugs and the growing disparity between rich and poor. Poverty, disease, famine, oppression and despair abound, joining to produce 17 million refugees, 20 million displaced persons and massive migrations of peoples within and beyond national borders. These are both sources and consequences of conflict that require the ceaseless attention and the highest priority in the efforts of the United Nations. A porous ozone shield could pose a greater threat to an exposed population than a hostile army. Drought and disease can decimate no less mercilessly than the weapons of war. So at this moment of renewed opportunity, the efforts of the Organization to build peace, stability and security must encompass matters beyond military threats in order to break the fetters of strife and warfare that have characterized the past. But armed conflicts today, as they have throughout history, continue to bring fear and horror to humanity, requiring our urgent involvement to try to prevent, contain and bring them to an end.

Since the creation of the United Nations in 1945, over 100 major conflicts around the world have left some 20 million dead. The United Nations was rendered powerless to deal with many of these crises because of the vetoes – 279 of them – cast in the Security Council, which were a vivid expression of the divisions of that period.

With the end of the cold war there have been no such vetoes since 31 May 1990, and demands on the United Nations have surged. Its security arm, once disabled by circumstances, it was not created or equipped to control, has emerged as a central instrument for the prevention and resolution of conflicts and for the preservation of peace. Our aims must be:

- To seek to identify at the earliest possible stage situations that could produce conflict, and to try through diplomacy to remove the sources of danger before violence results;
- Where conflict erupts, to engage in peacemaking aimed at resolving the issues that have led to conflict;
- Through peace-keeping, to work to preserve peace, however fragile, where fighting has been halted and to assist in implementing agreements achieved by the peacemakers;
- To stand ready to assist in peace-building in its differing contexts: rebuilding the institutions and infrastructures of nations torn by civil war and strife; and building bonds of peaceful mutual benefit among nations formerly at war;
- And in the largest sense, to address the deepest causes of conflict: economic despair, social injustice and political oppression. It is possible to discern an increasingly common moral perception that spans the world's nations and peoples, and which is finding expression in international laws, many owing their genesis to the work of this Organization.

This wider mission for the world Organization will demand the concerted attention and effort of individual States, of regional and non-governmental organizations and of all of the United Nations system, with each of the principal organs functioning in the balance and harmony that the Charter requires. The Security Council has been assigned by all Member States the primary responsibility for the maintenance of international peace and security under the Charter. In its broadest sense this responsibility must be shared by the General Assembly and by all the functional elements of the world Organization. Each has a special and indispensable role to play in an integrated approach to human security. The Secretary-General's contribution rests on the pattern of trust and cooperation established between him and the deliberative organs of the United Nations.

The foundation-stone of this work is and must remain the State. Respect for its fundamental sovereignty and integrity are crucial to any common international progress. The time of absolute and exclusive sovereignty, however, has passed; its theory was never matched by reality. It is the task of leaders of States today to understand this and to find a balance between the needs of good internal governance and the requirements of an ever more interdependent world. Commerce, communications and environmental matters transcend administrative borders; but inside those borders is where individuals carry out the first order of their economic, political and social lives. The United Nations has not closed its door. Yet if every ethnic, religious or linguistic group claimed statehood, there would be no limit to fragmentation, and peace, security and economic well-being for all would become ever more difficult to achieve.

One requirement for solutions to these problems lies in commitment to human rights with a special sensitivity to those of minorities, whether ethnic, religious, social or linguistic. The League of Nations provided a machinery for the international protection of minorities. The General Assembly soon will have before it a declaration on the rights of minorities. That instrument, together with the increasingly effective machinery of the United Nations dealing with human rights, should enhance the situation of minorities as well as the stability of States.

Globalism and nationalism need not be viewed as opposing trends, doomed to spur each other on to extremes of reaction. The healthy globalization of contemporary life requires in the first instance solid identities and fundamental freedoms. The sovereignty, territorial integrity and independence of States within the established international system, and the principle of self-determination for peoples, both of great value and importance, must not be permitted to work against each other in the period ahead. Respect for democratic principles at all levels of social existence is crucial: in communities, within States and within the community of States. Our constant duty should be to maintain the integrity of each while finding a balanced design for all.

II. Definitions

The terms preventive diplomacy, peacemaking and peace-keeping are integrally related and as used in this report are defined as follows:

- *Preventive diplomacy* is action to prevent disputes from arising between parties, to prevent existing disputes from escalating into conflicts and to limit the spread of the latter when they occur.
- *Peacemaking* is action to bring hostile parties to agreement, essentially through such peaceful means as those forseen in Chapter VI of the Charter of the United Nations.
- *Peace-keeping* is the deployment of a United Nations presence in the field, hitherto with the consent of all the parties concerned, normally involving United Nations military and/or police personnel and frequently civilians as well. Peace-keeping is a technique that expands the possibilities for both the prevention of conflict and the making of peace.

The present report in addition will address the critically related concept of post-conflict *peace-building* – action to identify and support structures which will tend to strengthen and solidify peace in order to avoid a relapse into conflict. Preventive diplomacy seeks to resolve disputes before violence breaks out; peacemaking and peace-keeping are required to halt conflicts and preserve peace once it is attained. If successful, they strengthen the opportunity for post-conflict peace-building, which can prevent the recurrence of violence among nations and peoples.

These four areas for action, taken together, and carried out with the backing of all Members, offer a coherent contribution towards securing peace in the spirit of the Charter. The United Nations has extensive experience not only in these fields, but in the wider realm of work for peace in which these four fields are set. Initiatives on decolonization, on the environment and sustainable development, on population, on the eradication of disease, on disarmament and on the growth of international law – these and many others have contributed immeasurably to the foundations for a peaceful world. The world has often been rent by conflict and plagued by massive human suffering and deprivation. Yet it would have been far more so without the continuing efforts of the United Nations. This wide experience must be taken into account in assessing the potential of the United Nations in maintaining international security not only in its traditional sense, but in the new dimensions presented by the era ahead.

III. Preventive Diplomacy

The most desirable and efficient employment of diplomacy is to ease tensions before they result in conflict – or, if conflict breaks out, to act swiftly to contain it and resolve its underlying causes. Preventive diplomacy may be performed by the Secretary-General personally or through senior staff or specialized agencies and programmes, by the Security Council or the General Assembly, and by regional organizations in cooperation with the United Nations. Preventive diplomacy requires measures to create confidence; it needs early warning based on information gathering and informal or formal fact-finding; it may also involve preventive deployment and, in some situations, demilitarized zones.

Measures to Build Confidence

Mutual confidence and good faith are essential to reducing the likelihood of conflict between States. Many such measures are available to Governments that have the will to employ them. Systematic exchange of military missions, formation of regional or subregional risk reduction centres, arrangements for the free flow of information, including the monitoring of regional arms agreements, are examples. I ask all regional organizations to consider what further confidence-building measures might be applied in their areas and to inform the United Nations of the results. I will undertake periodic consultations on confidence-building measures with parties to potential, current or past disputes and with regional organizations, offering such advisory assistance as the Secretariat can provide.

Fact-finding

Preventive steps must be based upon timely and accurate knowledge of the facts. Beyond this, an understanding of developments and global trends, based on sound analysis, is required. And the willingness to take appropriate preventive action is essential. Given the economic and social roots of many potential conflicts, the information needed by the United Nations now must encompass economic and social trends as well as political developments that may lead to dangerous tensions.

(a) An increased resort to fact-finding is needed, in accordance with the Charter, initiated either by the Secretary-General, to enable him to meet his responsibilities under the Charter, including Article 99, or by the Security Council or the General Assembly. Various forms may be employed selectively as the situation requires. A request by a State for the sending of a United Nations fact-finding mission to its territory should be considered without undue delay.

(b) Contacts with the Governments of Member States can provide the Secretary-General with detailed information on issues of concern. I ask that all Member States be ready to provide the information needed for effective preventive diplomacy. I will supplement my own contacts by regularly sending senior officials on missions for consultations in capitals or other locations. Such contacts are essential to gain insight into a situation and to assess its potential ramifications.

(c) Formal fact-finding can be mandated by the Security Council or by the General Assembly, either of which may elect to send a mission under its immediate authority or may invite the Secretary-General to take the necessary steps, including the designation of a special envoy. In addition to collecting information on which a decision for further action can be taken, such a mission can in some instances help to defuse a dispute by its presence, indicating to the parties that the Organization, and in particular the Security Council, is actively seized of the matter as a present or potential threat to international security.

(d) In exceptional circumstances the Council may meet away from Headquarters as the Charter provides, in order not only to inform itself directly, but also to bring the authority of the Organization to bear on a given situation.

Early Warning

In recent years the United Nations system has been developing a valuable network of early warning systems concerning environmental threats, the risk of nuclear accident, natural disasters, mass movements of populations, the threat of famine and the spread of disease.

There is a need, however, to strengthen arrangements in such a manner that information from these sources can be synthesized with political indicators to assess whether a threat to peace exists and to analyse what action might be taken by the United Nations to alleviate it. This is a process that will continue to require the close cooperation of the various specialized agencies and functional offices of the United Nations. The analyses and recommendations for preventive action that emerge will be made available by me, as appropriate, to the Security Council and other United Nations organs. I recommend in addition that the Security Council invite a reinvigorated and restructured Economic and Social Council to provide reports, in accordance with Article 65 of the Charter, on those economic and social developments that may, unless mitigated, threaten international peace and security.

Regional arrangements and organizations have an important role in early warning. I ask regional organizations that have not yet sought observer status at the United Nations to do so and to be linked, through appropriate arrangements, with the security mechanisms of this Organization.

Preventive Deployment

United Nations operations in areas of crisis have generally been established after conflict has occurred. The time has come to plan for circumstances warranting preventive deployment, which could take place in a variety of instances and ways. For example, in conditions of national crisis there could be preventive deployment at the request of the Government or all parties concerned, or with their consent; in inter-State disputes such deployment could take place when two countries feel that a United Nations presence on both sides of their border can discourage hostilities; furthermore, preventive deployment could take place when a country feels threatened and requests the deployment of an appropriate United Nations presence along its side of the border alone. In each situation, the mandate and composition of the United Nations presence would need to be carefully devised and be clear to all.

In conditions of crisis within a country, when the Government requests or all parties consent, preventive deployment could help in a number of ways to alleviate suffering and to limit or control violence. Humanitarian assistance, impartially provided, could be of critical importance; assistance in maintaining security, whether through military, police or civilian personnel, could save lives and develop conditions of safety in which negotiations can be held; the United Nations could also help in conciliation efforts if this should be the wish of the parties. In certain circumstances, the United Nations may well need to draw upon the specialized skills and resources of various parts of the United Nations system; such operations may also on occasion require the participation of non-governmental organizations.

In these situations of internal crisis the United Nations will need to respect the sovereignty of the State; to do otherwise would not be in accordance with the understanding of Member States in accepting the principles of the Charter. The Organization must remain mindful of the carefully negotiated balance of the guiding principles annexed to General Assembly resolution 46/182 of 19 December 1991. Those guidelines stressed, *inter alia*, that humanitarian assistance must be provided in accordance with the principles of humanity, neutrality and impartiality; that the sovereignty, territorial integrity and national unity of States must be fully respected in accordance with the Charter of the United Nations; and that, in this context, humanitarian assistance should be provided with the consent of the affected country and, in principle, on the basis of an appeal by that country. The guidelines also stressed the responsibility of States to take care of the victims of emergencies occurring on their territory and the need for access to those requiring humanitarian assistance. In the light of these guidelines, a Government's request for United Nations involvement, or consent to it, would not be an infringement of that State's sovereignty or be contrary to Article 2, paragraph 7, of the Charter which refers to matters essentially within the domestic jurisdiction of any State.

In inter-State disputes, when both parties agree, I recommend that if the Security Council concludes that the likelihood of hostilities between neighbouring countries could be removed by the preventive deployment of a United Nations presence on the territory of each State, such action should be taken. The nature of the tasks to be performed would determine the composition of the United Nations presence.

In cases where one nation fears a cross-border attack, if the Security Council concludes that a United Nations presence on one side of the border, with the consent only of the requesting country, would serve to deter conflict, I recommend that preventive deployment take place. Here again, the specific nature of the situation would determine the mandate and the personnel required to fulfil it.

Demilitarized Zones

In the past, demilitarized zones have been established by agreement of the parties at the conclusion of a conflict. In addition to the deployment of United Nations personnel in such zones as part of peace-keeping operations, consideration should now be given to the usefulness of such zones as a form of preventive deployment, on both sides of a border, with the agreement of the two parties, as a means of separating potential belligerents, or on one side of the line, at the request of one party, for the purpose of removing any pretext for attack. Demilitarized zones would serve as symbols of the international community's concern that conflict be prevented.

IV. Peacemaking

AUTHOR

Between the tasks of seeking to prevent conflict and keeping the peace lies the responsibility to try to bring hostile parties to agreement by peaceful means. Chapter VI of the Charter sets forth a comprehensive list of such means for the resolution of conflict. These have been amplified in various declarations adopted by the General Assembly, including the Manila Declaration of 1982 on the Peaceful Settlement of International Disputes and the 1988 Declaration on the Prevention and Removal of Disputes and Situations Which May Threaten International Peace and Security and on the Role of the United Nations in this Field. They have also been the subject of various resolutions of the General Assembly, including resolution 44/21 of 15 November 1989 on enhancing international peace, security and international cooperation in all its aspects in accordance with the Charter of the United Nations. The United Nations has had wide experience in the application of these peaceful means. If conflicts have gone unresolved, it is not because techniques for peaceful settlement were unknown or inadequate. The fault lies first in the lack of political will of parties to seek a solution to their differences through such means as are suggested in Chapter VI of the Charter, and second, in the lack of leverage at the disposal of a third party if this is the procedure chosen. The indifference of the international community to a problem, or the marginalization of it, can also thwart the possibilities of solution. We must look primarily to these areas if we hope to enhance the capacity of the Organization for achieving peaceful settlements.

The present determination in the Security Council to resolve international disputes in the manner foreseen in the Charter has opened the way for a more active Council role. With greater unity has come leverage and persuasive power to lead hostile parties towards negotiations. I urge the Council to take full advantage of the provisions of the Charter under which it may recommend appropriate procedures or methods for dispute settlement and, if all the parties to a dispute so request, make recommendations to the parties for a pacific settlement of the dispute.

The General Assembly, like the Security Council and the Secretary-General, also has an important role assigned to it under the Charter for the maintenance of international peace and security. As a universal forum, its capacity to consider and recommend appropriate action must be recognized. To that end it is essential to promote its utilization by all Member States so as to bring greater influence to bear in pre-empting or containing situations which are likely to threaten international peace and security.

Mediation and negotiation can be undertaken by an individual designated by the Security Council, by the General Assembly or by the Secretary-General. There is a long history of the utilization by the United Nations of distinguished statesmen to facilitate the processes of peace. They can bring a personal prestige that, in addition to their experience, can encourage the parties to enter serious negotiations. There is a wide willingness to serve in this capacity, from which I shall continue to benefit as the need arises. Frequently it is the Secretary-General himself who undertakes the task. While the mediator's effectiveness is enhanced by strong and evident support from the Council, the General Assembly and the relevant Member States acting in their national capacity, the good offices of the Secretary-General may at times be employed most effectively when conducted independently of the deliberative bodies. Close and continuous consultation between the Secretary-General and the Security Council is, however, essential to ensure full awareness of how the Council's influence can best be applied and to develop a common strategy for the peaceful settlement of specific disputes.

The World Court

The docket of the International Court of Justice has grown fuller but it remains an under-used resource for the peaceful adjudication of disputes. Greater reliance on the Court would be an important contribution to United Nations peacemaking. In this connection, I call attention to the power of the Security Council under Articles 36 and 37 of the Charter to recommend to Member States the submission of a dispute to the International Court of Justice, arbitration or other dispute-settlement mechanisms. I recommend that the Secretary-General be authorized, pursuant to article 96, paragraph 2, of the Charter, to take advantage of the advisory competence of the Court and that other United Nations organs that already enjoy such authorization turn to the Court more frequently for advisory opinions.

I recommend the following steps to reinforce the role of the International Court of Justice:

(a) All Member States should accept the general jurisdiction of the International Court under Article 36 of its Statute, without any reservation, before the end of the United Nations Decade of International Law in the year 2000. In instances where domestic structures prevent this, States should agree bilaterally or multilaterally to a comprehensive list of matters they are willing to submit to the Court and should withdraw their reservations to its jurisdiction in the dispute settlement clauses of multilateral treaties;

(b) When submission of a dispute to the full Court is not practical, the Chambers jurisdiction should be used;

(c) States should support the Trust Fund established to assist countries unable to afford the cost involved in bringing a dispute to the Court, and such countries should take full advantage of the Fund in order to resolve their disputes.

Amelioration through Assistance

Peacemaking is at times facilitated by international action to ameliorate circumstances that have contributed to the dispute or conflict. If, for instance, assistance to displaced persons within a society is essential to a solution, then the United Nations should be able to draw upon the resources of all agencies and programmes concerned. At present, there is no adequate mechanism in the United Nations through which the Security Council, the General Assembly or the Secretary-General can mobilize the resources needed for such positive leverage and engage the collective efforts of the United Nations system for the peaceful resolution of a conflict. I have raised this concept in the Administrative Committee on Coordination, which brings together the executive heads of United Nations agencies and programmes; we are exploring methods by which the inter-agency system can improve its contribution to the peaceful resolution of disputes.

Sanctions and Special Economic Problems

In circumstances when peacemaking requires the imposition of sanctions under Article 41 of the Charter, it is important that States confronted with special economic problems not only have the right to consult the Security Council regarding such problems, as Article 50 provides, but also have a realistic possibility of having their difficulties addressed. I recommend that the Security Council devise a set of measures involving the financial institutions and other components of the United Nations system that can be put in place to insulate States from such difficulties. Such measures would be a matter of equity and a means of encouraging States to coopcratc with decisions of the Council.

Use of Military Force

It is the essence of the concept of collective security as contained in the Charter that if peaceful means fail, the measures provided in Chapter VII should be used, on the decision of the Security Council, to maintain or restore international peace and security in the face of a 'threat to the peace, breach of the peace, or act of aggression'. The Security Council has not so far made use of the most coercive of these measures – the action by military force forseen in Article 42. In the situation between Iraq and Kuwait, the Council chose to authorize Member States to take measures on its behalf. The Charter, however, provides a detailed approach which now merits the attention of all Member States.

Under Article 42 of the Charter, the Security Council has the authority to take military action to maintain or restore international peace and security. While such action should only be taken when all peaceful means have failed, the option of taking it is essential to the credibility of the United Nations as a guarantor of international security. This will require bringing into being, through negotiations, the special agreements foreseen in Article 43 of the Charter, whereby Member States undertake to make armed forces, assistance and facilities available to the Security Council for the purposes stated in Article 42, not only on an ad hoc basis but on a permanent basis. Under the political circumstances that now exist for the first time since the Charter was adopted, the long-standing obstacles to the conclusion of such special agreements should no longer prevail. The rcady availability of armed forces on call could serve, in itself, as a means of detcrring breaches of the peace since a potential aggressor would know that the Council had at its disposal a means of response. Forces under Article 43 may perhaps never be sufficiently large or well enough equipped to deal with a threat from a major army equipped with sophisticated weapons. They would be useful, however, in meeting any threat posed by a military force of a lesser order. I recommend that the Security Council initiate negotiations in accordance with Article 43, supported by the Military Staff Committee, which may be augmented if necessary by others in accordance with Article 47, paragraph 2, of the Charter. It is my view that the role of the Military Staff Committee should be seen in the context of Chapter VII, and not that of the planning or conduct of peace-keeping operations.

Peace-Enforcement Units

The mission of forces under Article 43 would be to respond to outright aggression, imminent or actual. Such forces are not likely to be available for some time to come. Cease-fires have often been agreed to but not complied with, and the United Nations has sometimes been called upon to send forces to restore and maintain the cease-fire. This task can on occasion exceed the mission of peace-keeping forces and the expectations of peace-keeping force contributors. I recommend that the Council consider the utilization of peace-enforcement units in clearly defined circumstances and with their terms of reference specified in advance. Such units from Member States would be available on call and would consist of troops that have volunteered for such service. They would have to be more heavily armed than peace-keeping forces and would need to undergo extensive preparatory training within their national forces. Deployment and operation of such forces would be under the authorization of the Security Council and would, as in the case of peace-keeping forces, be under the command of the Secretary-General. I consider such peace-enforcement units to be warranted as a provisional measure under Article 40 of the Charter. Such peace-enforcement units should not be confused with the forces that may eventually be constituted under Article 43 to deal with acts of aggression or with the military personnel which Governments may agree to keep on stand-by for possible contribution to peace-keeping operations.

Just as diplomacy will continue across the span of all the activities dealt with in the present report, so there may not be a dividing line between peacemaking and peace-keeping. Peacemaking is often a prelude to peace-keeping – just as the deployment of a United Nations presence in the field may expand possibilities for the prevention of conflict, facilitate the work of peacemaking and in many cases serve as a prerequisite for peace-building.

V. Peace-keeping

Peace-keeping can rightly be called the invention of the United Nations. It has brought a degree of stability to numerous areas of tension around the world.

Increasing Demands

Thirteen peace-keeping operations were established between the years 1945 and 1987; 13 others since then. An estimated 528,000 military, police and civilian personnel had served under the flag of the United Nations until January 1992. Over 800 of them from 43 countries have died in the service of the Organization. The costs of these operations have aggregated some $8.3 billion till 1992. The unpaid arrears towards them stand at over $800 million, which represent a debt owed by the Organization to the troop-contributing countries. Peace-keeping operations approved at present are estimated to cost close to $3 billion in the current 12-month period, while patterns of payment are unacceptably slow. Against this, global defence expenditures at the end of the last decade had approached $1 trillion a year, or $2 million per minute.

The contrast between the costs of United Nations peace-keeping and the costs of the alternative, war – between the demands of the Organization and the means provided to meet them – would be farcical were the consequences not so damaging to global stability and to the credibility of the Organization. At a time when nations and peoples increasingly are looking to the United Nations for assistance in keeping the peace – and holding it responsible when this cannot be so – fundamental decisions must be taken to enhance the capacity of the Organization in this innovative and productive exercise of its function. I am conscious that the present volume and unpredictability of peace-keeping assessments poses real problems for some Member States. For this reason, I strongly support proposals in some Member States for their peace-keeping contributions to be financed from defence, rather than foreign affairs, budgets and I recommend such action to others. I urge the General Assembly to encourage this approach.

The demands on the United Nations for peace-keeping, and peace-building, operations will in the coming years continue to challenge the capacity, the political and financial will and the creativity of the Secretariat and Member States. Like the Security Council, I welcome the increase and broadening of the tasks of peace-keeping operations.

New Departures in Peace-keeping

The nature of peace-keeping operations has evolved rapidly in recent years. The established principles and practices of peace-keeping have responded flexibly to new demands of recent years, and the basic conditions for success remain unchanged: a clear and practicable mandate; the cooperation of the parties in implementing that mandate; the continuing support of the Security Council; the readiness of Member States to contribute the military, police and civilian personnel, including specialists, required; effective United Nations command at Headquarters and in the field; and adequate financial and logistic support. As the international climate has changed and peace-keeping operations are increasingly fielded to help implement settlements that have been negotiated by peacemakers, a new array of demands and problems has emerged regarding logistics, equipment, personnel and finance, all of which could be corrected if Member States so wished and were ready to make the necessary resources available.

Personnel

Member States are keen to participate in peace-keeping operations. Military observers and infantry are invariably available in the required numbers, but logistic units present a greater problem, as few armies can afford to spare such units for an extended period. Member States were requested in 1990 to state what military personnel they were in principle prepared to make available; few replied. I reiterate the request to all Member States to reply frankly and promptly. Stand-by arrangements should be confirmed, as appropriate, through exchanges of letters between the Secretariat and Member States concerning the kind and number of skilled personnel they will be prepared to offer the United Nations as the needs of new operations arise.

Increasingly, peace-keeping requires that civilian political officers, human rights monitors, electoral officials, refugee and humanitarian aid specialists and police play as central a role as the military. Police personnel have proved increasingly difficult to obtain in the numbers required. I recommend that arrangements be reviewed and improved for training peace-keeping personnel – civilian, police or military – using the varied capabilities of Member State Governments, of non-governmental organizations and the facilities of the Secretariat. As efforts go forward to include additional States as contributors, some States with considerable potential should focus on language training for police contingents which may serve with the Organization. As for the United Nations itself, special personnel procedures, including incentives, should be instituted to permit the rapid transfer of Secretariat staff members to service with peace-keeping operations. The strength and capability of military staff serving in the Secretariat should be augmented to meet new and heavier requirements.

Logistics

Not all Governments can provide their battalions with the equipment they need for service abroad. While some equipment is provided by troop-contributing countries, a great deal has to come from the United Nations, including equipment to fill gaps in under-equipped national units. The United Nations has no standing stock of such equipment. Orders must be placed with manufacturers, which creates a number of difficulties. A pre-positioned stock of basic peace-keeping equipment should be established, so that at least some vehicles, communications equipment, generators, etc., would be immediately available at the start of an operation. Alternatively, Governments should commit themselves to keeping certain equipment, specified by the Secretary-General, on stand-by for immediate sale, loan or donation to the United Nations when required.

Member States in a position to do so should make air- and sea-lift capacity available to the United Nations free of cost or at lower than commercial rates, as was the practice until recently.

VI. Post-conflict Peace-building

Peacemaking and peace-keeping operations, to be truly successful, must come to include comprehensive efforts to identify and support structures which will tend to consolidate peace and advance a sense of confidence and well-being among people. Through agreements ending civil strife, these may include disarming the previously warring parties and the restoration of order, the custody and possible destruction of weapons, repatriating refugees, advisory and training support for security personnel, monitoring elections, advancing efforts to protect human rights, reforming or strengthening governmental institutions and promoting formal and informal processes of political participation.

In the aftermath of international war, post-conflict peace-building may take the form of concrete cooperative projects which link two or more countries in a mutually beneficial undertaking that can not only contribute to economic and social development but also enhance the confidence that is so fundamental to peace. I have in mind, for example, projects that bring States together to develop agriculture, improve transportation or utilize resources such as water or electricity that they need to share, or joint programmes through which barriers between nations are brought down by means of freer travel, cultural exchanges and mutually beneficial youth and educational projects. Reducing hostile perceptions through educational exchanges and curriculum reform may be essential to forestall a re-emergence of cultural and national tensions which could spark renewed hostilities.

In surveying the range of efforts for peace, the concept of peace-building as the construction of a new environment should be viewed as the counterpart of preventive diplomacy, which seeks to avoid the breakdown of peaceful conditions. When conflict breaks out, mutually reinforcing efforts at peacemaking and peace-keeping come into play. Once these have achieved their objectives, only sustained, cooperative work to deal with underlying economic, social, cultural and humanitarian problems can place an achieved peace on a durable foundation. Preventive diplomacy is to avoid a crisis; post-conflict peace-building is to prevent a recurrence.

Increasingly it is evident that peace-building after civil or international strife must address the serious problem of land mines, many tens of millions of which remain scattered in present or former combat zones. De-mining should be emphasized in the terms of reference of peace-keeping operations and is crucially important in the restoration of activity when peace-building is under way: agriculture cannot be revived without de-mining and the restoration of transport may require the laying of hard surface roads to prevent re-mining. In such instances, the link becomes evident between peace-keeping and peace-building. Just as demilitarized zones may serve the cause of preventive diplomacy and preventive deployment to avoid conflict, so may demilitarization assist in keeping the peace or in post-conflict peace-building, as a measure for heightening the sense of security and encouraging the parties to turn their energies to the work of peaceful restoration of their societies.

There is a new requirement for technical assistance which the United Nations has an obligation to develop and provide when requested: support for the transformation of deficient national structures and capabilities, and for the strengthening of new democratic institutions. The authority of the United Nations system to act in this field would rest on the consensus that social peace is as important as strategic or political peace. There is an obvious connection between democratic practices – such as the rule of law and transparency in decision-making – and the achievement of true peace and security in any new and stable political order. These elements of good governance need to be promoted at all levels of international and national political communities.

VII. Cooperation with Regional
Arrangements and Organizations

The covenant of the League of Nations, in its Article 21, noted the validity of regional understandings for securing the maintenance of peace. The Charter devotes Chapter VIII to regional arrangements or agencies for dealing with such matters relating to the maintenance of international peace and security as are appropriate for regional action and consistent with the Purposes and Principles of the United Nations. The cold war impaired the proper use of Chapter VIII and indeed, in that era, regional arrangements worked on occasion against resolving disputes in the manner foreseen in the Charter.

The Charter deliberately provides no precise definition of regional arrangements and agencies, thus allowing useful flexibility for undertakings by a group of States to deal with a matter appropriate for regional action which also could contribute to the maintenance of international peace and security. Such associations or entities could include treaty-based organizations, whether created before or after the founding of the United Nations, regional organizations for mutual security and defence, organizations for general regional development or for cooperation on a particular economic topic or function, and groups created to deal with a specific political, economic or social issue of current concern.

In this regard, the United Nations has recently encouraged a rich variety of complementary efforts. Just as no two regions or situations are the same, so the design of cooperative work and its division of labour must adapt to the realities of each case with flexibility and creativity. In Africa, three different regional groups – the Organization of African Unity, the League of Arab States and the Organization of the Islamic Conference – joined efforts with the United Nations regarding Somalia. In the Asian context, the Association of South-East Asian Nations and individual States from several regions were brought together with the parties to the Cambodian conflict at an international conference in Paris, to work with the United Nations. For El Salvador, a unique arrangement – 'The Friends of the Secretary-General' – contributed to agreements reached through the mediation of the Secretary-General. The end of the war in Nicaragua involved a highly complex effort which was initiated by leaders of the region and conducted by individual States, groups of States and the Organization of American States. Efforts undertaken by the European Community and its member States, with the support of States participating in the Conference on Security and Cooperation in Europe, have been of central importance in dealing with the crisis in the Balkans and neighbouring areas.

In the past, regional arrangements often were created because of the absence of a universal system for collective security; thus their activities could on occasion work at cross-purposes with the sense of solidarity required for the effectiveness of the world Organization. But in this new era of opportunity, regional arrangements or agencies can render great service if their activities are undertaken in a manner consistent with the Purposes and Principles of the Charter, and if their relationship with the United Nations, and particularly the Security Council, is governed by Chapter VIII.

It is not the purpose of the present report to set forth any formal pattern of relationship between regional organizations and the United Nations, or to call for any specific division of labour. What is clear, however, is that regional arrangements or agencies in many cases possess a potential that should be utilized in serving the functions covered in this report: preventive diplomacy, peace-keeping, peacemaking and post-conflict peace-building. Under the Charter, the Security Council has and will continue to have primary responsibility for maintaining international peace and security, but regional action as a matter of decentralization, delegation and cooperation with United Nations efforts could not only lighten the burden of the Council but also contribute to a deeper sense of participation, consensus and democratization in international affairs.

Regional arrangements and agencies have not in recent decades been considered in this light, even when originally designed in part for a role in maintaining or restoring peace within their regions of the world. Today a new sense exists that they have contributions to make. Consultations between the United Nations and regional arrangements or agencies could do much to build international consensus on the nature of a problem and the measures required to address it. Regional organizations participating in complementary efforts with the United Nations in joint undertakings would encourage States outside the region to act supportively. And should the

Security Council choose specifically to authorize a regional arrangement or organization to take the lead in addressing a crisis within its region, it could serve to lend the weight of the United Nations to the validity of the regional effort. Carried forward in the spirit of the Charter, and as envisioned in Chapter VII, the approach outlined here could strengthen a general sense that democratization is being encouraged at all levels in the task of maintaining international peace and security, it being essential to continue to recognize that the primary responsibility will continue to reside in the Security Council.

VIII. Safety of Personnel

When United Nations personnel are deployed in conditions of strife, whether for preventive diplomacy, peacemaking, peace-keeping, peace-building or humanitarian purposes, the need arises to ensure their safety. There has been an unconscionable increase in the number of fatalities. Following the conclusion of a cease-fire and in order to prevent further outbreaks of violence, United Nations guards were called upon to assist in volatile conditions in Iraq. Their presence afforded a measure of security to United Nations personnel and supplies and, in addition, introduced an element of reassurance and stability that helped to prevent renewed conflict. Depending upon the nature of the situation, different configurations and compositions of security deployments will need to be considered. As the variety and scale of threat widens, innovative measures will be required to deal with the dangers facing United Nations personnel.

Experience has demonstrated that the presence of a United Nations operation has not always been sufficient to deter hostile action. Duty in areas of danger can never be risk-free; United Nations personnel must expect to go in harm's way at times. The courage, commitment and idealism shown by United Nations personnel should be respected by the entire international community. These men and women deserve to be properly recognized and rewarded for the perilous tasks they undertake. Their interests and those of their families must be given due regard and protected.

Given the pressing need to afford adequate protection to United Nations personnel engaged in life-endangering circumstances, I recommend that the Security Council, unless it elects immediately to withdraw the United Nations presence in order to preserve the credibility of the Organization, gravely consider what action should be taken towards those who put United Nations personnel in danger. Before deployment takes place, the Council should keep open the option of considering in advance collective measures, possibly includ-

ing those under Chapter VII when a threat to international peace
and security is also involved, to come into effect should the purpose
of the United Nations operation systematically be frustrated and
hostilities occur.

IX. Financing

A chasm has developed between the tasks entrusted to this Organization and the financial means provided to it. The truth of the matter is that our vision cannot really extend to the prospect opening before us as long as our financing remains myopic. There are two main areas of concern: the ability of the Organization to function over the longer term; and immediate requirements to respond to a crisis.

To remedy the financial situation of the United Nations in all its aspects, my distinguished predecessor repeatedly drew all the attention of Member States to the increasingly impossible situation that has arisen and, during the forty-sixth session of the General Assembly, made a number of proposals. Those proposals which remain before the Assembly, and with which I am in broad agreement, are the following:

– *Proposal one.* This suggested the adoption of a set of measures to deal with the cash flow problems caused by the exceptionally high level of unpaid contributions as well as with the problem of inadequate working capital reserves:
    (a) Charging interest on the amounts of assessed contributions that are not paid on time;
    (b) Suspending certain financial regulations of the United Nations to permit the retention of budgetary surpluses;
    (c) Increasing the Working Capital Fund to a level of $250 million and endorsing the principle that the level of the Fund should be approximately 25 per cent of the annual assessment under the regular budget;
    (d) Establishment of a temporary Peace-keeping Reserve Fund, at a level of $50 million, to meet initial expenses of peace-keeping operations pending receipt of assessed contributions;

(e) Authorization to the Secretary-General to borrow commercially, should other sources of cash be inadequate.

- *Proposal two.* This suggested the creation of a Humanitarian Revolving Fund in the order of $50 million, to be used in emergency humanitarian situations. The proposal has since been implemented.

- *Proposal three.* This suggested the establishment of a United Nations Peace Endowment Fund, with an initial target of $1 billion. The Fund would be created by a combination of assessed and voluntary contributions, with the latter being sought from Governments, the private sector as well as individuals. Once the Fund reached its target level, the proceeds from the investment of its principal would be used to finance the initial costs of authorized peace-keeping operations, other conflict resolution measures and related activities.

In addition to these proposals, others have been added in recent months in the course of public discussion. These ideas include: a levy on arms sales that could be related to maintaining an Arms Register by the United Nations; a levy on international air travel, which is dependent on the maintenance of peace; authorization for the United Nations to borrow from the World Bank and the International Monetary Fund – for peace and development are interdependent; general tax exemption for contributions made to the United Nations by foundations, businesses and individuals; and changes in the formula for calculating the scale of assessments for peace-keeping operations.

As such ideas are debated, a stark fact remains: the financial foundations of the Organization daily grow weaker, debilitating its political will and practical capacity to undertake new and essential activities. This state of affairs must not continue. Whatever decisions are taken on financing the Organization, there is one inescapable necessity: Member States must pay their assessed contributions in full and on time. Failure to do so puts them in breach of their obligations under the Charter.

In these circumstances and on the assumption that Member States will be ready to finance operations for peace in a manner commensurate with their present, and welcome, readiness to establish them, I recommend the following:

(a) Immediate establishment of a revolving peace-keeping reserve fund of $50 million;

(b) Agreement that one third of the estimated cost of each new peace-keeping operation be appropriated by the General

Assembly as soon as the Security Council decides to establish the operation; this would give the Secretary-General the necessary commitment authority and assure an adequate cash flow; the balance of the costs would be appropriated after the General Assembly approved the operation's budget;

(c) Acknowledgement by Member States that, under exceptional circumstances, political and operational considerations may make it necessary for the Secretary-General to employ his authority to place contracts without competitive bidding.

Member States wish the Organization to be managed with the utmost efficiency and care. I am in full accord. I have taken important steps to streamline the Secretariat in order to avoid duplication and overlap while increasing its productivity. Additional changes and improvements will take place. As regards the United Nations system more widely, I continue to review the situation in consultation with my colleagues in the Administrative Committee on Coordination. The question of assuring financial security to the Organization over the long term is of such importance and complexity that public awareness and support must be heightened. I have therefore asked a select group of qualified persons of high international repute to examine this entire subject and to report to me. I intend to present their advice, together with my comments, for the consideration of the General Assembly, in full recognition of the special responsibility that the Assembly has, under the Charter, for financial and budgetary matters.

X. An Agenda for Peace

The nations and peoples of the United Nations are fortunate in a way that those of the League of Nations were not. We have been given a second chance to create the world of our Charter that they were denied. With the cold war ended we have drawn back from the brink of a confrontation that threatened the world and, too often, paralysed our Organization.

Even as we celebrate our restored possibilities, there is a need to ensure that the lessons of the past four decades are learned and that the errors, or variations of them, are not repeated. For there may not be a third opportunity for our planet which, now for different reasons, remains endangered.

The tasks ahead must engage the energy and attention of all components of the United Nations system – the General Assembly and other principal organs, the agencies and programmes. Each has, in a balanced scheme of things, a role and a responsibility.

Never again must the Security Council lose the collegiality that is essential to its proper functioning, an attribute that it has gained after such trial. A genuine sense of consensus deriving from shared interests must govern its work, not the threat of the veto or the power of any group of nations. And it follows that agreement among the permanent members must have the deeper support of the other members of the Council, and the membership more widely, if the Council's decisions are to be effective and endure.

The Summit Meeting of the Security Council of 31 January 1992 provided a unique forum for exchanging views and strengthening cooperation. I recommend that the Heads of State and Government of the members of the Council meet in alternate years, just before the general debate commences in the General Assembly. Such sessions would permit exchanges on the challenges and dangers of the moment and stimulate ideas on how the United Nations may best serve to steer change into peaceful courses. I propose in addition that the

Security Council continue to meet at the Foreign Minister level, as it has effectively done in recent years, whenever the situation warrants such meetings.

Power brings special responsibilities, and temptations. The powerful must resist the dual but opposite calls of unilateralism and isolationism if the United Nations is to succeed. For just as unilateralism at the global or regional level can shake the confidence of others, so can isolationism, whether it results from political choice or constitutional circumstance, enfeeble the global undertaking. Peace at home and the urgency of rebuilding and strengthening our individual societies necessitates peace abroad and cooperation among nations. The endeavours of the United Nations will require the fullest engagement of all of its Members, large and small, if the present renewed opportunity is to be seized.

Democracy within nations requires respect for human rights and fundamental freedoms, as set forth in the Charter. It requires as well a deeper understanding and respect for the rights of minorities and respect for the needs of the more vulnerable groups of society, especially women and children. This is not only a political matter. The social stability needed for productive growth is nurtured by conditions in which people can readily express their will. For this, strong domestic institutions of participation are essential. Promoting such institutions means promoting the empowerment of the unorganized, the poor, the marginalized. To this end, the focus of the United Nations should be on the 'field', the locations where economic, social and political decisions take effect. In furtherance of this I am taking steps to rationalize and in certain cases integrate the various programmes and agencies of the United Nations within specific countries. The senior United Nations official in each country should be prepared to serve, when needed, and with the consent of the host authorities, as my Representative on matters of particular concern.

Democracy within the family of nations means the application of its principles within the world Organization itself. This requires the fullest consultation, participation and engagement of all States, large and small, in the work of the Organization. All organs of the United Nations must be accorded, and play, their full and proper role so that the trust of all nations and peoples will be retained and deserved. The principles of the Charter must be applied consistently, not selectively, for if the perception should be of the latter, trust will wane and with it the moral authority which is the greatest and most unique quality of that instrument. Democracy at all levels is essential to attain peace for a new era of prosperity and justice.

Trust also requires a sense of confidence that the world Organization will react swiftly, surely and impartially and that it will not be debilitated by political opportunism or by administrative or financial inadequacy. This presupposes a strong, efficient and independent international civil service whose integrity is beyond question and an assured financial basis that lifts the Organization, once and for all, out of its present mendicancy.

Just as it is vital that each of the organs of the United Nations employ its capabilities in the balanced and harmonious fashion envisioned in the Charter, peace in the largest sense cannot be accomplished by the United Nations system or by Governments alone. Non-governmental organizations, academic institutions, parliamentarians, business and professional communities, the media and the public at large must all be involved. This will strengthen the world Organization's ability to reflect the concerns and interests of its widest constituency, and those who become more involved can carry the word of United Nations initiatives and build a deeper understanding of its work.

Reform is a continuing process, and improvement can have no limit. Yet there is an expectation, which I wish to see fulfilled, that the present phase in the renewal of this Organization should be complete by 1995, its fiftieth anniversary. The pace set must therefore be increased if the United Nations is to keep ahead of the acceleration of history that characterizes this age. We must be guided not by precedents alone, however wise these may be, but by the needs of the future and by the shape and content that we wish to give it.

I am committed to broad dialogue between the Member States and the Secretary-General. And I am committed to fostering a full and open interplay between all institutions and elements of the Organization so that the Charter's objectives may not only be better served, but that this Organization may emerge as greater than the sum of its parts. The United Nations was created with a great and courageous vision. Now is the time, for its nations and peoples, and the men and women who serve it, to seize the moment for the sake of the future.

Index

271